CW00919234
POOLE
POTS
B'MOUTH
using pots
AT
POOLE

POOLE POTTERY

Top left: Jesse Carter, 1830-1926; top right: Owen Carter, 1862-1919; centre left: Charles Carter 1860-1934; centre right: Cyril Carter, 1888-1969; bottom left: John Adams, 1882-1953, portrait by R.R. Tomlinson (City Museum and Art Gallery, Stoke on Trent); bottom right: Harold Stabler, 1872-1945.

POOLE POTTERY

Carter & Company and their Successors 1873-2002

Leslie Hayward
Edited by Paul Atterbury

Richard Dennis, Somerset
2002

Acknowledgements

These pages owe much inspiration to my former colleagues, particularly to those of the 1950s when Poole Pottery was facing up to the challenge and opportunities of the future, whilst retaining strong and secure links with the past. I owe therefore a special debt of gratitude to those who assisted me at that time and provided the foundation upon which my later interest was to develop, in particular, Ruth Pavely, Leslie Elsden, Jack Such and Roy Holland.

I am also grateful to others who served with me, including Guy Sydenham, Ann Read, Jimmy Soper and Nellie Blackmore, for more recent help in recalling details of products, processes and events that have not always been available from surviving factory records.

My thanks are also due to those who worked in the formative years of Carter, Stabler & Adams and were already in retirement when my researches commenced. To Margaret Holder, Beatrice Bibbey and Ernest Bristowe, also Marjorie Batt, Myrtle Bond, Vera Wills and many other pre war paintresses who gave detailed accounts of their working lives.

Similarly with those who came later and have been equally generous in their continuing support. In particular Bob Jefferson, Tony Morris, Christine Tate, Carole Holden, Julia Williams, Ros Sommerfelt, Barbara Linley Adams and Alan Pepper, also David Walton and Yvonne Morris who have clarified many of the more obscure technical details for me.

I am grateful too for the kind assistance provided by friends and family not immediately connected with the pottery, including Tony Carter, Jennifer Opie, Lorna Young, Jasmin French, Barbara McLeish, Frank Tarrant, my wife Ursula and my daughters Rosalind and Alison.

The majority of the photographs were taken by Graham Miller, but some additional photography was undertaken by Farquharson Murless, Chris Hart, Mark Nicholson, Mike Legg and John Atkinson.

Above all I am indebted to Paul Atterbury for editing the information gained from these and other sources and for assisting me in the presentation of the relevant facts, a process in which his considerable experience has been a valuable asset.

Finally, I must place on record my appreciation for the contribution made in the production of this book, by the management and staff of the Poole Pottery today and by Richard Dennis and all the staff at Flaydemouse. In particular, for that made by Wendy Wort whose untiring efforts and quiet diplomacy have played such an important part.

L.H

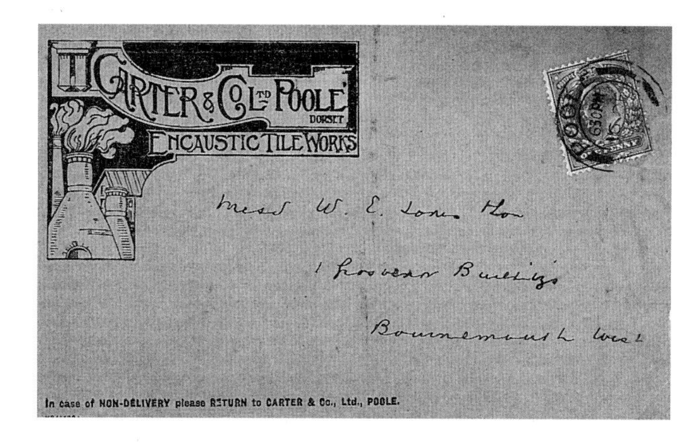

The publishers are grateful for the help and support willingly given by the following: Clive and Thelma Bailey, Teresa Bretherton and Colin Richards, John C. Clark, Tony Fern, Jimmy Hardy and John Runniff-Nutman, Jeremy Hulme, David and Julie Metcalfe and Jim and Dorothy Watson. We should also like to thank J.S.M. Scott for making available his extensive collection of tiles.

Photography by Graham Miller and Magnus Dennis

Production by Wendy Wort

Print, Design and Reproduction by Flaydemouse, Yeovil, England

Published by Richard Dennis, The Old Chapel, Shepton Beauchamp, Somerset TA19 OLE

ISBN 0 903685 86 8

British Library Cataloguing-in-Publication Data. A catalogue record for this book is available from the British Library

The end papers show a selection of tiles designed by Edward Bawden and used in the visitors' tea room opened in 1932.

Contents

Commemorative roundel made by Carter & Company for the coronation of King George V and Queen Mary

Late 19th century views of the East Quay, Poole, showing aspects of the three storey brick pottery set up by James Walker from 1861 and bought by Jesse Carter in 1873.

Chapter One

Introduction

Engraving showing the Patent Architectural Pottery, Hamworthy, in 1855.

Pottery making has been a feature of the Poole region for centuries, the result of large local deposits of various types of clays. These have been exploited since prehistory and regularly exported in bulk since the 18th century. Particularly famous are the fine white Dorset ball clays, whose qualities have long been appreciated by potters in Staffordshire and other centres of the ceramic industry. Less well known is the pottery actually made in the region which for centuries was essentially domestic and of largely local interest.

In the Victorian period this was radically changed by the establishment of a number of potteries in and around Poole making architectural ceramics. The dark clays that occurred in great quantity and variety to the north of Poole were found to be ideal for bricks and tiles, drain pipes, chimney pots and basic garden pottery, products that could reflect the increasing market demand for such wares in stoneware and terracotta. The making of this type of pottery had been pioneered by London companies such as Doulton and Blashfield, building on the tradition established in the late 18th century by Mrs. Coade's famous stone works. By the 1850s the making of garden and architectural terracotta had begun to spread to other centres such as Derbyshire, Yorkshire, the Black Country and Shropshire. It was at this point that Dorset began to be known for its pottery as well as for its clays.

In January 1855 a large celebration marked the official opening of the Patent Architectural Pottery in Hamworthy, a company set up by a partnership of local and Staffordshire men that was destined to make the Poole name well known throughout England. Writing some twenty years later, the ceramic historian Llewellyn Jewitt described some of the major products of this large and well equipped pottery: 'patent coloured and glazed bricks and mouldings, semi perforated and pressed: patent mosaic, tesselated, encaustic, vitreous and other glazed wall tiles: embossed and perforated tiles; quarries and fire-clay goods.' Clays used at Hamworthy came from Dorset, notably Purbeck and the Canford estate, from Surrey and from Cornwall, thanks to the opening, from 1847, of the railway lines that linked southern Dorset and the pottery's site near Poole's busy quays, to the national network. By this time the Architectural Pottery and its products were becoming well known, the result of displays and awards at International exhibitions in London, Dublin, Paris and elsewhere, a growing reputation that also encouraged the setting up of rival concerns.

In 1861 James Walker, the Architectural Pottery's chief technician, had left Hamworthy to establish another company on Poole's East Quay. This, known grandly as T.W. Walker's Patent Encaustic and Mosaic Ornamental Brick and Tile Manufactory and housed in an extensive three-storey brick building, concentrated on the making of a large range of tiles and similar products. However, despite Walker's grand ambitions, things did not go well. Twice during the 1860s the business was offered for sale and by 1873 Walker was bankrupt and the pottery had closed. The same year Jesse Carter, a successful Surrey-based builders' merchant and ironmonger, bought the semi-derelict pottery and re-started the business, initially with Walker as an employee, establishing in the process a link between pottery making at Poole and the Carter family that was to last until the 1960s. Seeing the manufacture of architectural ceramics as a potentially rewarding expansion of his other business interests, Jesse Carter moved to Poole with his wife and six children, two of whom, Charles and Owen, were to play their part in the subsequent development of the pottery. Initially he struggled to get the business going and produced a wide range of products, including cement and lime produced from Purbeck limestone, calcined in a kiln adjacent to the works and subsequently sold to local builders. At the same time he expanded this new area of interest by purchasing a share in a similar pottery in Worcester, an established producer of bricks, tiles and terracotta garden wares. By the 1880s, the East Quay works was well established and its growing reputation was not only beginning to overshadow its Hamworthy rival but also to challenge some of the major Staffordshire manufacturers such as Wedgwood. Increasingly, the company was known for its glazed architectural faience and decorative tiling, used extensively for pubs, hotels, restaurants and shops, but also important were mosaic flooring and mosaic advertising panels, domestic wares such as fire surrounds and painted tile panels. Little is known about the artists and designers working for the pottery at this time. Among the first were Edwin Turner who came to Poole in the early 1890s and his half-brother James Radley Young, who arrived in 1893. The modeller and sculptor William Unwin joined the company

Watercolour by Jasper Salway showing a postwar redevelopment scheme for the Poole Pottery, as carried out between 1946 and 1948. A new kiln shed was later built over the central garden area.

Photograph showing the East Quay, Poole, with the bottle ovens and the gas company's coal transporter beyond.

An aerial view of the Poole Pottery complex in the 1970s.

in 1896. All its products were featured in a series of well illustrated catalogues issued by the pottery from the 1880s, documents that steadily became more comprehensive and which included colour plates from the early 1900s. The continued success of the East Quay works enabled it to eclipse Hamworthy completely and in 1895 the Carter family were able to buy the Patent Architectural Pottery for £2000. From this point on the two companies worked together, becoming the cornerstones of a business that was to give the Poole name an important place in the history of pottery making in the 20th century.

In 1901 Jesse Carter retired, leaving the company, by then established in the premier league of British makers of architectural ceramics, in the hands of his sons Charles and Owen. In the same year a second site was purchased at Hamworthy, across the road from the old Architectural Pottery where, sometime after 1905, another pottery was established concentrating on the production of white and cream glazed wall tiles. Inevitably this became known as the White Works and it quickly contributed to the rising reputation, and the financial success, enjoyed by Carter & Company. At this time Hamworthy concentrated on floor tiles while faience, glazed and decorative tiles and terracotta were made at the East Quay works.

The dominant figure of the next two decades was Owen Carter. Increasingly interested by decorative pottery and perhaps inspired by the long association between Poole and William de Morgan, for whom the Architectural Pottery had been making blanks since the early 1870s, Carter learned to throw and developed a particular interest in glaze technology.

Working with Alfred Eason, the pottery's glaze technician and later works manager, he perfected a range of reduction-fired lustre glazes that were to be used both for tiles and for a new range of vases, dishes and other decorative wares. The move towards decorative pottery seemed to grow naturally from traditional areas of artistic production, such as tile painting, faience modelling and the making of ornamental garden wares, notably the ranges made for Liberty's from designs by Archibald Knox. The initial impetus for this new area of activity came from Owen Carter, but it was James Radley Young, head of the design department, who put Poole firmly on the road towards hand made and hand decorated domestic pottery. Young had left Poole in about 1901 to start his own pottery near Haslemere in Surrey but the venture was never a success and he returned to Dorset after a few years. However, while working on his own he developed distinct styles of decorating and glazing pottery that emphasised handcraft techniques and it was these styles that were to form the basis of a new range of ornamental wares.

Owen Carter's lustre wares were the start, augmented by beads and portrait tiles, but the major changes occurred during the First World War when Young's characteristic decorative ranges were developed, partly to help fill production gaps created by the great reduction in decorative tiling and other areas curtailed or limited by government controls. These included an unglazed range, using the basic tile clay with simple painted decoration, inspired by Roman, Egyptian, African and other primitive pottery forms, and two tin-glazed ranges, free-hand painted with flower sprigs or stripes. The soft, highly absorbent, grey-white tin glaze, a typical feature of the 17th and early 18th century pottery associated with Bristol and other production centres, had been recreated by Young and Eason before the war, but it was given added impetus by the arrival in Poole in 1914 of Belgian potters fleeing the invasion of their country, notably Joseph Roelants. Also important was the relationship that developed from 1914 between Poole and Roger Fry's Omega Workshops, which developed further the pottery's interest in handcraft techniques and brought it into contact with leading avant garde artists such as Duncan Grant and Vanessa Bell. Although the pottery that came from the Omega connection was limited in both financial and production terms, it established at Poole the habit of working closely with contemporary artists and designers, a tradition that has been an important part of the pottery's story to the present day. By 1917 production was sufficiently organised for the new ranges of decorative wares to be shown for the first time at the British Industries Fair. This display established a pattern for the future and underlined the contribution made by James Radley Young in moving Poole away from its traditional areas of production and in establishing at the pottery the nucleus of a team of throwers, paintresses and others skilled in the making of ornamental wares. However, the display also represented the climax of Young's period of influence. The same year he was called up to work as a draughtsman at the Poole shipyard and when he returned after the war the climate had already begun to change, a change hastened by the death in 1919 of Owen Carter.

By 1920 the production of ornamental wares was well established at the East Quay works, underlined by displays at exhibitions and favourable reports in the trade and consumer press. Typical was the following comment published in the *Journal for the Royal Society of Arts* in June 1920: 'The simple ware manufactured with skill and taste by Carter of Poole ... introduces to the public ceramics of good design colour and workmanship within the reach of all.' In 1921 Carter & Company issued the second catalogue of their ornamental wares which, while maintaining the styles developed by Young, indicated that the somewhat random design and production processes of the previous decade had been standardised to suit the needs of the retail market. However, the bulk of their business was still in the fields of architectural ceramics and their continued success with large scale contracts for tiling, ceramic marble and other building product ranges for home and overseas markets in effect underwrote the manufacture of the ornamental wares. Future developments were now in the hands of the next generation of Carters. Charles's son Cyril had started working as a representative in the London office before the First World War. After a number of locations, this office had been permanently established on the Albert Embankment in 1911 in a building that was, in its own way, to become as distinctive as the extensive premises of its neighbour, Royal Doulton. The manager was Alfred Carter's son, Arthur. Following war service, Cyril Carter returned to Poole, first to look after the floor tile works at Hamworthy and then, in about 1921, he moved to the ornamental and domestic wares. Until his retirement in 1928, when he was succeeded by Benjamin Elford, Owen's brother Charles remained as managing director for the whole Carter & Company enterprise, and maintained the tradition of firm but enlightened direction established by Jesse. Charles Carter was aware of the needs for change, particularly in the design field and he introduced Cyril to the designer and silversmith Harold Stabler, who already had some ceramic experience gained from the making of the pottery figures modelled by his wife, Phoebe. Stabler in turn introduced Cyril Carter to John Adams, a Staffordshire born and trained designer and technical potter who had been teaching in South Africa, and his wife Truda, also a designer of some standing.

The result of all this was the setting up in 1921 of Carter, Stabler & Adams as an independent but wholly-owned subsidiary of Carter & Company with the responsibility for creating, at the East Quay works, a successful business for the production of ornamental and domestic pottery. Carter, Stabler & Adams, or CSA as it was generally known, was to do this with notable success until 1963, when the company name was finally changed to Poole Pottery Limited, at the time of the takeover by Pilkington's Tiles.

The design changes introduced by the Stablers and the Adams revolutionised pottery making at Poole. The techniques of James Radley Young were initially maintained with the Delftware tin glaze painting process becoming the most characteristic feature of Poole, but a design explosion, initiated by Truda Adams, brought into being the characteristic Poole style of free-hand painting in bright colours of vivid patterns inspired by flowers and other natural motifs. These patterns, reflecting the more decorative aspects of Art Deco modernism, and moving steadily towards abstraction, were applied to an increasingly wide range of domestic pottery and gave the company its particular place in the market, defined by many critics as the successful marriage of art or studio pottery and commercial production. Success in the retail market was underlined by

Set of promotional postcards, issued in 1937, and showing Gertie Gilham throwing, Jimmy Soper turning, Leslie Elsden spraying, Ernest Hustler at the kiln, Jack Such handling, Christine Lucas and Ruth Pavely painting, and samples of ware.

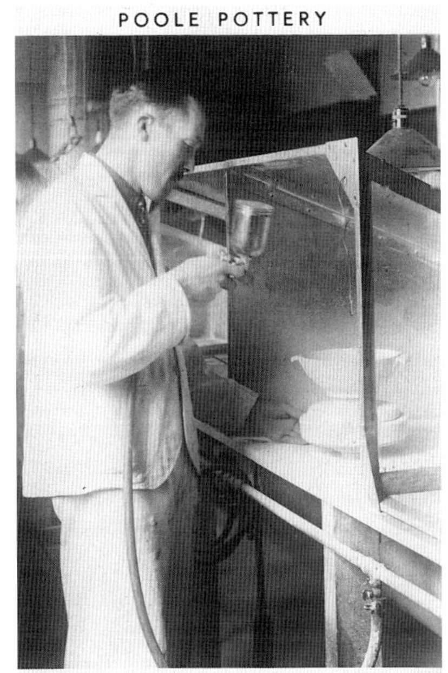

Visitors' tea room at Poole, opened in 1932, showing the Edward Bawden wall tiles, a John Adams pierced panel, Harold Stabler Studland tea wares and distinctive menu cover designed by Irene Fawkes.

Carter & Company stand at the Building Trades Exhibition, 1953, the focal point of which was Joseph Ledger's Europa panel (see page 175).

The Carter, Stabler & Adams stand at the British Industries Fair, 1947.

Seconds showroom at Poole, 1964.

Display of Poole Pottery at Barkers of Kensington, 1970, with a fine selection of Delphis.

Trevor Wright, Poole's managing director, 1976-1988, disposing of imperfect examples of the limited edition Jubilee loving cup of 1977.

displays at exhibitions at home and abroad, with notable examples being Paris in 1925 and Leipzig in 1927. At the same time, firm links were established between Poole and avant garde retailers such as Heal & Son, and the reputation the pottery was enjoying soon brought other artists to Dorset, such as Erna Manners, Dora Batty, Minnie McLeish, Edward Bawden and Olive Bourne. The painted wares soon became the pottery's mainstay, but also important were the ranges of figures, garden wares and vases modelled by Harold and Phoebe Stabler and the monochrome glazes and modern shapes developed by John Adams. It was Adams who, more than anyone, took Poole into the cool, modernist styles of the 1930s, underlined by architectural shapes and matt glazes in soft colours, and it was Adams who turned Poole into a major producer of tablewares. In the 1930s, the company was able to establish that critical balance between ornamental wares and tablewares that was the key to its reputation and its commercial success, a balance that has been maintained, to a greater or lesser extent, ever since. At the same time CSA established a lasting commitment to modernism and was able to prove then, and in subsequent decades, that there was a place in the market for contemporary styles. The pottery's lasting association with stylish modernism was underlined by its catalogues and other publications and by its advertisements. Also important was the popular appeal of the pottery itself, which made the most of its position at the heart of a seaside resort. From the early 1920s, pottery visits were encouraged with paintresses often acting as guides and a modern showroom was followed, in 1932, by the opening of a tea room in a setting lined with Edward Bawden tiles and equipped with contemporary tablewares designed first by Harold Stabler and then by John Adams.

The impetus for much of this came from Harold Stabler and Cyril Carter through their links with the various government-inspired organisations set up to improve standards of industrial design in Britain. Stabler was a founder member of the British Institute of Industrial Art and the Design and Industries Association, while Carter was a member of the Council for Art and Industry and on the selection committee for the exhibitions of modern design that it instigated during the 1930s, at Dorland Hall, at Burlington House and at the Victoria & Albert Museum. These activities and the valuable contacts that naturally followed from them, underwrote the CSA commitment of modernism and kept the pottery's products in the vanguard of contemporary design in the marketplace. Success brought its own problems. There was always a shortage of space and so the East Quay works was continually being enlarged, generally in a rather rudimentary way. A new factory was planned in the late 1930s by the architect Geoffrey Jellicoe, but the war came before work had started and brought all such schemes to an end. The Second World War scattered many of the hundred employees that had been working at the East Quay in the late 1930s and severely curtailed production. From 1942 the making of decorative wares for the home market was forbidden by the Board of Trade, and so, not having the developed export markets of larger potteries, Poole had to rely on utility wares for the home market and a very limited range of painted wares for export.

The ultimate test of Poole tableware: Sir Gordon Russell tries a Contour tea cup during a factory visit in 1964, watched by Robert Jefferson and Roy Holland.

Famous visitors: above, actress Eva Bartok with Lucien Myers at a Tea Centre exhibition in 1958 and right, TV comedian Harry Worth amusing Guy Sydenham in the craft section in 1966.

With very few employees many of the buildings that had been part of the company's rapid and often unplanned growth during previous decades were abandoned and, when peace returned in 1945, the pottery was barely alive. Harold Stabler had died in 1945 and John Adams was in failing health. However, Cyril Carter took up the fight and he persuaded the directors of Carter & Company to start all over again and to rebuild CSA into the major pottery it had been before the war. Massive investment resulted in a new factory, fully equipped with the latest plant including a Gibbons twin-tunnel electric kiln for biscuit and glost firing. Work started in the spring of 1946 and by 1948 large scale production was underway again, aimed now at developing export markets. The redevelopment programme was masterminded by Cyril Carter, with the support of Roy Holland, the newly recruited works director.

Initially the pottery relied on pre-war ranges, with the emphasis on the hand painted wares with their Truda Carter designs, and the John Adams tablewares. However, the retirement of John Adams in 1950 left a major gap which was partly filled by the appointment of Lucien Myers as managing director. This left the vital area of design unresolved. After one or two false starts a design team was established under the direction of Alfred Read and with his leadership, supported by Myers and Roy Holland, Carter, Stabler & Adams were soon able to re-establish their pre-war reputation as a pottery synonymous with modern design. While maintaining traditional styles of decoration and manufacture, Poole of the 1950s, with its abstract patterns and flowing shapes, was able to express probably better than any other British pottery, the contemporary taste for modern design. The styles associated with Alfred Read, and the other members of his design team, Ruth Pavely, Ann Read and Guy Sydenham, did much to restore Poole's pre-war eminence in the contemporary market, a position again underlined by exhibition displays and by reports in consumer and trade magazines.

The successful rebuilding of the ornamental ranges, including the traditional hand painted ware, was an achievement of the 1950s. However, tablewares, an increasingly important part of the Poole production, were still dependent largely upon pre-war shapes and the two-colour glaze effects developed by John Adams, now known as Twintone. It was with this in mind that the company appointed Robert Jefferson as its designer in 1958 and it was Jefferson who successfully took Poole into the modern consumer market of the 1960s with his oven-to-tablewares and his Contour and Compact tablewares. These new ranges maintained the Poole tradition for modernism and ensured that, as with previous decades, the pottery's products were at the forefront of contemporary design. Jefferson was also instrumental in establishing a new craft studio at Poole devoted to the design and manufacture of one-off and limited production ranges of predominantly experimental wares made to emphasise, in a new way, the handcraft traditions so deeply interwoven into the Poole story. These studio wares, designed and made largely by Jefferson, Guy Sydenham and, later, Tony Morris, were first exhibited in 1961 and were well received by press and public.

From quite an early date, these products of the new Poole Studio were sold under the Delphis name and their success encouraged the company to start a new craft section for the production of ranges of hand decorated wares developed from these pioneering studio pieces. A number of new paintresses were recruited, many with art school training, and they were encouraged to carry out individually conceived and hand painted decoration on a series of standard shapes. With its bright colours and abstract patterns, the Delphis range captured the spirit of the 1960s and was an immediate success. Once again, Poole had managed to maintain its modernist tradition into a new decade. Other ranges followed, notably Aegean and Guy Sydenham's more individual Atlantis wares, projecting collectively a contemporary style that carried Poole through the 1960s and into the 1970s. The popularity of these ranges, and the continuing support enjoyed by the traditional hand painted wares, ensured that the correct balance between ornamental and tablewares was maintained once again.

This all happened against a background of major changes. In 1963 Lucien Myers had left, to be succeeded as managing director by Roy Holland. The same year Cyril Carter retired from the CSA board at the age of seventy five and his departure two years later marked the end of decades of Carter influence at Poole. In 1964 Carter & Company, and all its subsidiary interests, became a part of Pilkington's Tiles of Manchester and in 1966 Robert Jefferson left having steered Poole into a commanding place in the new consumer-dominated market place.

The late 1960s, the 1970s and the 1980s were a period of diversification, with the Poole pottery an increasingly small part in an ever-expanding corporate empire. In 1970 Pilkington's appointed Trevor Wright as works director and as managing director in 1976 on the retirement of Roy Holland. There was, at this time, an awareness of the pottery's place in history, highlighted by the centenary in 1973, a major exhibition at the Victoria & Albert Museum in 1978 and the visit of Her Majesty the Queen and the Duke of Edinburgh a year later. The Delphis ranges continued through to the end of the 1970s and traditional hand painting carried on, supported by many new products. Notable additions were the Barbara Linley Adams stoneware sculptures, the cathedral and calendar plates of Tony Morris, rapidly expanding ranges of gift wares and a great enlargement of the tableware market, with new transfer-printed patterns applied to new shapes created by outsiders such as Robert Jefferson, Robert Welch and the Queensberry Hunt Partnership, along with factory based designers such as Elaine Williamson. This pattern was maintained until the early 1990s when another radical change took place. Following years of corporate control, Poole became an independent company as a result of a management buy-out in 1992 masterminded by Peter Mills. At the same time, David Queensberry took on the mantle of design director. So far the design emphasis has been on tablewares, with Poole taking the lead in the expanding casual dining market with new informal patterns based on hand-painting, sponging and other natural styles. In preparation now is the new generation of ornamental wares, to carry the Poole tradition into the 21st century.

Her Majesty the Queen with Leslie Hayward and Arnold Smith in the Poole museum during the Royal visit of 1979.

Chapter One

Carter & Company 1873-1921

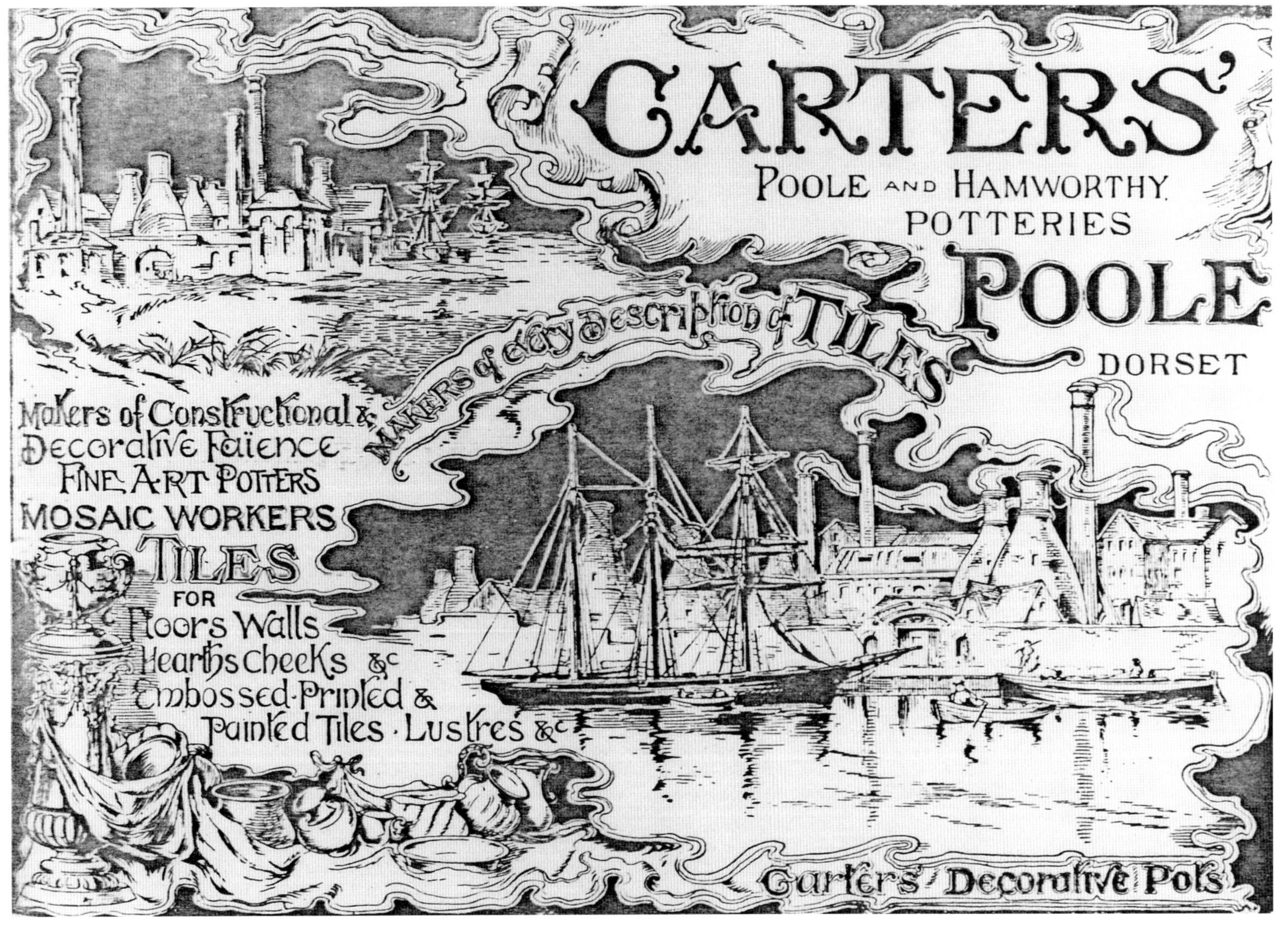

Advertisement for Carter & Company published in the April 1896 issue of *The Brickbuilder*.

Between 1873 when Jesse Carter bought the tile business started in the 1860s on Poole's East Quay by James Walker, and 1895 when he took over the Architectural Pottery Company in Hamworthy, production at Poole was concentrated on tiles and architectural ceramics. These included plain floor tiles in red, black, buff and other colours, encaustics, moulded and glazed faience, terracotta, garden wares, pots with embossed decoration, painted panels and mosaics. In 1887 a review in the magazine *Decoration* of that year's Building & Trades Exhibition said: 'Messrs. Carter & Co. of Poole had a very extensive and meritorious display of tiles; the great variety shown in the exhibition being well calculated to suit all requirements...' Continued expansion, and the resulting commercial success made Carter & Co. into one of Britain's largest tile businesses, well known particularly for its decorative faience frontages for shops and pubs and its painted panels. Many of these reflected the pottery's increasing interest in traditional ceramic styles such as maiolica, Della Robbia and Delftware, an interest developed by Jesse Carter's son Owen, the company's art and technical director. At the same time, through his friendship with the art potter William de Morgan, who made extensive use of blank tiles and other wares supplied by Carter's, Owen became fascinated by reduced lustre glazes. From the late 1890s until his death in 1919, Owen Carter devoted much of his time to the development of new ranges of decorative pottery, which included lustre wares made at Hamworthy alongside the floor tile production transferred from East Quay in 1895. By the time the White Works was opened at Hamworthy in 1905 for the manufacture of glazed wall tiles, the Poole factory had expanded its faience and terracotta departments, and in 1914 was able to accommodate a new decorative pottery unit which in time developed the handcraft ranges of 1917 onwards. Apart from his lustre decorated wares, which were said by *The Art Journal* in 1905 to: 'deserve a place among the well-known works of Maw, De Morgan and Lachenal' and the range of portrait tiles, Owen also expanded this area of production by the re-employment from 1906 of the thrower and designer James Radley Young. Later came the long line of female decorators who were to contribute so much to the Poole reputation over successive decades, the first of whom that can be identified with certainty is Lily Gilham. From the start, paintresses were encouraged to produce their own patterns and variations on the range of basic designs. Radley Young, who had first joined Carter's in 1893 and may have been involved in pot production before leaving in 1901 to develop his own styles and techniques while working until 1906 at the Hammer Vale Pottery near Haslemere, Surrey, played a major role in the development of decorative pottery at Poole. By that time lustre was in decline and his thrown shapes, initially in a buff vitreous earthenware body that was often left unglazed, had, from the start a characteristic Poole 'look'. He also used the grey semi-stoneware body that, combined with the opaque white tin-glaze, made possible the development of traditional Delftware decoration, with painting on to the raw, unfired glaze, the technique known always at Poole as 'in-glaze painting'. The first pattern ranges, simple sprigs, banding and lining in soft blues, greens, pinks and yellows, owed much to Belgian refugee potters such as Joseph Roelants and the influence of Roger Fry, Vanessa Bell and other Omega and Bloomsbury artists who worked closely with Carter & Co from about 1915. On this foundation, Owen Carter and Radley Young built a recognisable range of decorative wares, with names such as Moorish, Portuguese, and Monastic revealing the simple styles of pottery that inspired them, even if each piece was, in effect, a one-off. The pottery's products were widely sold in both local shops and major retailers such as Liberty and Heal & Son. Marketed initially under the Carter name, the products of this new artistic endeavour soon became known as Poole Pottery. By the end of the First World War Carters Handcraft Pottery was known and the factory was well on the way to becoming a major tourist attraction, with conducted tours by paintresses establishing another familiar Poole tradition.

Glazed white stoneware, moulded in the Queen Anne style. Probably designed and modelled by James Radley Young, 1893-1900. Height 12ins (30.5cm).
Pots with raised decoration were, from the 1880s, a natural corollary to the modelled and encaustic tiles Carter's were then making. In 1881 an advertisement in the *Poole and Bournemouth Herald* referred to 'tiles in green and amber glazes, so much used in buildings of the Queen Anne style,' a clear reference to the influence on Carter's of the revivalist form of architecture popularised by Norman Shaw and others working within the tradition of the Arts and Crafts movement.

CARTER & Co.
ENCAUSTIC TILE WORKS,
POOLE, DORSET.

PLATE 75.

Manchester Office:
100 Deansgate,
Manchester.

London Office:
43 Essex Street,
Strand, W.C.

Registered Telegraphic Address: "TILES," POOLE.

TERRA COTTA VASES IN BUFF, SALMON, OR RED.

FOR PRICES AND DIMENSIONS, SEE BACK.

Plate 75 from a trade catalogue issued by Carter & Company in about 1905, showing a range of terracotta vases.

Glazed faience capitol, heavily moulded in buff terracotta body. Probably modelled by William Unwin, 1900-1920. Length 23ins (58cm). Taken from the frontage of John Groves & Sons Ltd., Wine and Spirit Merchants in Holdenhurst Road, Bournemouth, during the course of demolition in 1977. Trustees of the Victoria & Albert Museum.

Page from a trade catalogue issued by Carter & Company in about 1908, showing tiled fire surrounds.

Plate 113 from a trade catalogue issued by Carter & Company in about 1908, showing tiling schemes.

Tiled panel designed and painted by James Radley Young, signed Carter & Co. Ltd., Poole. Built into the right-hand facade of a butcher and fishmonger's shop, part of which is now a bistro, constructed in brown and dark green faience for the original owners Jenkins & Sons, Parkstone, 1923.

Plate 34 from a trade catalogue issued by Carter & Company in about 1908, showing a range of moulded faience tiles.

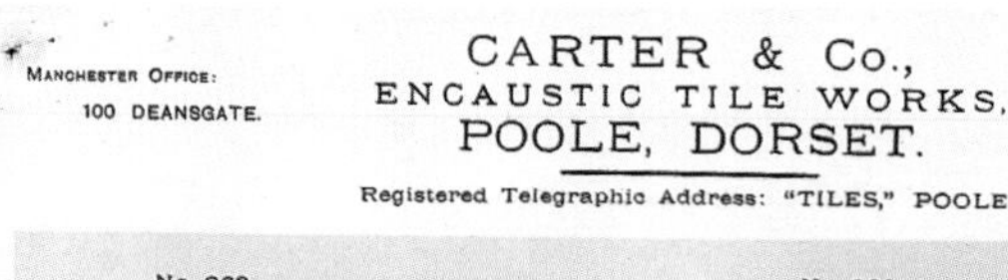

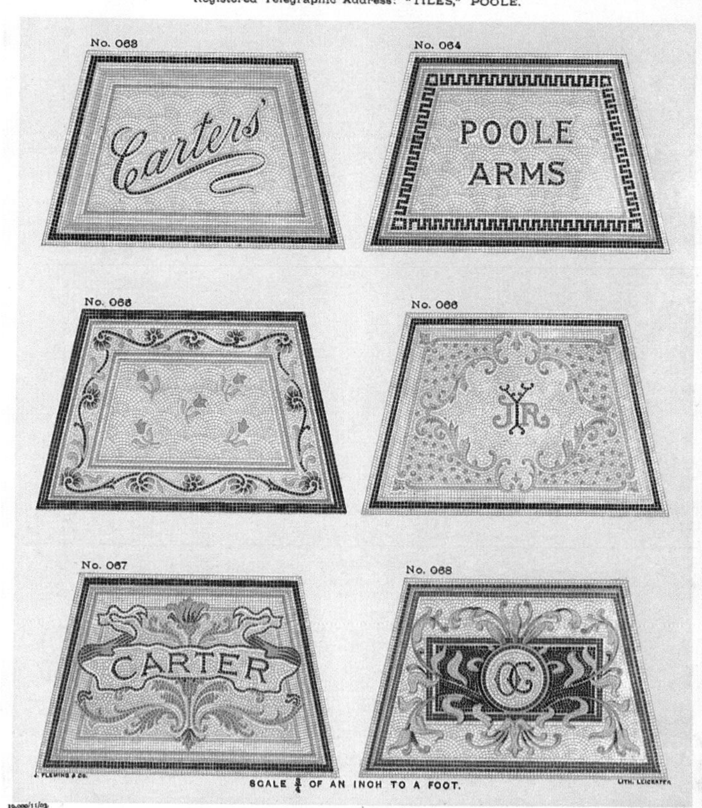

Plate 42 from a trade catalogue issued by Carter & Company in about 1908, showing mosaic panels.

Plate 100 from a trade catalogue issued by Carter & Company in about 1905, showing plain and encaustic floor tiling.

A page from a Carter pattern book of about 1900, showing a design for encaustic tiles.

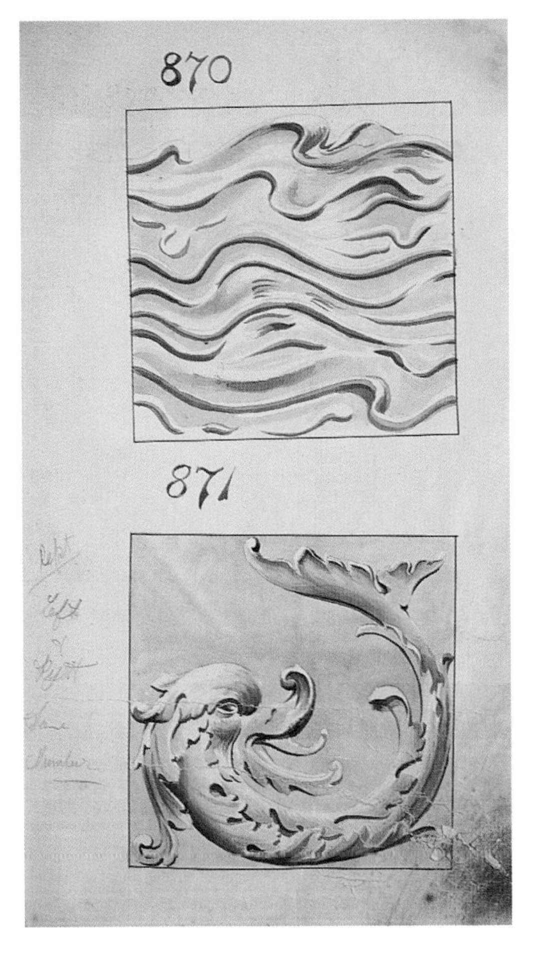

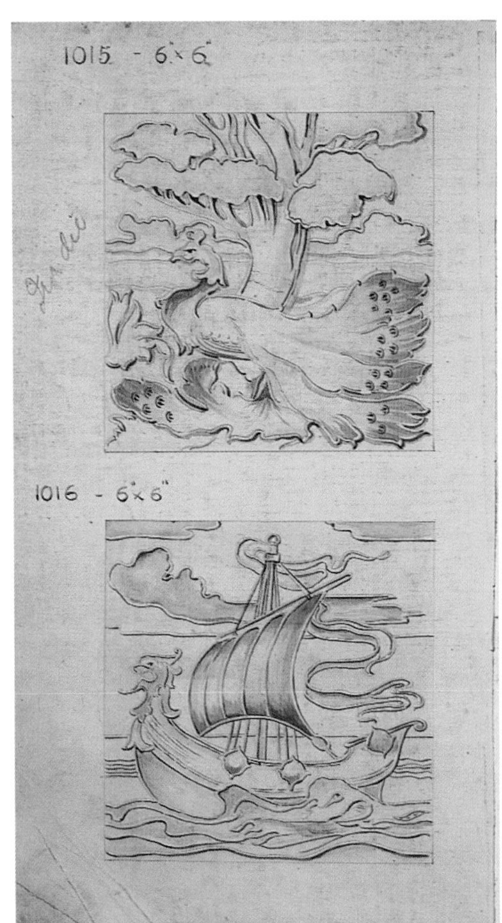

Watercolour designs for moulded and slip trailed faience tiles from a Carter pattern book of about 1900, with two examples of actual slip trailed tiles. The dolphin design, top left, is one of the earliest appearances of this familiar Poole symbol.

Celtic-style garden pot, 'The Rym'. Probably designed by Archibald Knox and from a series of garden wares for Liberty's, 1900-1910. Modelled by James Radley Young and moulded in a buff terracotta body, covered with white tin glaze. Height 11ins (28cm).

James Radley Young at the Hammer Vale Pottery, near Haslemere, Surrey, in about 1906. It was here that he experimented with the styles and decorative techniques that he was to develop fully after his return to Poole.

Photographs taken in the Carter factory in about 1910 showing above, faience workers making architectural mouldings and terracotta garden wares and right, slabbing-up tile panels.

Portrait tiles, plaques and teapot stand of World War I leaders, and of a young child of earlier date. Modelled from photographs in the Tremblay technique pioneered by Wedgwood in the mid 19th century; the surface of the white stoneware moulded tiles was covered with a coloured transparent glaze which settled more thickly into the recessed areas, and gave an accurate likeness to the photographic image. The Kitchener tile was modelled by John Emery, the remainder probably by William Unwin.

Top row, left to right: Joseph Jacques Césaire Joffre, Générale d'Armée; King Albert of the Belgians; Lloyd George; Sir John Grey, Foreign Secretary; Field Marshall Earl Roberts V.C. Bottom row, left to right: Field Marshall Lord Kitchener, with moulded inscription on back - 'Keramic copy of Bassano's portrait of Lord Kitchener by Carters of Poole Nov-1914-'; Field-Marshall Sir John French, Commander of the Expeditionary Force 1914; Evelyn Shepard aged three, with moulded inscription on back 'Carter & Co. Art Potters & Tile Makers, Poole & Hamworthy, Dorset', from a photograph loaned by her parents to Hedley Tilsed who was working for Carter's in 1910. Mr. Shepard was a wheelwright in Wareham where he lived with his family; Admiral Sir John Jellicoe in Captain's full dress uniform, from a portrait taken shortly after the Boxer rebellion in 1901; King George V. Other tiles in this series include a portrait of Gladstone, and one of Charles H. Lyell, Member of Parliament for Dorsetshire Eastern Division, 1904-1910. Lloyd George teapot stand 6ins (15cm).

Portrait plaque of Charles van Raalte, former Mayor of Poole and owner of Brownsea Island in Poole harbour, who died January 1908. Paper label on back 'In Memorium Charles van Raalte - Messrs. Carter of Poole have presented 500 of these Portrait Tiles to The Poole Borough League of Help and the proceeds will be devoted to its Fund'.

Portrait plaque of Dr. Alfred Russel Wallace OM, FRS, 1834-1913. Dr. Wallace was a nineteenth century naturalist, whose researches in Indonesia advanced the theory of evolution. This led to the publication of a joint paper with Darwin which was presented to the Linnean Society in 1858. He lived in Broadstone from 1902 until his death in 1913 when this tile was probably made.

Panel of lustre glazed tiles made for the Carter factory in about 1905, and still on display at the Poole pottery. This highly decorative panel shows the influence of both William de Morgan and the Art Nouveau styles then in vogue.

Red lustre glazed grey stoneware plaque designed and modelled in relief by James Radley Young, 1900-1917. Diameter 17ins (43cm).

Green lustre glazed grey stoneware urn shaped vase. Designed by Owen Carter, mark No.3, 1908. Height 9¼ins (23.5cm). Trustees of the Victoria & Albert Museum.

Lustre glazed grey stoneware vase and bowl, 1915-1918. Decorated with modelled and applied reliefs by Lily Gilham, mark No.5. The lustre glaze is here overfired or insufficiently reduced. Vase height 10¼ins (26cm).

Selection of lustre glazed grey and white stonewares designed by Owen Carter, 1900-1918. The plaque, candlestick and bowl, mark No.5. The moulded vase with gadrooned panels, mark No.3, plus date 1/1904. Tallest vase height 12½ins (32cm).

Selection of lustre glazed grey and white stoneware vases designed by Owen Carter, 1900-1918. From left to right: mark No.4, mark No.3, mark No.3 plus date 1903, mark No.3 plus date 2/1906, mark No.8 and 9, mark No.9, mark No.3 plus date XII/1905. A similar vase is illustrated in *The Art Journal*, 1905. Modelled relief decoration is by Lily Gilham, 1915-1918. Tallest vase height 14½ins (37cm).

Above: Unglazed pottery made from a fairly coarse grey/brown semi-vitrified tile body, thrown on the wheel and painted in Egyptian and Moorish styles with manganese brown oxide. Other colours including blue and yellow were also used, and vessels designed to hold liquids were smear glazed inside. Started by James Radley Young in 1914, the early war-time productions, on which the foot-rim and base was left unturned, were later consolidated into an identifiable range, and first exhibited at the British Industries Fair in 1917. All the pieces in this group are impressed with mark No.5, and two shapes - the tall vase No.124 and bowl No.107, are shown in the Carter Hand-craft Pottery catalogue of 1921. Tallest vase height 13ins (33cm).

Left: unglazed vase designed and thrown on the wheel by James Radley Young, 1915-1921, mark No.5, paintress insignia CF. Height 11ins (28cm).

Vase in buff stoneware covered with white tin glaze. Probably designed and made by Roger Fry and freely painted by Vanessa Bell for the Omega Workshops, 1914-1918. Traces of a painted insignia, probably the Omega symbol. Height 7¾ins (19.5cm). Trustees of the Victoria & Albert Museum.

Ewer and basin, grey stoneware covered with white tin glaze and freely painted in the Bloomsbury style. Probably by Vanessa Bell, 1915-1916. The ewer incised No.9 and the basin incised No.8. Both pieces impressed mark No.5. Ewer height 10ins (25.5cm).

Dish in grey stoneware covered with white tin glaze and freely painted in the Bloomsbury style, probably by James Radley Young, 1914-1921. Diameter 16¾ins (42.5cm).

Belgian Peasant Folk, modelled by Joseph Roelants, white stoneware covered with white tin glaze, mark partly obscured by glaze. Similar figures were shown at the British Industries Fair, 1917. Height of left-hand figure 8¾ins (22cm).

Group of tin glazed pottery, grey/white semi-stoneware body, 1915-1921. Hand painted in geometric designs on a light grey or tinted ground, or in the blue stripe 'Portuguese' style on a brownish earthenware ground. All impressed with mark No.5 except the large jug. The two handled vase is incised No.9 and three pieces are marked with the insignia of the paintress, spill vase MC, teapot CF and jam pot AH (Ann Hatchard). While the colouring of the Portuguese ware was principally a dull blue stripe, other colour schemes were also carried out. Large jug height 9½ins (24cm).

Above: The Carter & Company stand at the British Industries Fair, 1921.

Left: Lion advertising paperweight in buff stoneware. Made throughout the period 1905-1920, also glazed in transparent blue, green and possibly other colours. Given to customers by the firm's representatives as a goodwill token. Length 4½ins (11.5cm).
A lion was also made in an upright seated position, closely based on the lion *séjant* designed by Alfred Stevens (a local man born in Blandford, Dorset) for the forecourt railings of the British Museum in 1852.

Selection of tin glazed pottery, grey/white semi-stoneware body, 1915-1921. Hand painted in decorative panels, geometric designs and floral sprigs on a light grey or tinted ground. The bowl, potpourri and covered jar are impressed with mark No.5. The unmarked fruit plate, made and painted by Joseph Roelants, was given to J.M.J. Dacombe as a token of gratitude for his help in finding accommodation for the Roelants family when they arrived in Bournemouth as refugees from Belgium in late 1914. Mr. Dacombe was a business acquaintance of the Carters and was instrumental in securing employment for Joseph Roelants at Poole Pottery. Potpourri height 10¼ins (26cm).

Selection of tin glazed pottery, grey/white semi-stoneware body, 1915-1921. Hand painted in floral sprigs on a light grey or tinted ground, all impressed with mark No.5, except the two candlesticks, which are unmarked, and tall vase covered with a pale green alumina-type glaze and incised with the mark No.3, 3/1904. This vase was left in the biscuit state until 1917 when it was glazed and painted and given as one of a pair to John Holland in recognition of his 25 years service as a tile decorator. Four pieces are marked with the insignia of the paintress - spill vase CF, bulbous vase and low candlestick MC, and jam pot LG. The modelled and applied relief decoration on the shallow bowl is by Lily Gilham. Tall vase height 13¾ins (35cm).

Chapter Two

Transitional Wares of the Early 1920s

Selection of grey semi-stonewares, 1921-1922, showing continuity with the designs of James Radley Young painted on the unfired glaze. The early C.S.A. wares were left with an unglazed base until sometime in 1922 when a clear transparent glaze was first applied.
Left to right: jug 303/GL, painted by Ethel Barratt, mark No.10; jug T306/CX, painted by Ann Hatchard, mark No.10, plus FM incised (possibly made for Fortnum & Mason - a known early customer); vase D336/CT, mark No.10, G incised. A similar vase was shown in the first C.S.A. London exhibition held at Regent House, Kingsway, and illustrated in *The Pottery Gazette*, February 1st, 1922; lamp vase, mark No.10; vase 334/EA, mark No.11. This style of decoration is thought to have originated with the semi-matt green glazed ware named 'Monastic', made by Carters Hand-craft Pottery and shown at the British Industries Fair in 1920; jug B401/BQ, painted by Ethel Barratt, mark No.10, B-I-F incised; vase 353/BU, mark No.11; vase 336/HV, painted by Ethel Barratt, mark No.11. The lamp vase height 11ins (28cm).

The years that followed the end of the First World War were a period of transition for Carter & Co. A growing reputation lead to an increased demand for the ranges of decorative pottery developed by Owen Carter and James Radley Young, and so a programme of expansion was started. Apart from increasing the number of their retail outlets and establishing a showroom and shop, Carters also began to show their decorative wares regularly at the British Industries Fairs and other trade events. Reports in *The Pottery Gazette* and other journals were often favourable, referring to 'quaint and homely' shapes and 'appropriately simple' decorations, along with 'glistening lustre vases'. These reports, for the Fairs held in 1917, 1918 and 1920, also indicate the range of Carter's production, which included tiling in Dutch styles, 'admirable statuettes', vases for electric standards, candlesticks, the Portuguese striped wares, garden pottery and even dog troughs. The writers also commented on the traditional inspiration for both matt and glazed wares, mentioning Greek, Moorish, Egyptian, Eastern, Antique and Anglo-Dutch styles. Progress was hindered by the sudden death of Owen Carter in 1919, with the management of the company falling upon the shoulders of his brother Charles, a man lacking Owen's creative flair but, despite this setback, Carters issued their first Handcraft Pottery catalogue in 1920. Written by the critic Joseph Thorp and with illustrations of simple sprigged, banded and striped wares in both glazed and unglazed styles, this also included a clear statement of intent: 'In our Handcraft Pottery we aim at achieving simplicity of shape and decoration, and at giving individuality to each pot. In no case are the shapes moulded, but they are each thrown by the potter, no two pieces being identically the same; even when pots are somewhat similar in shape the decoration is varied, and all the designs are hand-painted.' A second catalogue, with a simpler text and more illustrations of a greater variety of ware, was issued in 1921, and the same year Carters had a notably impressive stand at the British Industries Fair. Aware of the need for dynamic leadership if the pottery was to maintain its impetus, Charles Carter discussed the matter with Harold Stabler, designer, artist and silversmith, and husband of the sculptor and potter Phoebe Stabler. It was Harold Stabler who encouraged the Stoke-on-Trent born potter John Adams to come to Poole and step into the gap. For Adams it was a new and exciting challenge after a period spent teaching in South Africa, and so he moved to Dorset with his wife Truda, herself an artist and designer, to form a new partnership with Carter and the Stablers. In 1921 Carter, Stabler & Adams was formed as a new company, a subsidiary of Carter & Co, to develop and expand the foundation laid down by Owen Carter and James Radley Young.

Selection of red bodied earthenwares, 1922-24. 'Portuguese' stripe and geometric border designs originated by James Radley Young, modified by Truda Adams and hand painted on the grey glaze. Left to right: vase 348/R, mark No.11; vase 462/BV, mark No.15; vase 337/PX, mark No.11; vase 346/EO, painted by Ruth Pavely, mark No.15; vase 206/LL, painted by Ethel Barratt, mark No.15; plate 282/FG, painted by Ethel Barratt, mark No.15; bowl 444/CA, painted by Ethel Barratt, mark No.15. Largest vase height 10½ins (26.5cm).

Selection of grey semi-stonewares, 1921-1922, with small and medium sized sprigs, hand painted on the grey glaze. Left to right: covered jar T371/FJ, pattern designed by Cissie Collett, paintress insignia CK, mark No.10; vase 202/HJ, pattern designed by Cissie Collett, painted by Ann Hatchard, mark No.11; miniature pot 583/B; vase 335/H, pattern designed by Cissie Collett, mark No.11; jug 303/AR, pattern designed by Erna Manners, painted by Ethel Barratt, mark No.11, a similar jug was illustrated in *The Studio Year Book of Decorative Art*, 1922; fruit stand 464/AM, fuchsia pattern designed by Erna Manners, painted by Ethel Barratt. Jug height 7½ins (19cm).

Selection of unglazed ware, 1921 to the early 1930s. Hand painted with brown and terracotta slips on a grey/brown high-fired biscuit, and smear glazed inside. The designs, originating from those of James Radley Young, 1914-1921, in most cases have been modified by Truda Adams, the painting becoming smoother and more refined. Left to right: pot 570/EL, mark No.14; jug 484/VX, mark No.11; plant pot 922/SD. The pattern, which includes gold, was painted by Ruth Pavely, mark No.21. A note in the pattern book states 'Reserved for Liberty's'; jug 944/HZ, painted by Ruth Pavely, mark No.21; vase 337/HI, painted by Lily Pedley, mark No.21; jug 484/UW, painted by Hilda Trim, mark No.21. Largest jug height 14½ins (37cm).

Interior of bowl of fruit stand 464/AM showing the fuchsia pattern designed by Erna Manners and painted by Ethel Barratt, 1921-1922. Diameter 6½ins (16.5cm).
Since 1990, /ED, /EE, /YO, and similar patterns designed by Truda Adams, have been wrongly described as fuchsia in sale catalogues and other literature. The Erna Manners pattern /AM is the only design with the fuchsia name ever used at the Poole factory.

Selection of red bodied earthenwares, 1922-1924, with simple or small sprig patterns. Left to right: vase 724/H, pattern designed by Cissie Collett and painted on grey glaze by Ruth Pavely, mark No.15; spill vase 206/YY, pattern designed by Truda Adams and painted on clear glaze over white slip by Ruth Pavely, mark No.11; vase 755/TM, painted on grey glaze by Ethel Barratt, mark No.15; spill vase 207/WT, painted on clear glaze over white slip by Gertie Warren, mark No.11; spill vase 205/FE, pattern designed by Cissie Collett and painted on grey glaze by Lily Pedley, mark No.11. Largest spill vase height 10ins (25.5cm).

CHAPTER THREE

Carter, Stabler & Adams in the Mid 1920s

The three partner directors in the new company were Charles Carter's son Cyril, whose enthusiasm and management skills were a firm foundation for rapid growth, John Adams, officially Managing Director but really responsible for design and technical development and Harold Stabler, who acted as an external design consultant. Born in Stoke-on-Trent, John Adams had spent his early life in the ceramic industry there before moving to South Africa to become Head of the Technical College School of Art in Durban. An inspired shape designer, particularly of tablewares, and a great glaze technician, Adams was largely responsible for the pottery's successful and rapid development through the 1920s and 1930s. In fact, pattern and, to a much lesser extent, shape design was from the start largely in the hands of Truda Adams who, like her husband, had been trained at the Royal College of Art in London. It was her vibrant and colourful style, with its hints of the Ballets Russes, French Art Deco and contemporary abstraction, that made Poole pottery so distinctive, along with similar work by her colleagues such as Erna Manners, Minnie McLeish and others. The designs were interpreted on the pots by skilled paintresses such as Ann Hatchard, Cissie Collett, Margaret Holder and Ruth Pavely, key figures in a steadily expanding team well able to make the most of a steady pattern of technical improvement. The most important of these was the change, in 1922, to a red earthenware body matched with a semi-matt grey glaze. Two years later this was further improved by the use of a white slip ground with a semi-matt clear glaze. This remained the standard body at the pottery until 1934, when the red earthenware was replaced by white, used until 1937 with a pink slip and a semi-matt white glaze, and then with the white glaze alone. These later changes were probably inspired by the increasing emphasis on tableware production, for which the red body was unsuitable. The rapid success of the new Carter, Stabler & Adams partnership was underlined by exhibitions and by frequent appearances of their products in publications such as *The Pottery Gazette* and *The Studio Year Book of the Decorative Arts*. The partnership was, in effect, launched by an exhibition held early in October 1921 at Regent House, Kingsway, London, well received by *The Pottery Gazette*: 'The decorations are for the most part simple, sound and practical, thoroughly befitting the shapes to which they are applied... the ingenious juxtaposition of one or two simple colours...' The Poole stand at the British Industries Fair in 1922 was also impressive, a pattern that was maintained through the 1920s, with highlights being the displays at the British Empire Exhibition at Wembley in 1924, the Exposition Internationale des Arts Decoratifs et Industriels, held in Paris in 1925 and the Exhibition of Industrial Art, Leipzig, 1927. By this time, Poole had established its reputation as one of Britain's leading artistic potteries with a product range synonymous with decorative modernism, and with a distinctive hand-painted style applied equally successfully to ornaments and fancies, tablewares, tiles and nursery wares.

Red bodied earthenware, 1925-1934. Vase 203/NY, with the grape pattern designed by Erna Manners in 1921 and painted on clear glaze over white slip by Margaret Holder, mark No.21. Height 8¼ins (21cm). A similar vase was shown at an exhibition of modern pottery at the Beaux Arts Gallery, Old Bond Street, London, in October 1923, and illustrated in *The Pottery Gazette*, November 1, 1923, and in *The Studio Year Book of Decorative Art*, 1924.

Selection of red bodied earthenwares, 1925-1934, with the grape pattern designed by Erna Manners in 1921, modified and adapted by Truda Adams, and hand painted on clear glaze over white slip. Left to right:vase 985/TR, mark No.21; candlestick 931/TR, painted by Nellie Bishton, mark No.11; vase 424/TR, painted by Ruth Pavely, mark No.21. Larger vase height 7¼ins (18.5cm).

Selection of red bodied earthenwares, with patterns designed by Truda Adams and hand painted on clear glaze over white slip.
Left to right: vase 594/ED, painted by Marian Heath, 1927-1934, mark No.21; fruit dish 495/EE, painted by Eileen Prangnell, 1926-1934, mark No.21; biscuit barrel 230/ED, painted by Hilda Hampton, 1930-1934, mark No.28; vase 212/XE, painted by Ann Hatchard, 1924 or later, mark No.11 and painted white slip spot; cake basket 274/EE, painted by Ruth Pavely, 1925-34, mark No.21; fruit stand 464/YO, painted by Ann Hatchard, 1924-1934, mark No.19; vase 968/YO, painted by Iris Skinner, 1930-1934, mark No.21. Largest vase height 10½ins (26.5cm).
This group of wares illustrates the use of alternative pattern codes when an original design is modified and adapted to different shapes. Since 1990, these patterns have been wrongly described as fuchsia. The only Poole fuchsia pattern is the Erna Manners /AM design, shown on page 32.

Red bodied earthenwares: dish 528/SL, pattern designed by Truda Adams and painted on clear glaze over white slip by Mary Brown, 1928-1934, mark No.21; dish 666/OF, pattern designed by Erna Manners in 1921 and painted on grey glaze by Ann Hatchard, 1922-1924, mark No.11. Diameter 14½ins (37cm).

Red earthenwares, 1922-1924, with patterns designed by Truda Adams and hand painted on grey glaze: vase 715/OR, painted by Gertie Warren, mark No.15. A similar vase was illustrated in *The Studio Year Book of Decorative Art*, 1924; floating bowl 492/JL, painted by Ann Hatchard, mark No.11. Vase height 8½ins (21.5cm).

Red bodied earthenwares, 1924 or later, with patterns designed by Truda Adams and hand painted on clear glaze over white slip. Left to right: fruit plate 495/RH, painted by Ann Hatchard, mark No.11. A similar plate was shown in the Ideal Home Exhibition, 1927; floating bowl 493/OM/ON, painted by Margaret Holder, mark No.11; fruit plate 495/ZU, painted by Ethel Barratt, mark No.11. Floating bowl diameter 14ins (35.5cm).

Group of wares with patterns by three designers. Left to right: red earthenware plate 413/NN with pattern designed by Truda Carter and painted on clear glaze over white slip by Margaret Holder, 1930-1934, mark No.28 and hexagon impressed; red earthenware jam pot 286/XD with the pattern Robin in the Rain designed by Minnie McLeish and painted on clear glaze over white slip by Gertie Warren, 1924-1927, mark No.11 and painted white slip spot; white earthenware dish 909/PL with pattern designed by Truda Carter and painted on white glaze by Ruth Pavely, 1934-1937, mark No.29; red earthenware bowl 296/BG with pattern Cocky Ollie Bird (a name used only in the factory) designed by Truda Adams and painted on clear glaze over white slip by Ruth Pavely, 1930-1934, mark No.28. The same pattern painted on plate D282, with a different border, was illustrated in *Design in Modern Industry*, the Year Book of the Design and Industries Association, 1922; red earthenware plate 694/XO with pattern designed by John Adams and painted on clear glaze over white slip by Ann Hatchard about 1924, mark No.11 and painted white slip spot. Illustrated in *The Studio Year Book of Decorative Art*, 1923. Diamater of large dish 10¾ins (27.5cm)..

Pages from a Poole factory pattern book of the 1920s showing an original version of the grape pattern, signed by Erna Manners and dated 1921, Bloomsbury style designs adapted by Truda Adams, a version of the deer pattern, and designs showing Truda Adams' development of abstract and stylised floral patterns.

Display of Poole pottery shown at Regent House, Kingsway, London, in October 1921.

Red earthenware dish 528/VU, the Persian Deer, designed by Truda Adams and painted on clear glaze over white slip by Gertie Warren, 1924-1927, mark No.11, and painted white slip spot. Diameter 14¾ins (37.5cm). A similar dish was shown in the British Empire Exhibition, Wembley, 1924, the International Exhibition of Modern, Decorative and Industrial Arts, Paris, 1925, the Ideal Home Exhibition, 1927 and the Exhibition of Industrial Art, Leipzig, 1927.

Red earthenware plate 694/SG, handpainted on the grey glaze, 1923-1924, mark No.11. An early example of tableware, with a pattern book notation 'Pattern reserved to Mrs Grace Wood New York'. Grey semi-stoneware vase D216/JQ, handpainted on the grey glaze by Ernest Banten, 1921, mark No.10, S incised. Ernest Banten is the only male painter whose mark has been identified. It is known however that E.E. Stickland, a Carter & Co. tile artist who transferred briefly to the pottery in 1929, Leslie Elsden and a younger member of the Way family, also painted pots in the 1920s, but not on piecework as was the case with the girls.

POTTERY—BRITISH

I

II

III

IV

V

VI

An illustration from *The Studio Year Book*, 1924, showing a range of Poole pottery including a slipware dish (bottom row, centre).

Chapter Four

Harold and Phoebe Stabler

Harold Stabler in his studio, mid 1930s. The hare model, far right on shelf, was the mascot of London's country buses and was specially made for the London Passenger Transport Board.

Phoebe Stabler in her garden at Hammersmith. The figure of a Piping Boy and Picardy Peasant were modelled by her and produced at Poole in the early 1920s.

The friendship between the Carters and Harold and Phoebe Stabler, which probably started in 1918, proved to be crucial to the subsequent history of the Poole pottery. Born in 1872 in Westmorland, Harold Stabler trained initially as a wood and stone carver, and then as a metal worker and silversmith In 1898 he became director of the Keswick School of Art, the start of a long career in art education, notably as Head of the Arts and Crafts Department at the Sir John Cass Institute in London, from 1907 to 1937. In 1906 he married Phoebe McLeish, a sculptor and designer, and from then on the couple were regular exhibitors at the Royal Academy, the Arts and Crafts Exhibition Society and similar institutions, with a growing reputation for work in silver, bronze and other metals, stone-carving and enamels. From about 1911, Mrs. Stabler developed a series of pottery figures with richly coloured glazes, fired first in a commercial London pottery and then in a kiln in their Hammersmith garden. First exhibited in 1912 these models, which included the Lavender Woman, Picardy Peasants, Bath Towel and Children with Bull, were subsequently produced under licence by a number of manufacturers, including Royal Doulton, Royal Worcester and the Ashtead Pottery. However, the range reached its full development at Poole in the early 1920s, when the Stabler models associated the pottery firmly with the revival of interest in ceramic sculpture. Some of these figures were also independently made in larger sizes in lead, cement and stone as garden sculptures. Figures and models apart, the Stablers played a formative role in the development of the distinctive styles of Poole pottery in the 1920s and 1930s, their contributions including large scale architectural work, such as the war memorials for Durban and Rugby School, and the series of roundels, all in richly coloured faience, the development of a new range of terracotta and glazed garden ornaments, a series of stylish Art Deco ornaments and vases to show off John Adams' monochrome glazes and the first characteristic Poole tableware range. Equally important was their influence in other areas. They introduced other designers to the pottery, notably Dora Batty, Phoebe's sister Minnie McLeish and, most important of all, John and Truda Adams. Harold Stabler, long a member of the Art Workers Guild, was also a founder member of the British Institute of Industrial Art and was on the first council of the Design and Industries Association when it was founded in 1915. It was through channels such as these that he was able to bring the pottery to the attention of figures and organisations such as Ambrose Heal, Frank Pick of London Underground and W. H. Smith, and to place it and its products in the forefront of modern industrial design in Britain.

The Rugby School War Memorial, designed by Harold and Phoebe Stabler and made in Della Robbia ware, 1922.

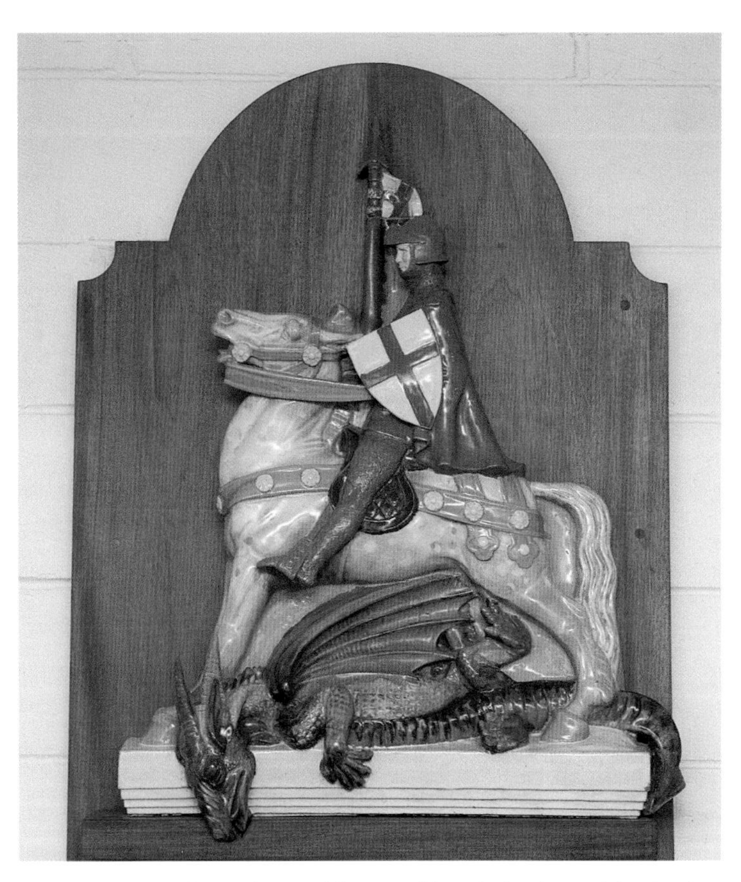

The St. George figure designed by Harold and Phoebe Stabler for the Rugby Memorial.

The Durban War Memorial, in Della Robbia ware, designed by H.L.G. Pilkington and modelled by Harold Stabler, 1925, was among the most important examples of architectural pottery made at Poole.

Group of faience panels modelled by Harold and Phoebe Stabler and displayed in the British Empire Exhibition, Wembley, 1924. Subsequently installed in the mortuary chapel at the Mary Abbots Kensington Infirmary but returned to Poole and re-erected in 1989 prior to the redevelopment of the Kensington site.

The Bull designed by Harold and Phoebe Stabler in 1914. Buff stoneware clay, press moulded, mark No.11. HAROLD & PHOEBE STABLER incised on side of base. Made at Poole from 1922 to the early 1930s. Height 13ins (33cm).
This figure was exhibited in the Arts and Crafts Society's exhibitions at the Royal Academy in 1916 and 1924, the British Industries Fair in 1923, the International Exhibition of Modern, Decorative and Industrial Arts, Paris, 1925, and the Mansard Gallery exhibition, Heal & Son, 1925. The Bull was also featured in a painting by H. Davis Richter, RI, ROI, RBC, for one of the dining rooms in the restaurant on C deck of the Cunard liner Queen Mary, and illustrated in the souvenir brochure for the ship's launching ceremony.

The Piping Boy designed by Phoebe Stabler, 1914-1918. Buff stoneware clay, press moulded, mark PHOEBE STABLER. Height 14¾ins (37.5cm). Made at Poole from about 1920 to the early 1930s. Widely exhibited in the early 1920s, this popular figure was made in a number of sizes, materials and finishes. Trustees of the Victoria & Albert Museum.

Left and centre: Picardy Peasants designed by Phoebe Stabler in 1911. Buff stoneware clay, press moulded, mark No.11. PHOEBE STABLER impressed on side of base (woman only). Made at Poole from 1922 to the early 1930s. Second left: The Lavendar Woman designed by Phoebe Stabler, 1911. Buff stoneware clay, press moulded mark No.11. Made at Poole from 1922 to the early 1930s. These popular figures were widely shown at Arts and Crafts Society exhibitions, at British Industry Fairs, at Wembley in 1924 and at Industrial Art Exhibitions at the Victoria & Albert Museum. Both were also issued in their HN figure series by Royal Doulton - Picardy Peasants from 1913 to 1938, and Lavender Woman from 1913 to 1936 - in a number of colour variations and with the title Madonna of the Square. Far right: the Bath Towel, two figures designed by Phoebe Stabler in about 1922. Buff stoneware clay, press moulded, mark No.11. Figures in a similar style were produced at the same time from Stabler models by the Ashtead Pottery, Surrey. Picardy Peasant woman height 10¼ins (26cm).

Harpy Eagle designed by Harold Stabler, 1916. Buff stoneware clay, press moulded, mark No.12. HAROLD STABLER 1916 incised on side of base. Height 26ins (66.5cm). Made at Poole from about 1924 to the early 1930s. A similar figure was shown in the International Exhibition of Modern, Decorative and Industrial Arts, Paris, 1925. Trustees of the Victoria & Albert Museum.

The Piping Fawn, a roundel designed by Phoebe Stabler, 1914. Buff stoneware clay, press moulded, mark H.S.P. LONDON impressed within a rectangle with an image of Hammersmith Bridge (Harold and Phoebe Stabler's personal backstamp). PHOEBE STABLER 1914 incised on front. Diameter 15ins (38cm). Made at Poole from about 1920 to the early 1930s, in plain and coloured glazes. A similar roundel in lead was shown in the Arts and Crafts Society's exhibition at the Royal Academy, 1916 and 1920, in pottery. Trustees of the Victoria & Albert Museum.

Shy, designed by Phoebe Stabler, 1914-1918. Buff stoneware clay, press moulded, mark PHOEBE STABLER impressed. Height 15¼ins (39cm). Possibly fired at Poole, 1920-1921 but not shown in Carter, Stabler & Adams catalogues. Trustees of the Victoria & Albert Museum.

Bird on Stump. Buff stoneware clay, press moulded, mark No.11. Printed in black ink 'original model designed and executed by Harold Stabler POOLE 1932'. Height 6ins (15cm).

The Buster Girl, by Phoebe Stabler, introduced about 1922. Buff stoneware clay, press moulded, mark No.11. PHOEBE STABLER incised on side of base. Centre: Fighting Cock, designed by Harold Stabler, 1923-1924. Buff stoneware clay, press moulded, mark No.11. This figure was later issued in the slip cast terracotta stoneware body. Right: the Buster Boy, designed originally by Phoebe Stabler in 1916 and introduced in about 1921. Buff stoneware clay, press moulded, mark No.11. Phoebe Stabler incised on side of base. Height of Fighting Cock 7½ins (19cm).

The Galleon, designed by Harold Stabler about 1925. Red faience architectural ware. Height 20ins (51cm).This model was adopted as an unofficial symbol of the pottery and featured at exhibitions, and in catalogues and advertisements. As a result, it was widely exhibited in the 1920s and 1930s and was made in a number of sizes and versions. Named THE HARRY PAGE along the bows, this name is derived from that of Henry Paye who is said to have been a local pirate but held high office under the Crown. See Ship Plates page 59.

Medallion No.574/MJ, designed by Harold Stabler about 1921. Spring flowers in glazed Della Robbia colours on buff terracotta. Mark HS moulded. Height 14½ins (37cm). A companion piece, comprising summer flowers in a basket, was also made.

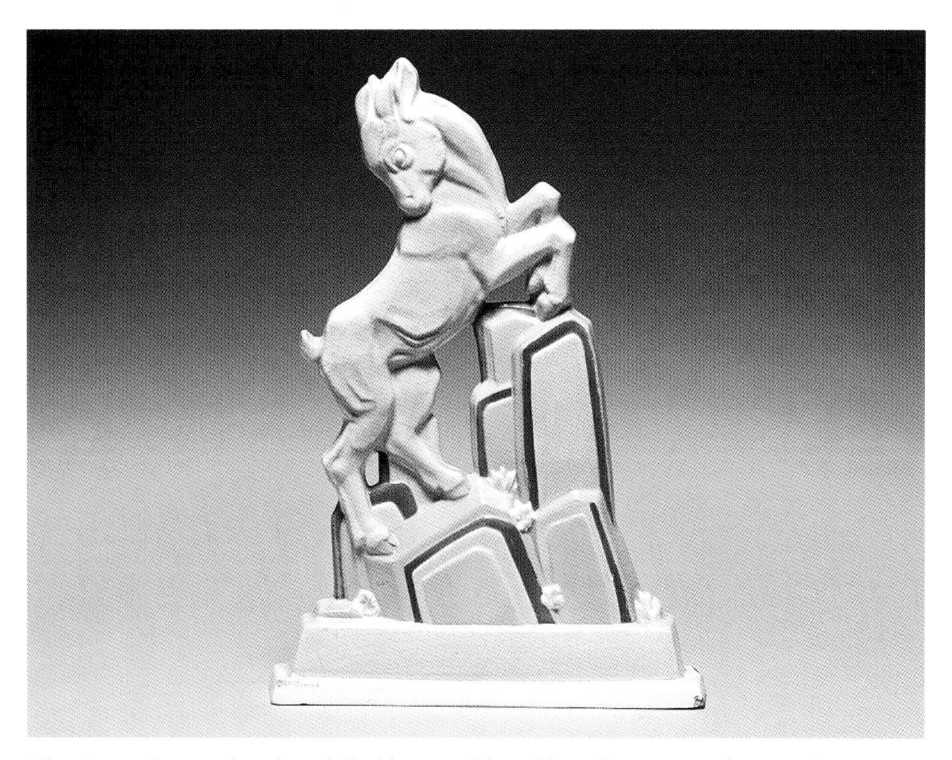

The Goat, designed and modelled by Harold Stabler. Slip cast in white earthenware, mark No.11 and H.S. moulded. Height 16ins (40.5cm). The companion figure, the Bear, can be seen on the right.

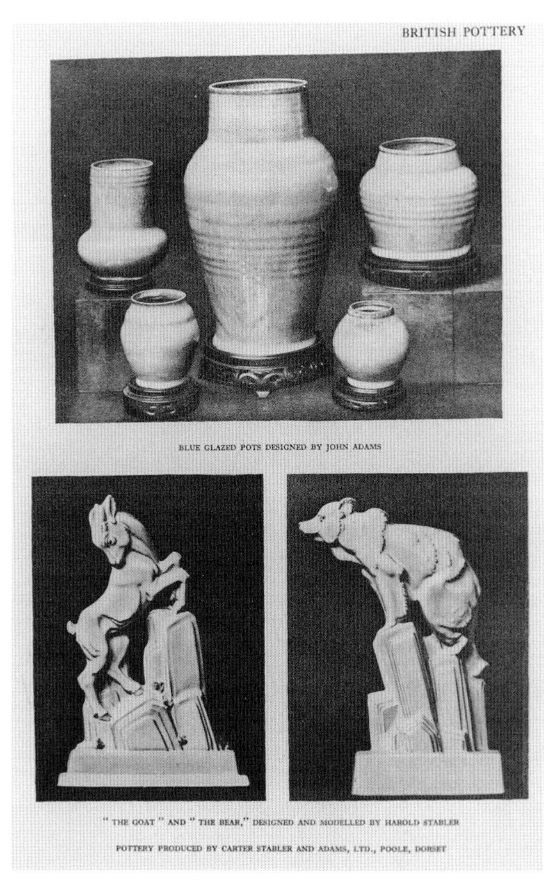

BRITISH POTTERY

BLUE GLAZED POTS DESIGNED BY JOHN ADAMS

"THE GOAT" AND "THE BEAR," DESIGNED AND MODELLED BY HAROLD STABLER

POTTERY PRODUCED BY CARTER STABLER AND ADAMS, LTD., POOLE, DORSET

Illustration from *The Studio Year Book*, 1927, showing Harold Stabler's Goat and Bear figures, with blue glazed pots by John Adams.

Studland tea and coffee ware designed by Harold Stabler, 1930, with apple green and sapphire blue glazes by John Adams. The patterned version, GPA, designed by Truda Carter and painted by Eileen Prangnell, mark No.19. Height of coffee pot $6^1/_2$ins (16.5cm). The Studland shape, which included dinner ware, was also made in other glazes and patterns. A coffee set was shown in The Thirties exhibition at the Hayward Gallery in 1979 and was illustrated in the catalogue.

Vase 865 designed by Harold Stabler about 1925, slip cast white earthenware covered with tangerine re-active glaze, mark CSA POOLE incised. Vases 811, designed by John Adams about 1925, slip cast white earthenware covered with tangerine re-active and white vellum glazes, mark No.21. Height $6^3/_4$ins (17cm).

Rabbit book-ends and eagle, designed by Harold Stabler in about 1930. Slip cast white earthenware covered with vellum white glaze, mark No.11. Height of eagle $7^1/_4$ins (18.5cm).

A page from Harold Stabler's sketch book, about 1925.

Slip cast angular and faceted shapes in white earthenware, designed by Harold Stabler, 1925-1926. Left to right: bowl 874 covered with Zulu black vellum glaze, mark No.19; electric lamp standard covered with orange (uranium) glaze, mark No.23; vase 199 covered with orange (uranium) glaze, mark No.14, 1930-1932. Probably designed by John Adams who would also have developed the specialist glazes used on these wares; bowl 838 in tangerine re-active glaze, mark No.11. Height of lamp $14^3/_4$ins (37.5cm).

The Francis Cup, designed by Harold Stabler in 1927 for a Cambridge College, showing the clear links between Stabler's metal work and his designs for Poole.

CHAPTER FIVE

Carter, Stabler & Adams in the Late 1920s

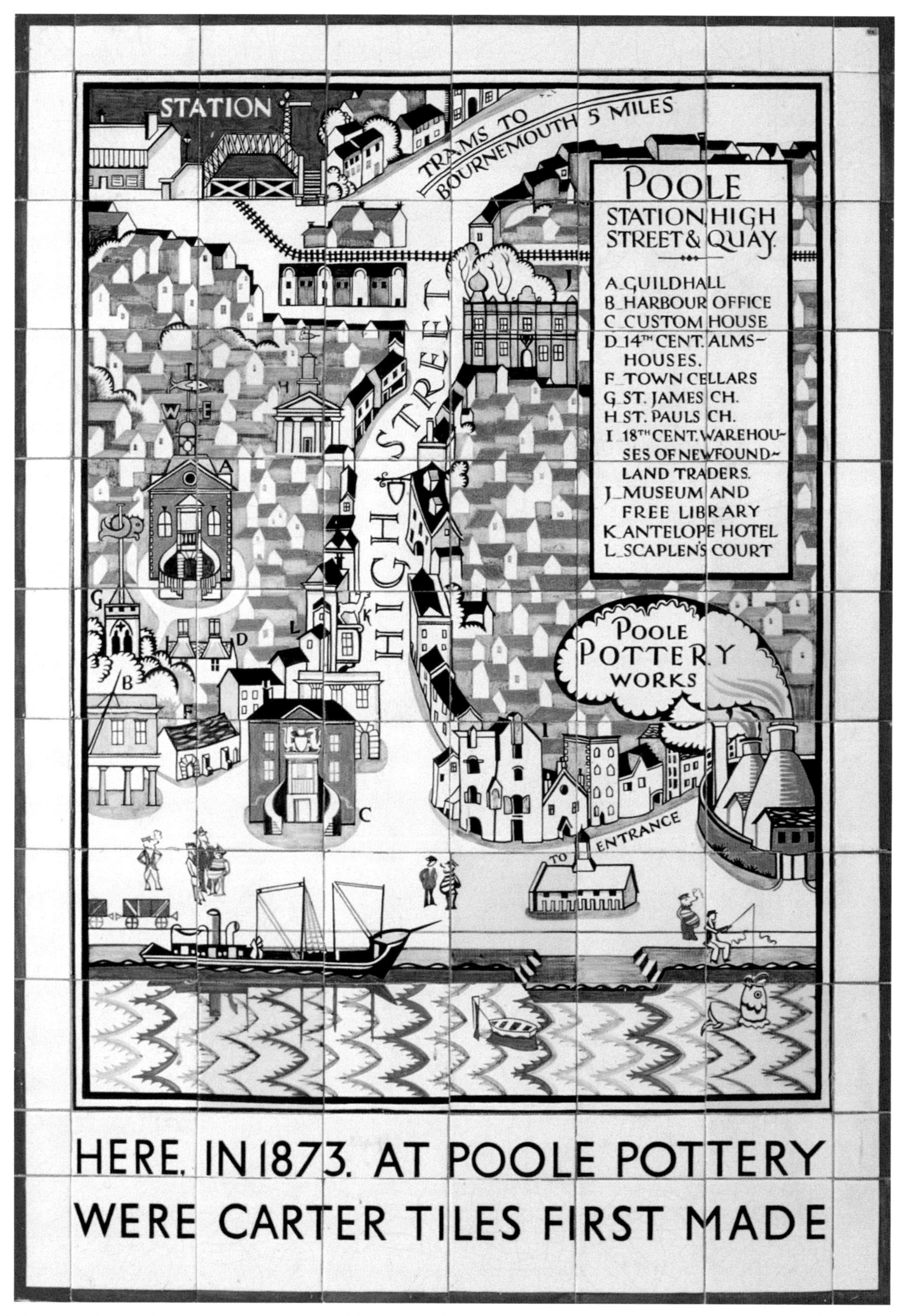

Tile panel, c1930, painted with the map of Poole designed by Edward Bawden, and first used in the promotional brochure, *Pottery Making at Poole*, designed by him and printed at the Curwen Press. First issued in about 1922, this was revised and repeated at least twice. Sited for many years on the staircase leading to the pottery showroom and now in the factory museum. A similar tile panel in which a bus was illustrated was formerly to be seen in the Bournemouth bus station at the departure point for Poole.

Poole paintresses by the sea.
Left: Ann Hatchard, Eileen Prangnell, Irene Hayes, Marjorie Batt and Gertie Warren, in 1927; right: Marjorie Cryer, Ruth Gough, Hilda Hampton, Lily Pedley, Marian Heath, Doris Marshall, Mary Brown and Ruby Cooper, in 1930.

Following their success at Paris in 1925 where they were awarded a Diploma of Honour, Carter, Stabler & Adams developed further their policy of using exhibitions to promote their products. Displays at Heal's Mansard Gallery and regular trade shows at the Gieve Gallery in Old Bond Street and elsewhere enhanced the pottery's reputation for decorative hand-painting and a distinctive style that matched individuality with quantity production. The design principles behind the ware were underlined by a critic writing in *The Pottery Gazette* in 1927: 'The idea of the firm seems to be not to copy Staffordshire, but to get just as far away from the Staffordshire productions as might be implied by the distance which geographically separates Staffordshire from Dorset. The Poole productions are none the worse for this.' Another report the same year referred to the newly issued catalogue No.5: 'it has a distinct "Poole" appearance, a stamp of the craftsman's genius.' The factory's reputation for style and originality was also reflected by its literature and publicity material. From the mid 1920s Poole advertisements adopt a modern but elegant graphic style with the extensive use of a hand-drawn letterform along with simple woodcut-style illustrations. Some of these were drawn by Edward Bawden, the most important of a number of artists associated with Poole during this period. Apart from his graphic work, seen at its best in the little booklet entitled *Pottery Making at Poole*, Bawden also designed ranges of tiles. Others artists making their mark included the sculptor, Harold Brownsword and the artist, Olive Bourne, famous for her stylised figures and portraits. Best known is the Leipzig Girl design, taking its name from the Leipzig International Exhibition of 1927, where Poole had an impressive display. Events such as these underlined the important role played by Cyril Carter in establishing, and maintaining the Poole reputation, via bodies such as The Design and Industries Association, and via his many contacts in the design and retail worlds. However, the key figures remained John Adams, now developing further his Chinese and Persian Blue and other monochrome glazes, probably the tangerine and mirror black, and pushing the pottery steadily towards tablewares, and his former wife, Truda, now married to Cyril Carter, whose floral designs were becoming increasingly abstract and vibrant. Under her direction, Poole was moving far closer towards a definite association with Art Deco styles than most other British potteries, a trend made clear in the lavish 1930 catalogue, the final, and most comprehensive of the series of illustrated booklets that had spanned the 1920s. Critics were not slow to appreciate this. Poole products appeared with increasing frequency in *The Studio Year Books of Decorative Arts* and similar, modern-minded publications. A report in *The Pottery Gazette* in April 1929 summarised the company's achievements: '...its object is to bridge the gulf that lies between the productions of the studio potter and the mass-production factories. A complete range of samples needs to be seen to appreciate what has been achieved within the last generation at the Poole Pottery; better still, a visit to the pottery, its designing rooms and decorating shops, affords most convincing testimony of the freshness of outlook which actuates the firm's principals and workers.' This freshness took a number of forms, from the colourful modernism of Truda Carter's designs, drawing increasingly upon the styles and patterns of French Art Deco, to the angular simplicity of Harold Stabler's new vases, complemented by Adams' new glazes. The popularity of the Poole styles, which seemed to satisfy many sections of the market, brought new paintresses to the decorating shops. Many of these girls, whose skills were regularly on display to the increasing number of visitors to the pottery, were encouraged to monogram their work. This practice, by now a well-established Poole tradition, has given the pottery a lasting appeal to generations of collectors.

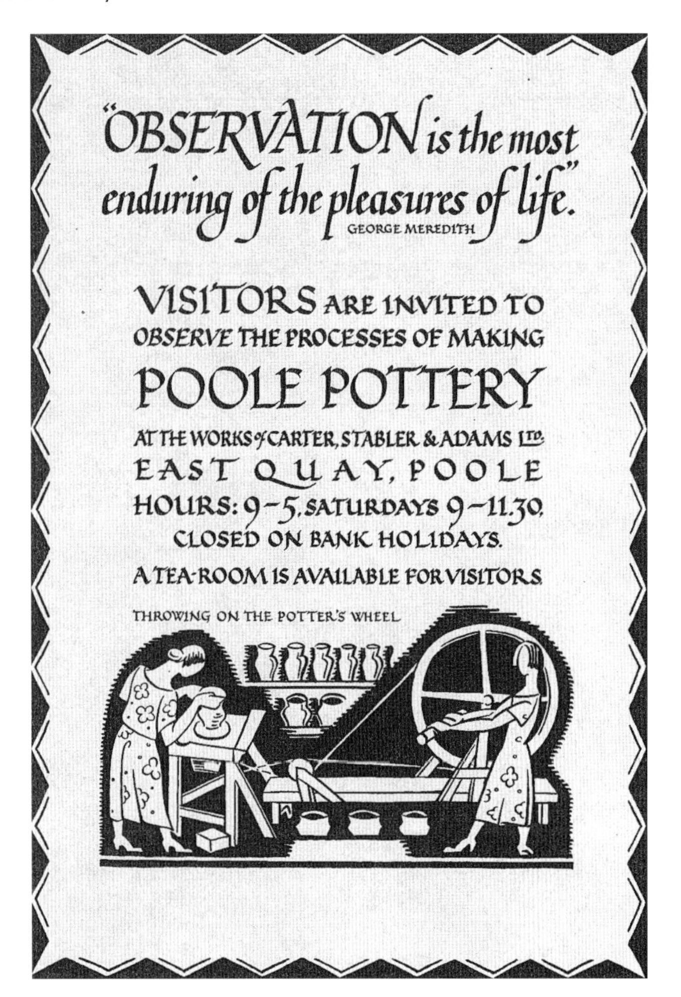

Advertisements and other promotional literature issued by Carter, Stabler & Adams during the 1920s and early 1930s showed a clear typographic house style and often featured charming woodcut-style illustrations by Edward Bawden and other artists. The colour illustration is from the back cover of a booklet promoting holidays in the Poole region.

INFALLIBLE JUDGMENT
may not always be possessed by the adjudicators at international exhibitions, so modesty forbids us to be unduly elated by the success of POOLE POTTERY at the greatest Decorative Art Exhibition of modern times held at Paris, April-November, 1925. We are much more concerned that the new ideas now being worked out shall surpass the work already done. BUT IT IS NONE THE LESS GRATIFYING that the International Jury at the
EXPOSITION DES ARTS DECORATIFS
at Paris awarded Poole Pottery a Diplôme d'Honneur and a gold medal, while those associated with the art and technical sides of the work received a
DIPLOME D'HONNEUR
A GOLD MEDAL
A SILVER MEDAL AND
A BRONZE MEDAL

CARTER, STABLER & ADAMS, LTD
POTTERS · POOLE · DORSET

Above: part of the Poole display at the Paris exhibition of 1925, illustrated in *The Pottery Gazette*, September 1925.
Left: advertisement in characteristic style issued by Carter, Stabler & Adams to celebrate their success at the Paris exhibition of 1925.

Below: exhibition of Poole pottery at the Gieve Gallery, Old Bond Street, London, September 1926.

Red bodied earthenwares, 1926-1930, with patterns designed by Truda Adams and hand painted on clear glaze over white slip. Left to right: vase 684/ZW, painted by Truda Rivers, mark No.21. A similar vase was shown in the Gieve Gallery exhibition, London, 1926, and at the Ideal Home Exhibition, 1927; vase 948/LE painted by Mary Brown, mark No.21. *The Pottery Gazette*, March 1, 1928, described this pattern as 'a freely painted design in the 18th century Strasburg manner, and with a lovely vellum-like glazed surface'; vase 684/YT, painted by Ruth Pavely, mark No.14. Shown in the Ideal Home Exhibition, 1927. Tallest vase height 16½ins (42cm).

Red bodied earthenwares, 1927-1930, with patterns designed by Truda Adams, hand painted on clear glaze over white slip: vase 947/JC, mark No.21; plate 283/JC, mark No.28. Vase height 12ins (30.5cm). The related pattern on the plate is also painted on the reverse side of the vase.

Carter & Company stand at the Building Trades Exhibition, 1928, with a mosaic version of the Truda Adams/JC pattern and a Harold Stabler galleon.

Red earthenware vase 429, 1922-1924, peacock pattern designed and painted on grey glaze by Truda Adams, mark No.11. Height 10½ins (26.5cm).

Vase 621/NT, red earthenware, 1924-1930, shape and pattern designed by Truda Adams and hand painted on clear glaze over white slip. Mark No.11, painted white slip spot. Height 10½ins (26.5cm). A similar vase, shown at the British Industries Fair, 1923, the International Exhibition of Modern Decorative and Industrial Arts, Paris, 1925, and in the Gieve Gallery exhibition, London, 1926.

Blue-bird patterns designed by Truda Adams. Left to right: red earthenware spill vase 206/PB, painted on clear glaze over white slip by Marjorie Batt, 1927-1934, mark No.21; red earthenware vase 202/PN, painted on clear glaze over white slip by Mary Brown, mark No.21 and U.M.L. No.30 1929; white earthenware vase 166/HE, painted on white glaze by Myrtle Bond, 1937-1942, mark No.28; red earthenware vase 439/HE, painted on clear glaze over white slip by Phyllis Ryall, 1930-1934, mark No.28; red earthenware spill vase 564/FX, painted on clear glaze over white slip by Eileen Prangnell, 1926-1934, mark No.21; white earthenware vase 117/BEA, painted on white glaze by Hilda Hampton, 1937-1945, mark No.29. This version of the pattern was designed exclusively for J. E. Beale Ltd., a leading department store in Bournemouth. Tallest vase height 9½ins (24cm).

Patterns designed by Olive Bourne, 1926-1927. Left to right: white earthenware dish 909/GZ, painted on Alpine white glaze by Gwen Haskins, 1952-1953, mark No.36; red earthenware dish 779/AC, painted on clear glaze over white slip, probably by Margaret Holder, 1926-1927, mark No.21; white earthenware plate 120-10ins/CM Sugar for the Birds painted on Alpine white glaze by Betty Gooby, 1958-1959, mark No.39. Dish diameter 12ins (30.5cm).

Red earthenware dish, 910/HD, the 'Leipzig Girl', pattern designed by Olive Bourne and painted on clear glaze over white slip by Margaret Holder, 1926-1927, mark No.11. Diameter $17^1/_2$ins (44.5cm). A similar dish was shown at the International Exhibition of Industrial Art, Leipzig, 1927.

The Poole display at the International Exhibition of Industrial Art, Leipzig, 1927.

Below left: Olive Bourne designs from a 1920s pattern book including, centre, Sugar for the Birds. Below right: vase 911/HF, decorated with an Olive Bourne design, shown in the Poole catalogue No.5, 1927.

Four branch candelabra No.250, slip cast white earthenware covered with sky blue vellum glaze, 1947-1949, mark No.29. A similar candelabra was shown at the British Industries Fair, 1947.

Candelabra designed by John Adams, 1928-1929. Single branch No. 963, slip cast white earthenware covered with white vellum glaze, mark No.21. A similar candelabra was shown at the British Industries Fair, 1931; three branch No. 249. slip cast white earthenware covered with sapphire blue glaze, mark No.21. A similar candelabra was shown at the British Industries Fair, 1947; two branch No. 964, slip cast white earthenware covered with sky blue vellum glaze, 1947-1949, mark No.29. Height of the three-branch candelabra 8½ins (21.5cm).

Love birds book-end No.808, designed by John Adams. Slip cast celadon stoneware, painted underglaze, mark No.25. A similar book-end was shown in the Gieve Gallery exhibition, London, 1930. The Ship, designed by Harold Stabler and modelled by Harry Brown. Slip cast white earthenware, mark No.22. A similar figure was shown in the Gieve Gallery exhibition, London, 1926. Also made with the lettering POOLE POTTERY on the base for use in shop window displays. The Ship book-end No.815, slip cast white earthenware covered with sapphire blue glaze, mark No.25. Springbok book-end No.831, designed by John Adams. Slip cast white earthenware, spray glazed by Leslie Elsden, mark No.29. Ship height 10¾ins (27.5cm).

Love Birds in the coloured Picotee glaze version with an oval base, modelled by Harry Brown and issued as an ornament about 1935.

Three Wise Monkeys book-end, designed by Hugh Llewellyn (Headmaster, Poole Borough School of Art) 1922-1923. Press moulded with buff stoneware clay and glazed by Ernest Banten, mark No.11. Height 7¼ins (18.5cm). This figure was later issued in a slip cast terracotta stoneware body.

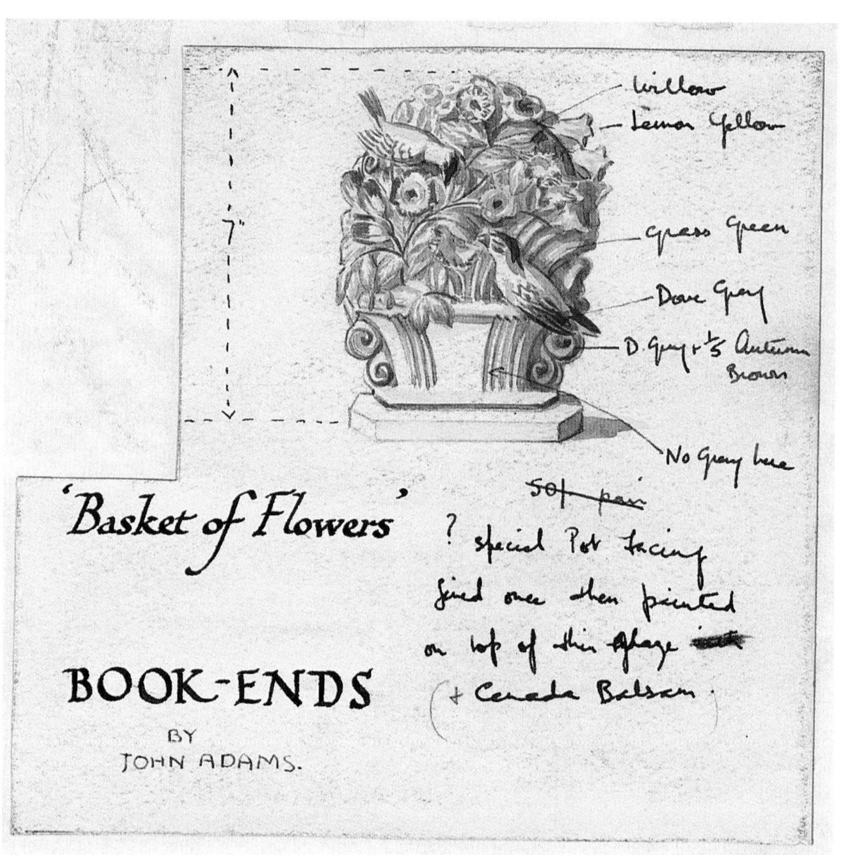

Factory pattern book page showing the design for the Basket of Flowers book-end, made from about 1931.

Harold Brownsword models, 1928-1930: candlestick 986, slip cast white earthenware, mark No.11.The Knight book-end 835. Slip cast celadon stoneware, painted underglaze, mark No.21. Elephant book-end 813, slip cast white earthenware (also made in stoneware), mark No.11. A similar book-end was shown in the exhibition of Industrial and Decorative Art, Monza, 1930. Height of The Knight book-end 8ins (20.5cm). Harold Brownsword, FRBS (1885-1964) was a student of the Hanley School of Art and a Royal exhibitioner, taking top place in 1908. A Travelling Scholar RCA (Sculpture) for five years, he became sculptor teacher at the Regent Street Polytechnic School of Art, London, in 1914, and held the post of Headmaster from 1938 until 1950. One of his notable works was the 1914-1918 War Memorial in Hanley, Stoke-on-Trent.

Range of wares decorated with Chinese blue glaze, from Poole catalogue No.6, 1930.

Group of Chinese blue glazed wares designed and developed by John Adams in the 1920s. Red earthenware covered with re-active glazes. Left to right: ginger jar 201, 1928-1934, mark No.21; vase 616, 1922-1923, mark No.11; vase 877, 1926-1927, mark No.11; vase 594, 1922-1924, mark No.11; spill vase 205, 1927-1934, mark No.21. Tallest vase height 8¼ins (21cm). An early version of Chinese blue glazed wares was shown in the exhibition at Regent House, Kingsway, London in October 1921.

Chapter Six

Carter, Stabler & Adams in the 1930s

The 1930s represents the pinnacle of Poole's achievements under the inspired direction of Carter, Stabler & Adams. The hand-painted wares were still the mainstay of the Poole 'look' but new designs emphasised modernism with their abstraction, geometry, softer colours and tinted grounds. Another period feature was the increased use of stylised birds and animals. By contrast, Arthur Bradbury's drawings of ships with local associations, finely painted onto large dishes by Margaret Holder and other senior paintresses, represented a more traditional development, and one that was to remain a characteristic Poole feature for several decades. Bradbury, a well-known sailor, painter and local maritime enthusiast, was drawn into the Poole net by Cyril Carter in 1931. However, of greater importance in terms of the pottery's standing was the dramatic increase in the range and variety of wares. Writing in 1950, John Adams noted how much Poole had been influenced during the late 1920s and 1930s by fashion and by changing attitudes and lifestyles. Smaller flats and houses, and the increasing use of domestic equipment such as refrigerators inspired many new products, including trays and other specialised food wares, cigarette boxes and ashtrays, wall vases, bookends, table lamps, biscuit barrels, storage jars, vases for flower arranging and many other items for table use or table decoration, made with traditional painted patterns or with the new glaze effect finishes. Linked to this was the increased production of tablewares as a major part of the Poole range, made possible by the change, in 1934, from the traditional red body to a fine white earthenware, a necessary step in the general upgrading of the Poole product. The first identifiable tableware range was Studland, designed by Harold Stabler and made from 1930, initially in apple green and sapphire blue. However, it was John Adams who really took Poole into the tableware market, with a series of designs from about 1932 that linked the pottery inextricably with popular modernism. First came Purbeck, but more important was Streamline of 1935-1936, the most characteristic Poole shape and one that was to carry the Poole name around the world over several decades. Parallel with the development of Streamline, and even more crucial in the creation of an instantly recognisable style, was the emergence of the two-colour technique, with its long list of paired coloured glazes. Applied initially to tablewares, two-colour soon became the mainstay of the popular Poole image, and was used for vases and bowls, now formalised into a definable shape range, and for a new series of ornaments which included shells, fishes and yachts, generally designed by John Adams. Adams, working with Ernest Baggaley, was responsible for the creation of the two-colour glazes, along with many of the other monochromes and glaze effects that characterised so much of the output of the 1930s. His experiments led him to produce stonewares with various high temperature glazes, but more important were the various ranges of glaze effect wares, often allied with distinctively modern shapes designed either by Adams himself or by Truda Carter. Notable were the ridged and banded Everest wares, with their semi-matt finish and white and pastel shades, launched in 1932, similar in inspiration to Keith Murray's designs for Wedgwood. Everest was well received, one critic writing in 1932: 'They have never produced more perfect pieces.' The same year saw the introduction of Picotee ware, distinguished by sprayed bands in a controlled range of subtle colours on a magnolia base. This represented the first use of glaze spraying via the aerograph technique, and it was soon developed by Leslie Elsden for the decorating of ornamental wares and figures. Both Everest and Picotee were also made as tablewares. Even more striking was Plane Ware, a series of shapes with wing-like handles and attachments finished in polar white and other plain colours. By contrast, traditional techniques such as combing, slip trailing and glaze dripping were also introduced. In 1934 Sylvan Ware was launched, a range of vases, bowls, candlesticks and other shapes decorated with blends of plain and broken coloured glazes. The Sylvan finish was later applied to other wares. Sylvan was promoted by a leaflet showing shapes and colours, establishing a pattern for the future that replaced the large general catalogues. Modern ranges were shown at the Arlington Gallery in London in 1933, the first of a number of displays there along with the regular appearances at the British Industries Fairs at Olympia, but more influential were the Poole displays at the series of exhibitions organised by the British Institute of Industrial Art, at Dorland Hall in 1933, at the Royal Academy in 1935 and at the Victoria & Albert Museum the same year, as part of the English Pottery Old and New exhibition. Cyril Carter was a key figure on the various planning committes, along with other leading potters and designers such as Gordon Forsyth and Harry Trethowan. He was also one of the selectors for the ceramics display at the Paris International Exhibition of 1937, along with Forsyth, W.B. Honey, Geoffrey Pilkington and others, where Poole had an impressive display, featuring a variety of monochrome wares and glaze effects. The modernist style such wares represented was reflected by company literature and publicity, with its striking use of modern sans serif lettering, and in its exhibition stands and showroom displays. Sometimes Poole and Carter issued joint advertisements, indicating a level of co-operation that was important to both companies. Typical was the commission for the Cunarders Queen Mary and Queen Elizabeth, involving Carter tiling and Poole monochrome-glazed wares. While modernism seems to have been the driving force at Poole during the 1930s, the company did not ignore its more traditional markets. There was a great increase in the number of bird and animal figures, often decorated in naturalistic colours, and the range included dogs, rabbits and sets of birds and ducks and others. Of equally traditional inspiration was the ever-expanding range of brooches, which included painted plaques and relief models based on flowers, birds and animals, mostly designed by Truda Carter. Floral and fruit patterns, again mostly by Truda Carter, were also used to decorate Streamline tablewares, trays and other modernist domestic wares

Animal and Bird Designs

Factory pattern book page showing a Truda Carter bird design, AS, and related flower design AT, with AU and AV sprigs.

Red earthenware vase 946/LZ, The Bush-Velt designed by John Adams, painted on clear glaze over white slip by Ruth Pavely, 1927-1934, mark No.21. Height $15^3/_4$ins (40cm). Shown as the frontispiece to the Poole catalogue No.6, 1930.

Red earthenware vase 916/EZ, with pattern designed by John Adams and painted on clear glaze over white slip by Ann Hatchard, 1927-1934, mark No.21. Height 15ins (38cm).

Red bodied earthenwares, hand painted on clear glaze over white slip: vase 911/SK with pattern designed by Truda Adams and painted by Ruth Pavely, 1927-1934, mark No.11; dish 211/FW, the moulded shape designed by Harold Stabler and the leaping stag pattern designed by John Adams, painted by Mary Brown about 1930, mark No.11. Dish diameter $11^1/_2$ins (29cm). A similar dish was shown at the British Industries Fair, 1931.

Red bodied earthenwares, with patterns designed by Truda Adams and hand painted on clear glaze over white slip, 1925-1934. Left to right: vase 958/ZV, the shape designed by Harold Stabler, painted by Ann Hatchard, mark No.11; vase 337/ZV, painted by Mary Brown, mark No.21; vase 202/JS, painted by Ann Hatchard, mark No.21. Tallest vase height $9^{3}/_{4}$ins (24.5cm).

Red bodied earthenwares with patterns designed by Truda Adams and hand painted on clear glaze over white slip, 1925-1934. Left to right: vase 337/FK/CF, painted by Ruth Pavely, mark No.21; dish 662/SY, painted by Ann Hatchard, mark No.21; vase 213/EW painted by Mary Brown, mark No.21. Dish diameter 12ins (30.5cm).

Group of wares with patterns designed by Truda Carter. From left to right: red earthenware vase 443/TZ, painted on clear glaze over white slip by Winifred Collett, 1930-1934, mark No.28; white earthenware vase 599/TZ, painted on white glaze by Phyllis Ryall, 1934-1937, mark No.28; red earthenware vase 440/TZ, painted on clear glaze over white slip by Eileen Prangnell, 1930-1934, mark No.28; red earthenware vase 439/SZ, painted on clear glaze over white slip by Marian Heath, 1930-1934, mark No.28; red earthenware vase 959/QB, painted on clear glaze over white slip by Vera Bridle, 1930-1933, mark No.28; red earthenware vase 199/QB, painted on clear glaze over white slip, 1930-1934, mark No.28. Tallest vase height $8^{1}/_{4}$ins (21cm).

Poole Pottery stand at the British Industries Fair, 1931.

Ship Plates

Dishes 909 in white earthenware. The patterns designed by Leslie Ward, 1936, were adapted and painted by Margaret Holder, mark No.19. Diameter 10¾ins (27cm). Several dishes were made including one (in the same series) of Corfe Castle. It is unlikely that these became part of the commercial range. Leslie Ward was a teacher at Bournemouth's Drummond Road Art School and a prominent member of Bournemouth Arts Club. He was well known for his lithography and etchings of old Poole views.

Self portrait by Arthur Bradbury, whose drawings were used for the ship plates.

A factory design for the Waterwitch plate, based on a Bradbury drawing.

Group of four ship plates, thrown on the wheel in the original dish shape, and hand-painted in the traditional manner. Top left: white earthenware dish 528, Port of Poole, Empire Airways 1940. From a drawing by Arthur Bradbury, painted by Ruth Pavely, 1941. Diameter 15$^1/_2$ins (39.5cm). The Empire flying boats provided scheduled services from Poole Harbour from 1939 to 1948. About six dishes with this design were made, and one was presented to Harry Hopkins when, in 1941 as President Roosevelt's special envoy, he left Poole after visiting London to finalise the details of the historic Lend-Lease Agreement. Top right: white earthenware dish 528, Sir Francis Chichester's Gypsy Moth IV, 1967. Drawn and painted by Pat Summers, 1967, mark No.48. Made to commemorate the single-handed round the world voyage of Sir Francis Chichester. Bottom left: red earthenware dish 909, James, Poole, 1386. From a drawing by Arthur Bradbury, painted by Ruth Pavely, 1933, mark No.21. John of Gaunt sailed for Spain in 1386 to obtain the crown of Castile. His fleet of 57 ships included the James of Poole. Bottom right: red earthenware dish 528 Waterwitch, built by Meadus of Poole, 1871, 207 tons, Master Capt. C.H. Deacon. From a drawing by Arthur Bradbury, painted by Margaret Holder, 1932, mark No.28. A similar dish was shown at the exhibition British Industrial Art in Relation to the Home, Dorland Hall, 1933. Built partly of oak, taken from one of the old 'wooden walls' battleships, the Waterwitch was the last square rigged vessel (Barquentine) to sail in trade under the British flag. She was a well-known coastal trader carrying china clay from Cornwall to ports on the East coast and returning with cargoes of coal. An occasional visitor to Poole harbour for consignments of ball clay, she sailed for the Baltic in April 1939, to join her new owners in Estonia.

Ship plate inscribed Brig General Wolfe, Newfoundland Trader, Poole, 1797. The reverse is inscribed, 'This Dish was made and painted at the Poole Pottery in the year 1939. Ship drawn by Arthur Bradbury, painted by Ruth Pavely.' Diameter 15ins (38cm). The General Wolfe, on passage to Newfoundland from Poole, was taken on the 19th October 1797 by a French privateer. Only the mate William Wellstood, a man named Hussey, and a lad, were left on board with twelve Frenchmen, drafted over as crew. On 5th November the three Englishmen overpowered their captors, took possession of all the arms, and succeeded in bringing the brig into Cork harbour.

Group of six ship plates hand jollied in white earthenware in the shape of a flat, shape 6 plaque, and handpainted on Alpine white glaze after designs by Arthur Bradbury. Diameter 12½ins (32cm). Made from 1974, these plates can still be commissioned from the Pottery. Top row, left to right: The Ship of Harry Paye, Poole, 1400, painted by Karen Hickisson, 1977, mark No.29. Admiral Henry Paye, a resident of Poole, was associated with Lord Berkley, in command of the fleet of the Cinque Ports; Primrose, Poole, 1588, painted by Susan Russell, 1979, mark No.29. A vessel of 120 tons, the Primrose was engaged in the Newfoundland trade during the reign of Queen Elizabeth I; Sea Adventure, Poole 1694, painted by Susan Russell, 1986, mark No.29. Sea Adventure, commanded by Captain Peter Joliffe, went to the assistance of a Weymouth ketch which had been seized by a French privateer. This bold action against a much larger vessel, forced the privateer to quit his prize and to founder on the shore near the village of Lulworth. Joliffe was given a medal by the Lords Commissioners of the Admiralty. Bottom row, left to right: H.M. Sloop Viper, built at Poole by Tito Durell, 1746, mark No.29. This ship was the first man-o'-war to be built in the county of Dorset for the Admiralty. In June 1747 she silenced and dismantled a battery and took, or burnt, 33 coasters at Cedeyra near Cape Ortegal, Spain; Poole Whaler, 1783, painted by Karen Hickisson, 1979, mark No.29. Ships from Poole took part in the Southern Whale Fishery in 1781 and 1783, following the damage inflicted on the North American trade by the War of Independence; the Brig General Wolfe, Newfoundland Trader, Poole 1797, painted by Carolyn Beckwith, 1987, mark No.29.

Group of six ship plates made and painted as above but not exclusively from the drawings of Arthur Bradbury. The 1957 version of the Mayflower painted by Ruth Pavely on a round dish, diameter 12ins (30.5cm). Top row, left to right: Egeria, built by Wanhill, Poole, 1865. From a drawing by Arthur Bradbury, painted by Susan Russell, mark No.29 and No.62. In the Egeria's maiden race, she beat the schooner Aline, 216 tons, designed by Camper and Nicholson. The pride of Poole's yachting fleet, she won the Queen's Cup no less than six times to become one of the most successful British yachts of all time; Polly, Poole Trawler, 1906, from a drawing by Arthur Bradbury, painted by Susan Russell, 1986, mark No.29. Built by W. Allan, Hamworthy, Poole, the Polly was owned by Richard Hayes and was one of the fastest sailing vessels in the Poole Fleet of trawlers; Schooner Bluenose from a drawing by Patricia Summers, painted by Susan Pottinger, 1977, mark No.29. Replica of a former schooner with the same name, this 100ft. vessel was in the 1970s based in Canada, and worked the charter business in the Caribbean Antilles. Bottom row, left to right: The Golden Hind, from a drawing by Margaret Holder, painted by Janice Dowding, 1979, mark No.29. When Francis Drake set sail on December 13th, 1577 with five small ships to make a voyage around the world, his flagship was the Pelican, afterwards re-named Golden Hind. This vessel had no connection with the Port of Poole, and the plate was first made as a special commission in 1939; Mayflower passing Old Harry Rocks, Poole, on her way to Plymouth, 1620. Drawn and painted by Ruth Pavely, BEM, at Poole Pottery, 1957. The Mayflower, 1620, from a drawing by Tony Morris, 1970, painted by Janice Dowding, 1978, mark No.29.

Geometric and Abstract Floral Designs

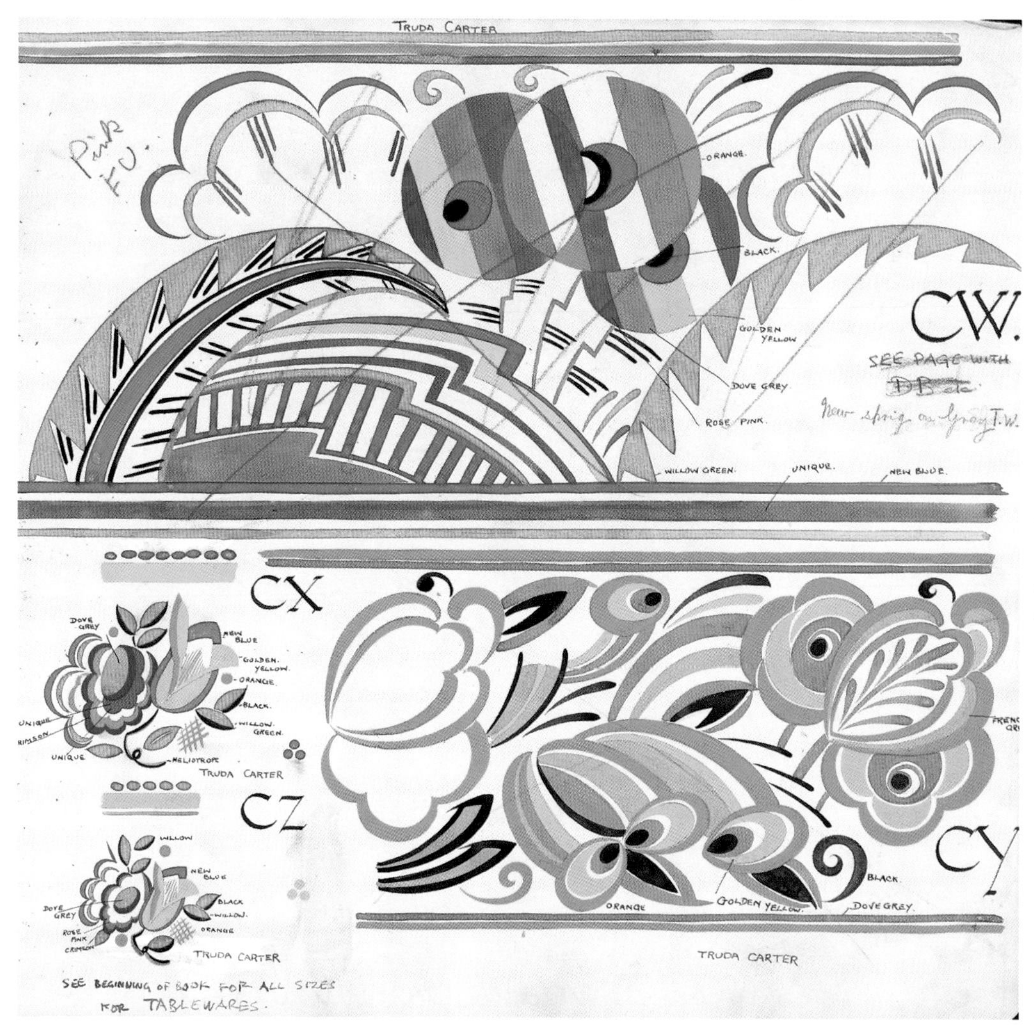

Factory pattern book page showing semi-abstract designs by Truda Carter.

Group of wares with designs by Truda Carter. Left to right: red earthenware vase 439/UB, painted on clear glaze over white slip by Clarice Heath, 1931-1934, mark No.28; white earthenware vase 596/YE, painted on white glaze by Marjorie Batt, 1934-1935, mark No.28; white earthenware vase 266/HZ, painted on white glaze by Myrtle Bond, 1934-1937, mark No.19; white earthenware vase 199/YE, painted on white glaze by Rene Hayes, 1934-1937, mark No.19; red earthenware vase 203/KN, painted on clear glaze over white slip by Ruth Pavely, 1930-1934, mark No.28. Tallest vase height 9¼ins (23.5cm).

Red bodied earthenware dish 291/BY with pattern designed by Truda Carter and painted on clear glaze over white slip by Vera Bridle, 1929-1932, mark No.21 and hexagon impressed. Diameter 9½ins (24cm).

Red bodied earthenwares with patterns probably designed by Truda Carter and hand painted about 193. Vase 947/, painted on grey pot facing glaze, hexagon impressed, mark No.21; ginger jar 201/PR(G) painted on clear glaze over white slip by Marian Heath, mark No.19. Vase height 11¾ins (30cm).

Red bodied earthenwares with patterns designed by Truda Carter and hand painted on clear glaze over white slip, 1930-1934. Left to right: vase 437/BD painted by Ann Hatchard, mark No.21; vase 973/BT, painted by Ann Hatchard, mark No.21; vase 966/EP painted by Hilda Hampton, mark No.28. This vase was given to Mr. & Mrs. R.H. Lewis as a wedding gift in 1932 by Benjamin Elford, Chairman and Managing Director of Carter & Company. Tallest vase height 10¼ins (26cm).

A group of wares with patterns designed by Truda Carter. Left to right: red earthenware vase 337/CE, painted on clear glaze over white slip by Ruth Pavely, 1930-1934, mark No.28; white earthenware vase 337/GEP, painted on white glaze by Eileen Prangnell, 1934-1937, mark No.18; red earthenware vase 966/CT, painted on clear glaze over white slip by Ruth Pavely, 1929-1934, mark No.21; red earthenware vase 970/BX, painted on clear glaze over white slip by Ann Hatchard, 1929-1934, mark No.21. Tallest vase height 10ins (25.5cm).

Group of red earthenwares with patterns designed by Truda Carter and hand painted on clear glaze over white slip. Left to right: vase 333/VY, painted 1929-1934, mark No.21; vase 333/BX, painted by Eileen Prangnell, 1929-1934, mark No.18; vase 333/FK, painted by Ann Hatchard, 1929-1934, mark No.21. Tallest vase height 9½in (24cm).

A group of wares with patterns designed by Truda Carter. Left to right: white earthenware vase 970, the pattern painted on pastel pink glaze by Ruth Pavely, 1935-1936, mark No.18; red earthenware vase 337/UE, painted on clear glaze over white slip by Margaret Holderabout 1930, mark No.21; red earthenware vase 472, the pattern painted on clear glaze over white slip by Margaret Holder, 1929-1930, mark No.21, and hexagon impressed. Tallest vase height 10ins (25.5cm).

Wares with patterns designed by Truda Adams: white earthenware vase 598/VY, painted on white glaze by Marjorie Batt, 1934-1935, mark No.28; red earthenware vase 115/TY, painted on clear glaze over white slip by Grace Burge, 1928-1929, mark No.19; white earthenware jug 318/VY, painted on white glaze by Hilda Trim, 1934-1937, mark No.28. Height of taller vase 9ins (23cm).

Red earthenwares with patterns designed by Truda Adams and hand painted on clear glaze over white slip, 1926-1934: jardinière 954/ZA, painted by Ann Hatchard, mark No.11; jug 897/ZB, painted by Mary Brown, mark No.21. A similar jug was shown at the Ideal Home Exhibition, 1927. Jardinière height 11 1/4ins (28.5cm).

Group of red bodied earthenwares with patterns designed by Truda Adams and hand painted on clear glaze over white slip, 1928-1934. Left to right: vase 973/EB, painted by Mary Brown, mark No.21; vase 966/BX, painted by Mary Brown, mark No.21; vase 271/HQ, painted by Marian Heath, mark No.21; vase 911/GX painted by Ruth Pavely, mark No.11; vase 979 (pattern code omitted), painted by Ruth Pavely, mark No.28. Largest vase height 9 3/4ins (24.5cm).

Group of red bodied earthenwares with patterns designed by Truda Carter and hand painted on clear glaze over white slip, 1930-1934. Left to right: vase 462/CU, painted by Ruth Pavely, mark No.28; spill vase 207/CO painted by Ann Hatchard, mark No.21; vase 203/CO, painted by Eileen Prangnell, mark No.21; vase 202/LN, painted by Eileen Prangnell, mark No.21; bowl 632/LP, painted by Ann Hatchard, mark No.21. Spill vase height 10ins (25.5cm).

A group of red earthenwares with patterns designed by Truda Carter and hand painted on clear glaze over white slip. Left to right: vase 429, the pattern painted by Margaret Holder, mark No.21 and hexagon impressed; jug 303/LW, painted by Doris Marshall, 1929-1934, mark No.18; vase 916/E, painted by Ruth Pavely, mark No.18; vase 429/BC, painted by Ann Hatchard, mark No.21. Tallest vase height 14ins (35.5cm).

A group of wares with patterns designed by Truda Carter. Left to right: white earthenware jardinière 679/CQ, painted on pastel grey glaze by Ruth Pavely about 1937, mark No.18; white earthenware bowl 171/KJ, painted on white glaze by Ruth Pavely about 1937, mark No.29; red earthenware vase 916/NZ, painted on grey pot facing glaze by Ann Hatchard about 1930, mark No.21; red earthenware vase 212/LJ, painted on clear glaze over white slip by Ann Hatchard, 1929-1934, mark No.21. This vase is a rare example of a shape known to have been designed by Truda Adams, dating from 1921. Tallest vase height 15ins (38cm).

Red bodied earthenware vase 946/HY with pattern designed by Truda Carter and painted on clear glaze over white slip by Ann Hatchard, 1929-1934, mark No.21. Height 15¾ ins (40cm).

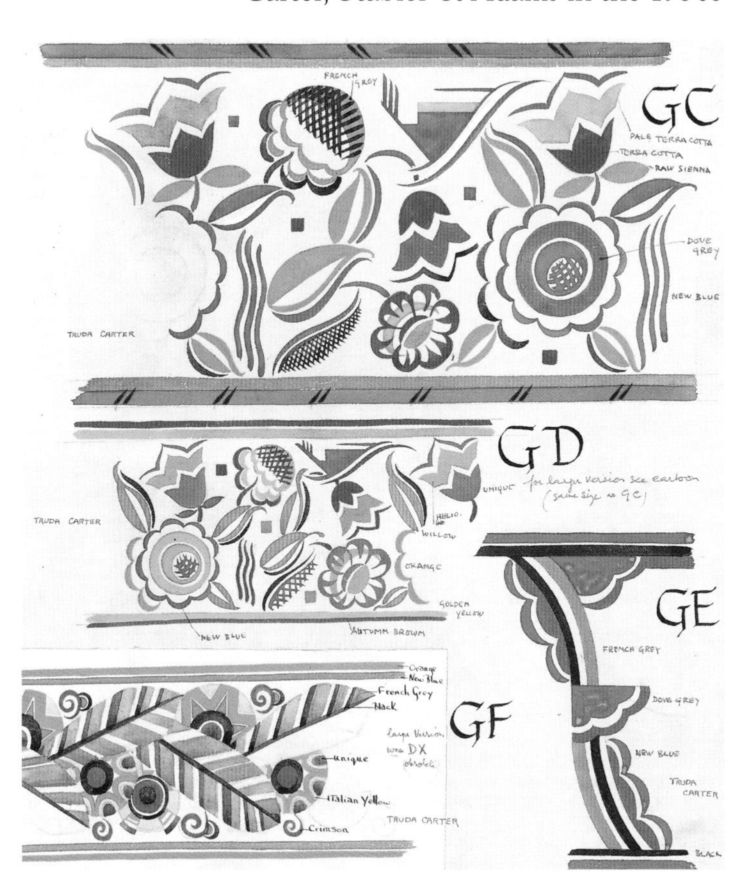

Factory pattern book page with Truda Carter, G series, stylised floral designs.

Wares with patterns designed by Truda Carter. Left to right: white earthware vase 846/ZN, painted on white glaze by Ruth Pavely, 1937-1941, mark No.28; red earthenware covered jar 946/HX, painted on clear glaze over white slip by Ann Hatchard, 1929-1934, mark No.21; red earthenware vase 949/Q, painted on clear glaze over white slip by Margaret Holder, 1929-1934, mark No.21. Largest vase height 16¼ins (41.5cm).

Red bodied earthenwares with patterns designed by Truda Carter and hand painted on clear glaze over white slip, 1930-1934. Left to right: vase 973/OL, painted by Mary Brown, mark No.21; vase 337/PU, painted by Ann Hatchard, mark No.21; vase 201/AX, painted by Ann Hatchard, mark No.21; dish 909, mark No.21. Dish diameter 10 3/4ins (26cm).

A group of wares with patterns designed by Truda Carter. From left to right: red earthenware vase 508/ZI, painted on clear glaze over white slip by Phyllis Ryall, 1930-1934, mark No.19; red earthenware vase 805/OS, painted on clear glaze over white slip by Eileen Prangnell, 1930-1934, mark No.28; red earthenware bowl 434/GPA, painted on clear glaze over white slip by Marjorie Batt, 1930-1934, mark No.28; white earthenware vase 199/GEP, painted on white glaze by Doris Marshall, 1934-1936, mark No.19; red earthenware tumbler 951/GPA painted on clear glaze over white slip by Ruth Pavely, 1930-1934, mark No.28. Tallest vase height 6ins (15cm).

Group of wares with patterns designed by Truda Carter. From left to right: red earthenware vase 115/TP, painted on clear glaze over white slip by Vera Bridle, 1930-1933, mark No.19; red earthenware jam pot base 285/SN, painted on clear glaze over white slip by Dorothy James, 1930-1934, mark No.19; white earthenware jug 319/WI, painted on pastel green glaze by Phyllis Ryall, 1935-1936, mark No.28, and a painted green spot; red earthenware vase 400/TJ, painted on clear glaze over white slip by Marjorie Batt, 1930-1934, mark No.28; white earthenware vase 596/AP, painted on white glaze by Marjorie Batt, 1934-1935, mark No.28; red earthenware vase 443/XA, painted on clear glaze over white slip by Phyllis Ryall, 1930-1934, mark No.15; red earthenware vase 969/HQ, painted on clear glaze over white slip by Dorothy James, 1930-1934, mark No.21; white earthenware vase 208/MA, painted on white glaze by Gladys Hallett, 1937-1941, mark No.29. Tallest vase height 9ins (23cm).

Group of wares with patterns designed by Truda Carter. From left to right: white earthenware vase 113/CL, painted on white glaze by Doris Marshall, 1934-1936, mark No.19; red earthenware floating-flowers bowl 744/WK, painted on clear glaze over white slip by Myrtle Bond, 1929-1934, mark No.21; white earthenware vase 966/BL, painted on white glaze by Norah Preston, 1937-1941, mark No.28; white earthenware vase 170/ZG, painted on white glaze by Vera Wills, 1937-1941, mark No.28; white earthenware vase 987/LT, painted on white glaze by Phyllis Allen, 1934-35, mark No.19; red earthenware bowl 565/EN, painted on clear glaze over white slip by Eileen Prangnell, 1929-1934, mark No.21; red earthenware powder bowl 956/ZY, painted on clear glaze over white slip by Marian Heath, 1929, mark No.21. Painted inscription under lid R.I.B.I. BOURNEMOUTH 1929. Made for the Rotary International Britain and Ireland conference, 1929. Tallest vase height 9½ins (24cm).

Group of wares with patterns designed by Truda Carter. From left to right: red earthenware plant pot 925/YQ, painted on clear glaze over white slip by Ruth Pavely, 1930-1934, mark No.21 and No.24. Made expressly for B. Altman of 5th Avenue, New York; white earthenware vase 112/V, painted on white glaze by Eileen Prangnell, 1934-1937, mark No.19; white earthenware vase 598/V, painted on white glaze by Ruth Pavely, 1937-1946, mark No.19; white earthenware vase 988/V, painted on white glaze by Phyllis Allen, 1934-1935, mark No.19; red earthenware vase 599/BM, painted on clear glaze over white slip by Marjorie Batt, 1933, mark No.28 and M.BATT/1933 painted. Largest vase height 9ins (23cm).

Tinted Pastel Grounds and Pale Colours

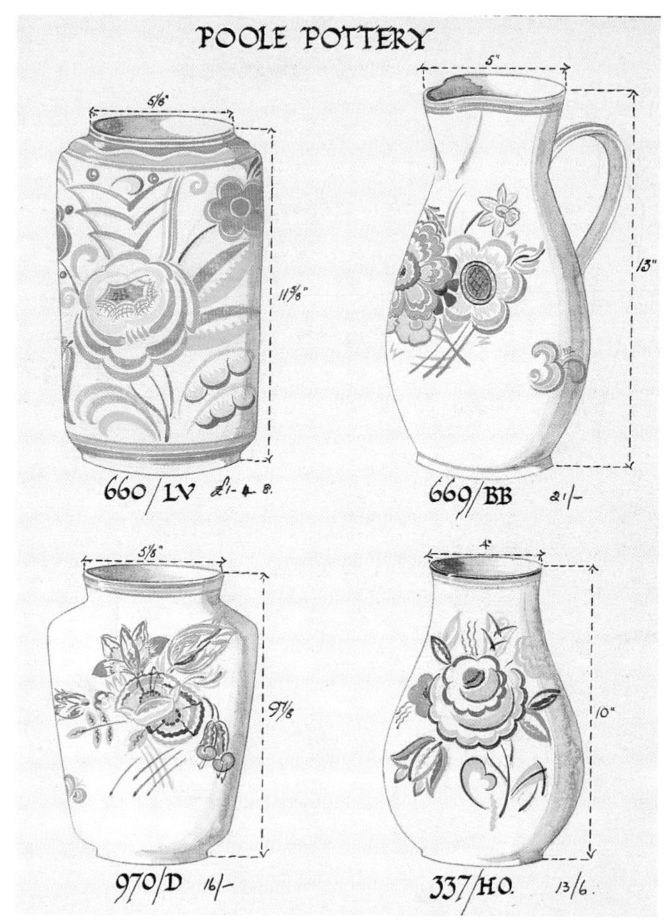

Factory pattern sheets showing designs for tinted grounds, 1935-1936.

White earthenware vase 598/WQ painted on pastel pink glaze, 1935-1936, the pattern probably designed by Truda Carter. Trustees of the Victoria & Albert Museum.

Advertisement from *The Pottery Gazette* for January 1935, showing a short-lived Poole Pottery showroom.

Left: Wares with patterns designed by Truda Adams: white earthenware vase 966/XD, painted on white glaze by Ruth Pavely, 1934-1937, mark No.28; red earthenware dish 662/BK painted on clear glaze over white slip by Mary Brown, 1928-1934, mark No.21; red earthenware vase 966/BS, painted on clear glaze over white slip by Ann Hatchard, 1928-1934, mark No.21. Dish diameter 12¼ins (31cm).

Right: Red bodied earthenwares with patterns designed by Truda Carter and hand painted on clear glaze over white slip, 1930-1934: dish 662/KI, painted by Ruth Pavely, mark No.28; vase 429/BR painted by Ann Hatchard, mark No.21; vase 946/WOODPECKER, designed and (probably) painted by Truda Carter. Shown at the British Art in Industry Exhibition at the Royal Academy, January 1935, mark No.21. Tallest vase height 15¼ins (39cm).

Factory pattern book page showing Truda Carter D series designs, c1934.

Drip, Everest, Plane and Other 1930s Ware

A group of high fired wares, 1930-1935. Left to right: grey stoneware bowl, the outside covered with an iron brown and black tenmoku glaze designed by John Adams. The pattern in soluble greys designed by Truda Carter and painted by Ruth Pavely, mark No.16. White stoneware vase designed by John Adams and covered with a crackled turquoise blue glaze developed by John Adams and Ernest Legg, mark No.19. Buff stoneware vase covered with a thick mottled glaze designed by John Adams, mark No.21. Bowl diameter $7^{1}/_{2}$ins (19cm). A large number of stoneware pieces designed by John Adams, Truda Carter and Harold Stabler were shown in the British Institute of Industrial Art exhibition at the Dorland Hall, Regent Street, London in 1933.

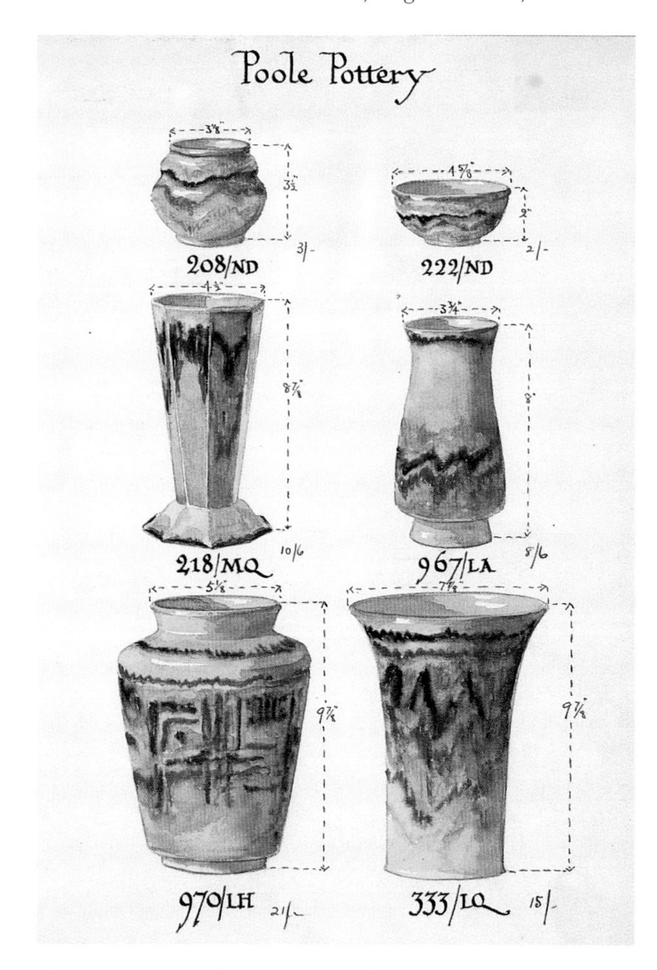

Factory pattern sheet of the early 1930s showing splashed glaze designs by John Adams.

A selection of white earthenwares designed by John Adams, 1930-1933. The thrown Everest vase shape 702, slip colour code 14, and mark No.19 and No.30, was turned and bottle blown on the lathe with pastel coloured slip bands; the tea cup, saucer and jug, mark No.19, slip cast and glazed in apple green and magnolia. These wares were illustrated in *The Pottery Gazette*, 1933; Purbeck coffee pot, shape No.365, tea cup and saucer with apple green, sapphire blue and magnolia glazes. The coffee pot mark No.19 and X painted; Plane ware vase, shape 861 P, magnolia glazed and decorated with applied pastel grey flange-type wings, mark No.19 and No.26, with glaze code 5 painted. Coffee pot height $9^{1}/_{4}$ins (23.5cm).

Everest ware illustrated in *The Pottery Gazette*, 1933.

Everest Belgrave table lamp 825, the name and slip colour code 20, printed in black ink inside foot rim, mark No.19. Height 7ins (18cm).

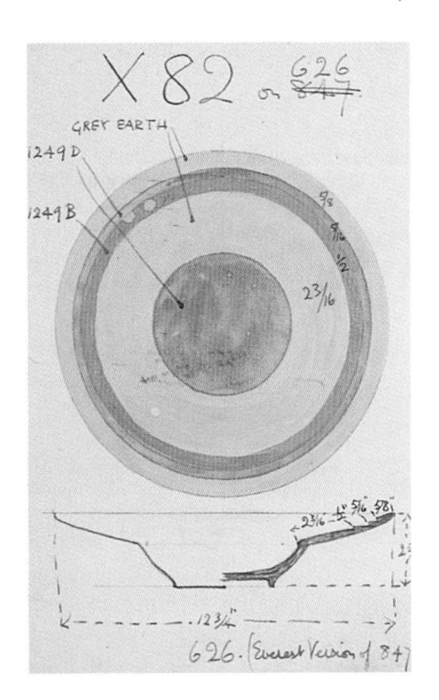

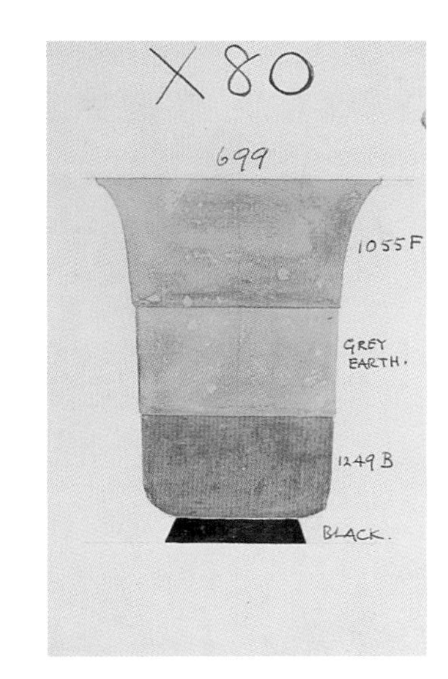

Plane ware plant pot, 280 P, mark No.28 and 26 with glaze code 5 painted. Height 6¾ins (17cm).

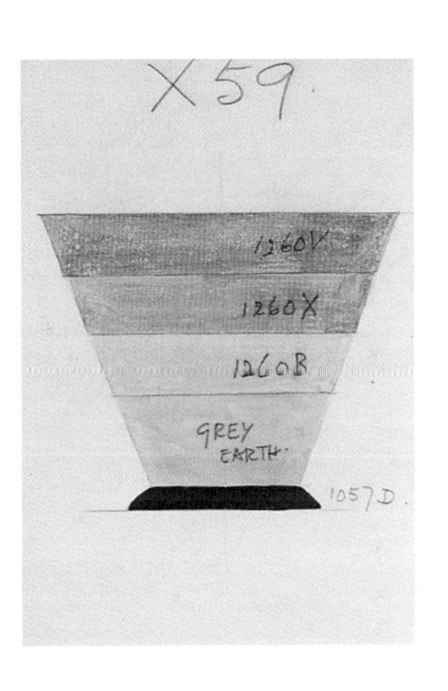

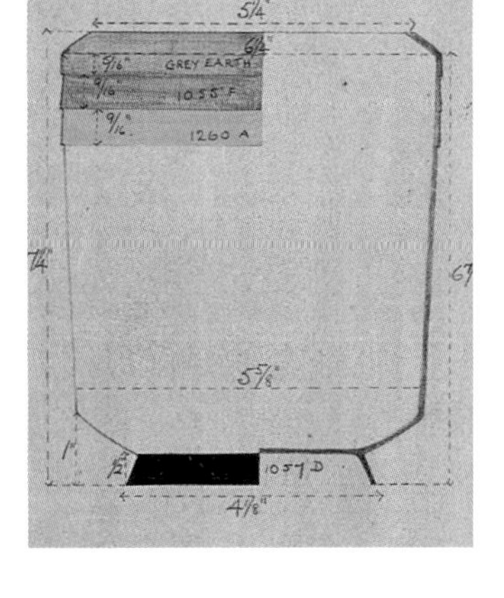

Above and left: factory pattern cards showing Everest shapes and colourways. Below: factory shape cards for Plane ware.

Belgrave white earthenware electric clock case, covered with a pastel grey glaze in the Everest style, 1935, mark No.19. Height 7ins (18cm).

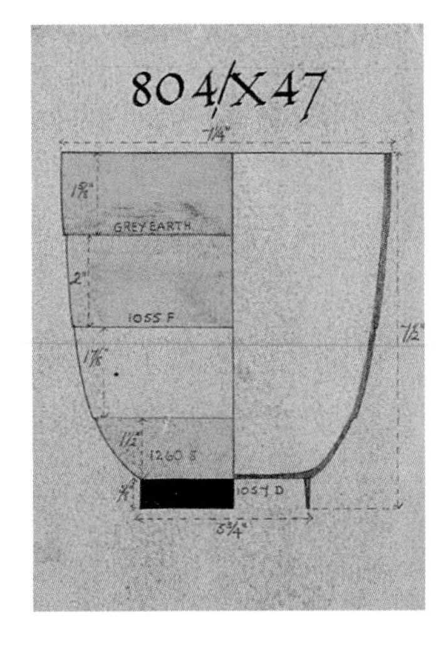

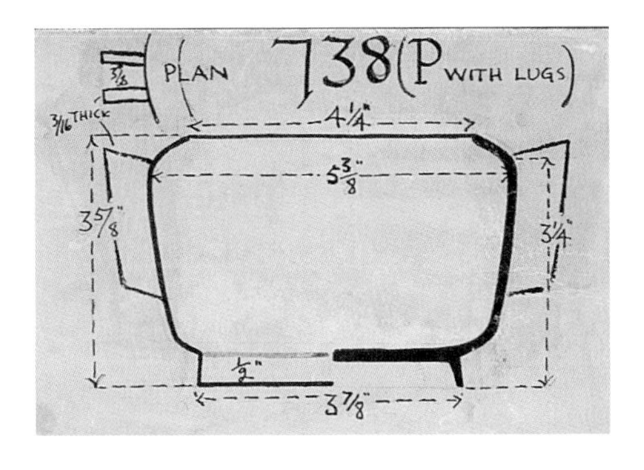

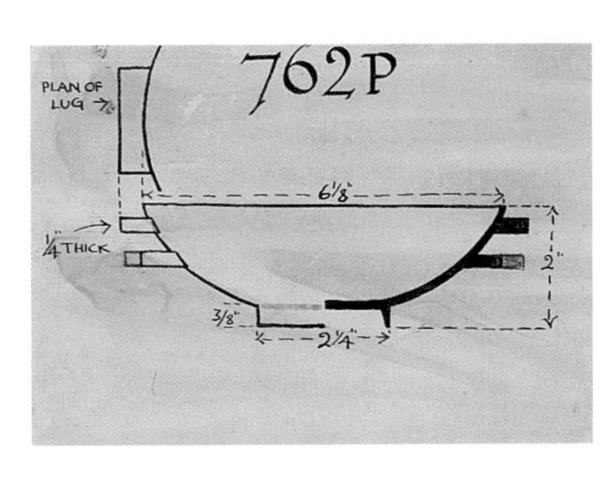

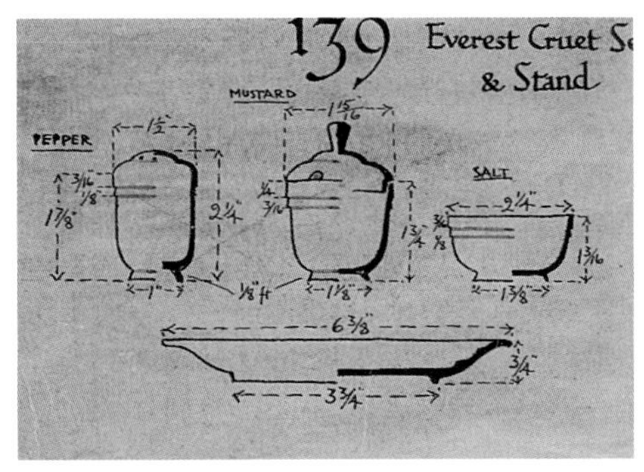

Monochrome & Glaze Effect Wares

A VARIETY OF
POOLE POTTERY
KNOWN AS SYLVAN WARE

DECORATIVE POTS & BOWLS

PLAIN COLOURS

The pieces on page one give a good indication of the delicacy of colour achieved at Poole. The jug is No. 837, $10\frac{7}{8}$" high (No. 669, 13" high), and obtainable both in Sylvan Ware and plain colours. The bowl is No. 844, $10\frac{7}{8}$" wide, also Sylvan or plain colours. The pot is No. 668, $8\frac{1}{4}$" high—a smaller pot No. 768 is $6\frac{5}{8}$" high; both sizes are made in Sylvan Ware and plain colours.

PASTEL GREY
PASTEL PINK
PASTEL GREEN
PASTEL BLUE
SAPPHIRE BLUE
APPLE GREEN
ZULU BLACK
& MAGNOLIA WHITE

SYLVAN EFFECTS

M 70
M 38
M 72
M 36
M 24
M 22
M 7

Above
Posy Bowl No. 175 and Posy Ring No. 188

PLANT POT No. 141. $8\frac{1}{4}$" high × $8\frac{7}{8}$" wide in Sylvan Glazes or Plain colours. A smaller version is No. 140 $7\frac{1}{4}$" high × 8" wide.
THESE POTS WERE MADE SPECIALLY FOR THE "QUEEN MARY"

Pages from a Sylvan ware promotional leaflet of about 1934 showing the range of glaze colours and effects and, below, the shapes available.

Red earthenware vase and dish with slip trailed and combed decoration, designed by John Adams and executed by Jimmy Soper, 1926-1930, mark No.19 and a swastika impressed on dish. Length of dish 14³/4ins (37.5cm).

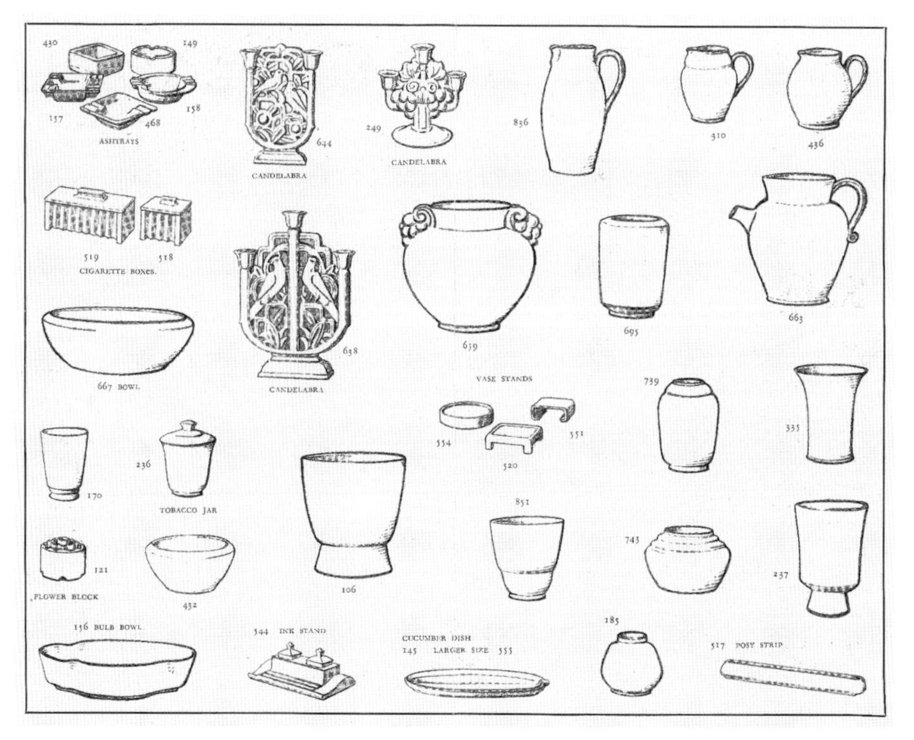

A range of hand thrown and slip cast white earthenwares covered with semi matt glazes in plain colours and broken Sylvan effects, designed and developed by John Adams, 1934-1937: tankard 649, M70, mark No.29; plant pot 179, M73, mark No.28; vase 770, M38, mark No.19; jug 669, M22, mark No.28; ashtray 158, M24, mark No.29; tray M24, mark No.19; ink stand 544, apple green, mark No.29; tobacco jar 236, M36, mark No.28 and 'Brunt Baccy Taunton 1937' incised in script. Jug height 13ins (33cm).

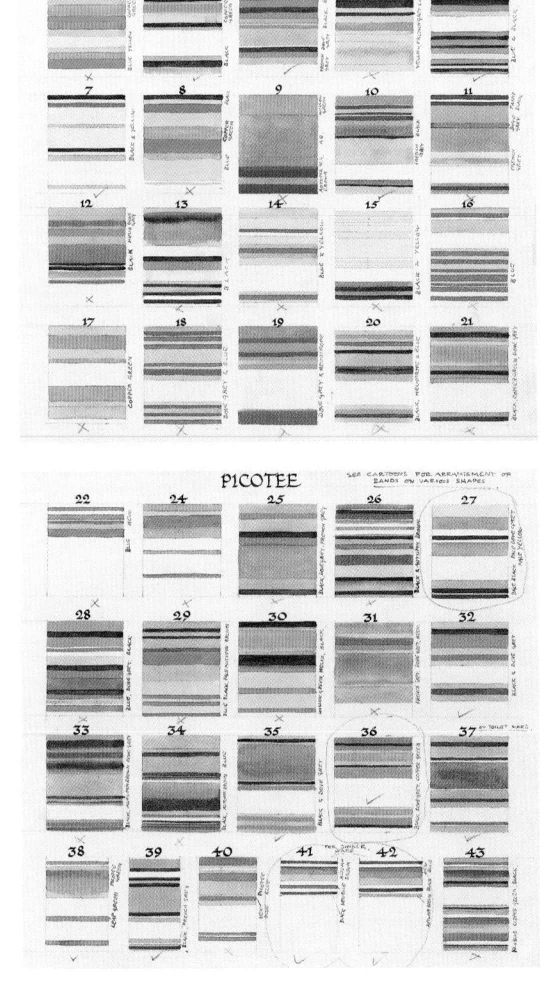

Factory pattern sheets showing the coloured banding used on Picotee wares in the 1930s.

A group of Picotee ware: sweet stand 883/8, mark No.11; salad bowl 496/2, mark No.28; jam pot 287/26, mark No.28; cheese dish 955/2, mark No.21. Salad bowl diameter 10¼ins (26cm).

Advertisement from *The Pottery Gazette*, 1st June 1932, announcing Picotee ware.

Miscellaneous Wares

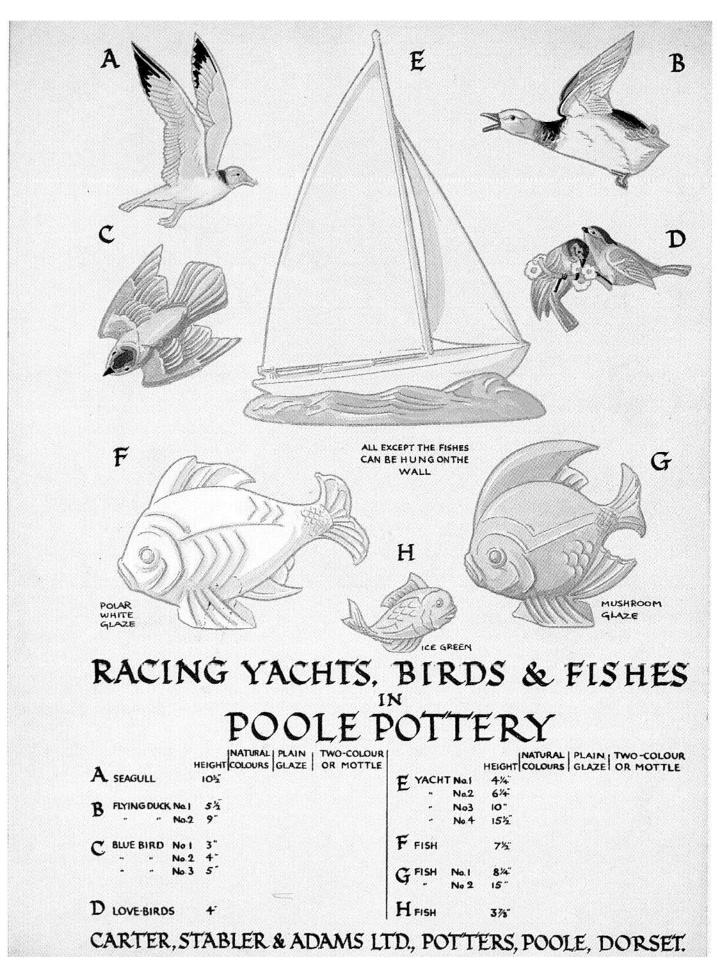

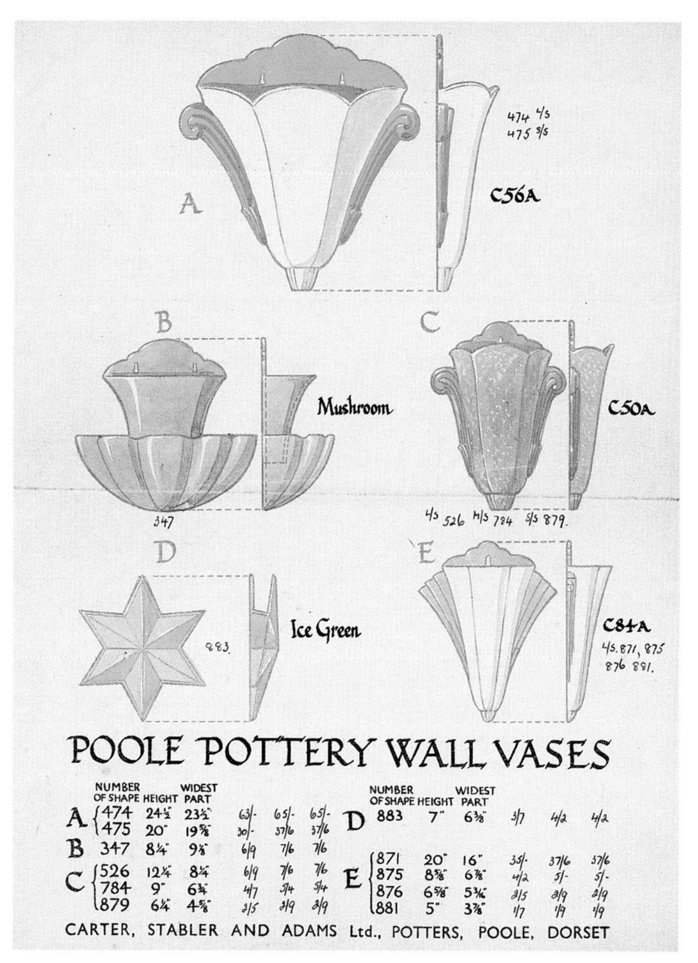

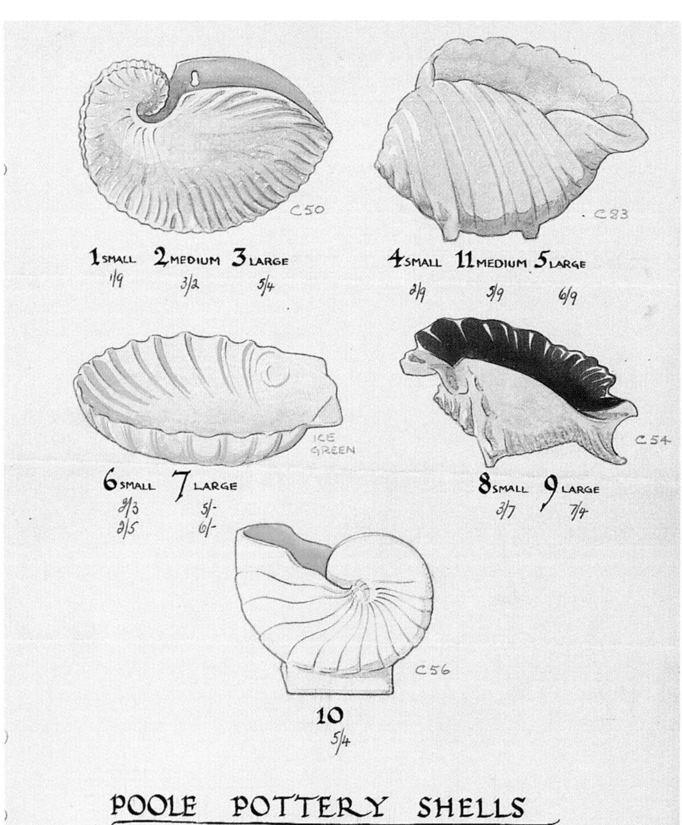

Factory pattern sheets of the late 1930s, showing yacht, bird and fish models, wall vases, shell models and bowls in Picotee and two colour glaze effects.

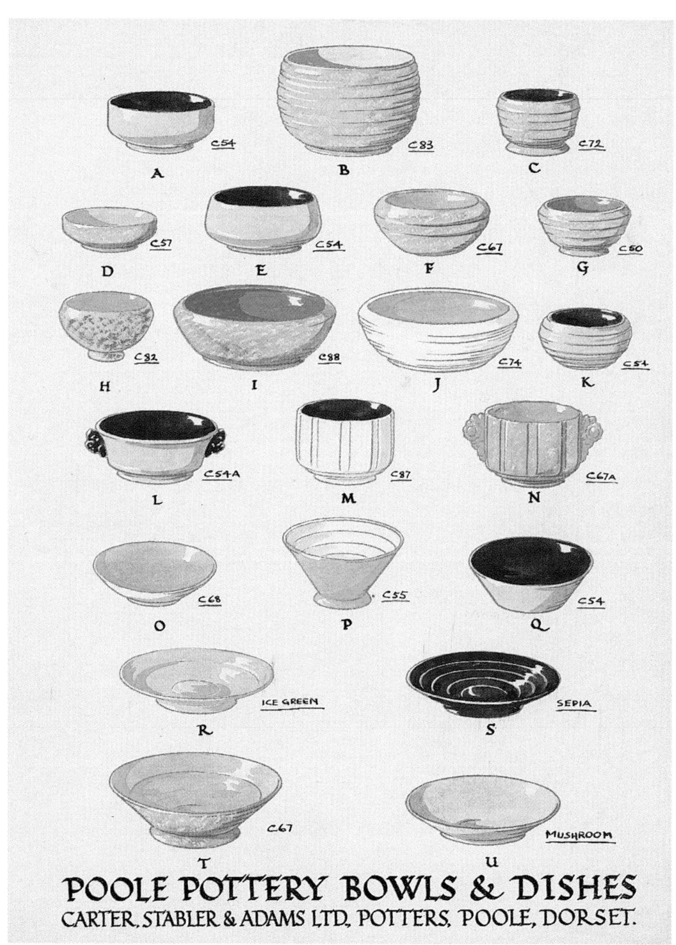

A selection of wares in two colour and Picotee glaze effects on white earthenware. The shells designed by John Adams and probably modelled by Harry Brown, 1936-1937. The other items, while not attributed, probably resulted from the same partnership. From left to right: shell 307/1 with peach bloom and seagull vellum glazes, mark No.34 and glaze code C97 stamped. Illustrated in *The Pottery Gazette*, November, 1947; ashtray 542 with ice green and seagull vellum glazes, mark No.29 and glaze code C57 stamped; fish 314 with Picotee green and new blue glazes applied with an air brush, mark No.29; shell 308/1 with ice green and mushroom vellum glazes, mark No.34 and glaze code C96 stamped; candlestick 974 with celadon and magnolia glazes, mark No.33, glaze code C56 and sprayer's mark stamped. Fish height 8½ins (21.5cm).

Sylvan ware probably designed by John Adams and modelled by Harry Brown, 1933-1937: candelabra 639 with broken glaze effect M24, mark No.19 and New Forest stamped; fish on stand, probably broken glaze effect M24, mark No.19; red stoneware ashtray 239, modelled by Harold Brownsword, 1928-1929, covered with a powder blue glaze, mark No.11 and hexagon impressed. A similar candelabra was exhibited at the British Industries Fair, 1947. Fish on stand height 17ins (43cm).

A group of wall mounted white earthenware birds and ducks, designed and modelled by John Adams assisted by Harry Brown, 1936-1939. Air brush sprayed with Picotee reduced strength glazes. Seagulls 816/3, 816/2 and 816/1, all mark No.39; lovebirds 832, mark No.19; bluebirds 807/1, 807/2 and 807/3, all mark No.19; flying ducks 812/1, 812/2 and 812/3, all mark No.29. Large duck length 11¾ins (30cm).

Model of a schooner and four racing yachts, probably designed by John Adams and modelled by Harry Brown, 1937-1938. Spray glazed in magnolia and shagreen (two colour glaze effect C65) on white earthenware. Left: The Egeria, built by Wanhill of Poole in 1865 and six times winner of the Queen's Cup, mark No.19 and sprayer's mark stamped; four racing yachts 814/4, mark No.19; 814/2, mark No.29; 814/1, mark No.29; 814/3, mark No.19 and sprayer's mark stamped. All models, except 814/4, were designed to be either free standing or wall mounted. Similar racing yachts were exhibited at the Arlington Gallery, London, 1938, and at the British Industries Fair, 1939 and 1947. Tallest yacht height 15½ins (39.5cm).

Right: A white earthenware vase and two bowls probably designed by John Adams, 1936-1938. Mantelpiece vase 472, made in 1947-1949, and sprayed in peach bloom and seagull Twintone glazes C97 in 1953-1954, mark No.29. A similar vase was illustrated in *Pottery & Glass*, July 1950; bowl 369, sprayed in blue pool glaze by Leslie Elsden, mark No.19 and BLUE POOL stamped; bowl 889 sprayed in magnolia and shagreen Twintone glazes C65, mark No.29. A similar bowl was exhibited at the British Industries Fair, 1947; red earthenware vase 872 designed by Harold Stabler for a vellum white or tangerine glaze finish, 1925-1926, covered with clear glaze over a white slip and a painted design by Ruth Pavely, about 1930-1932, mark No.11. This shape, in each of the original glaze finishes, was shown at the Gieve Gallery exhibition, London, 1926. Mantelpiece vase height 7¾ins (19.5cm).

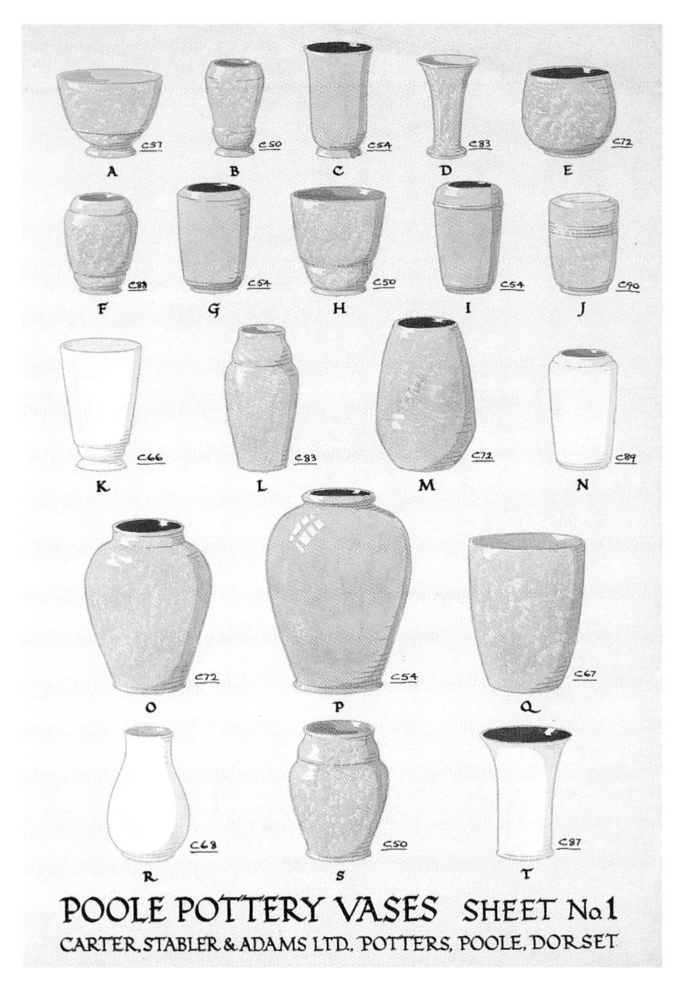

Factory pattern sheets of the late 1930s showing the vase range.

White earthenware pierced tray 486, air brush sprayed with Picotee glazes in shades of autumn brown and Italian yellow. Decoration code P3 (1948), mark No.29. Length 12ins (30.5cm). A similar tray was shown at the British Industries Fair, 1947.

A selection of white earthenware, wall mounted dogs' heads probably designed and modelled by Harry Brown, 1938-1939. Picotee glazed and air brush sprayed with reduced strength glazes: terrier 823, mark No.19; Alsation 817, mark No.19; red setter 819, mark No.19 and sprayer's mark painted; greyhound 820, mark No.19. Alsation height 4$^{1}/_{2}$ins (11.5cm).

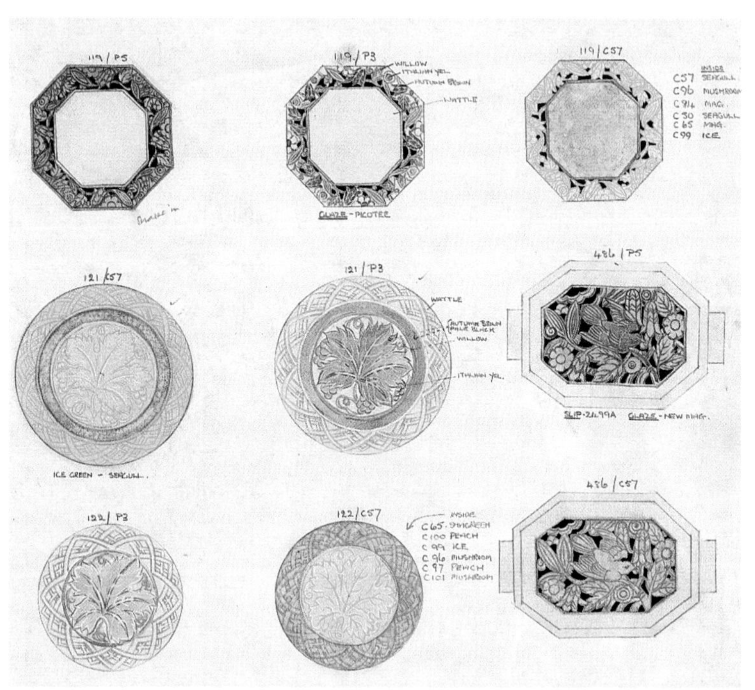

Factory pattern sheets of the late 1930s showing trays.

White earthenware vase FM905400 thrown on the wheel, covered with a pink slip and clear glaze and painted by Ruth Pavely about 1935, mark No.19 and 1850c painted. Height 9½ins (24cm). One of a series of ribbed vases and bowls made for Fortnum & Mason.

Grey stoneware bowl 838 designed by Harold Stabler and covered on the outside with a thick mirror black glaze developed by John Adams about 1930, mark No.19 and No.16. Diamater 5ins (12.5cm).

White earthenware vase 858 covered with magnolia white glaze (a smaller version of a vase designed by Harry Trethowan about 1935), mark No.19 and stencilled MAGNOLIA WHITE. Height 9ins (23cm).

White earthenware vase slip cast and covered with a mottled shagreen glaze, one of several made for the Cunard liner, the Queen Elizabeth, 1938-1939, mark No.19. Height 25½ins (65.5cm).

One of the large Poole vases set in niches on the main staircase of the Queen Elizabeth.

First class swimming pool on the Cunard liner, Queen Mary, showing the Carter tiling scheme. (University Archives, University of Liverpool).

Poole Pottery and the Quay, painted by Eustace Nash in the 1930s. Nash, 1887-1969, a well known member of the Poole and East Dorset Art Society, produced a number of paintings of quay scenes.

Pierced faience wall panel, probably designed by John Adams, 1932, and mounted at the head of the tea room stairway above the tile and pottery showrooms.

Joint Carter and Carter, Stabler & Adams advertisement showing the visitors tea room and tiles with scenes by Edward Bawden, a pierced leaping deer panel attributed to John Adams and Studland shape tableware by Harold Stabler. Illustration from *The Studio Year Book*, 1934.

Brooches

A selection of Truda Carter patterns adapted for brooches. Left to right, first row: B1 bird with grapes, 1939-1953; B5 square perforated, 1939-1953, mark No.34; B2 bird with flowers, 1939-1953, mark No.34. Second row: B4 rectangular perforated, 1939-1953; B57 rectangular /RR, painted by Ruth Pavely, 1939-1942, mark No.34; B6 round perforated, 1939-1953. Third row: B54 broad octagon /EK, painted by Audrey Miles, 1939-1942, mark No.34; B56 medium octagon /FU painted, 1939-1953, mark No.34; B54 broad octagon /FU painted, 1939-1953, mark No.34. Fourth row, left: B53 narrow octagon /CZ, painted by Hazel Allner, 1946-1953, mark No.34; right: B53 narrow octagon /LL painted by Audrey Miles, 1939-1942, mark No.34. Fifth row: B54 broad octagon /CZ painted by Hazel Allner, 1946-1953, mark No.34; B51 largest round /ZC painted, 1939-1945, mark No.34; B52 oval /UB painted, 1939-1953, mark No.34. Sixth row: Dolphin, c1990 (a trial made for Disneyland but not put into production); terrier head, 1940-1953, mark No.34; 401 Dolphin 1968-1994; 402 seahorse 1979-1982. Size of centre brooch, top row, $2\frac{1}{4}$ins (6cm).

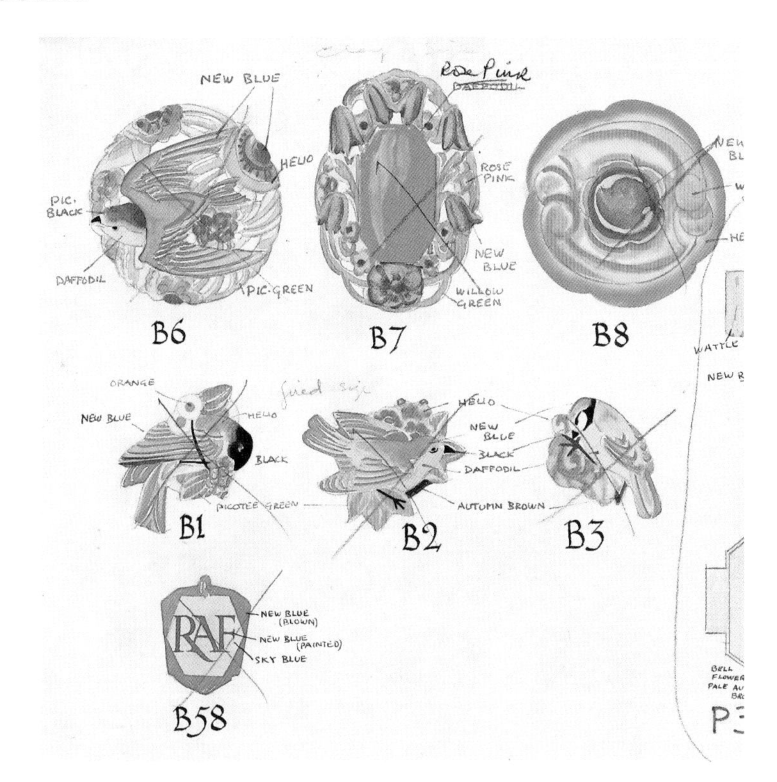

Above and below: factory designs for brooches, 1939-1940.

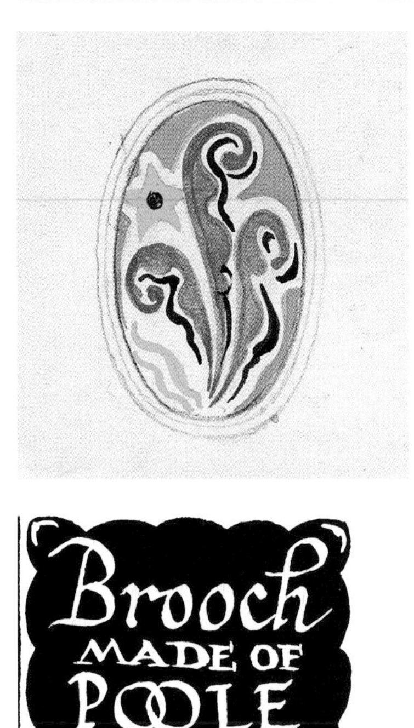

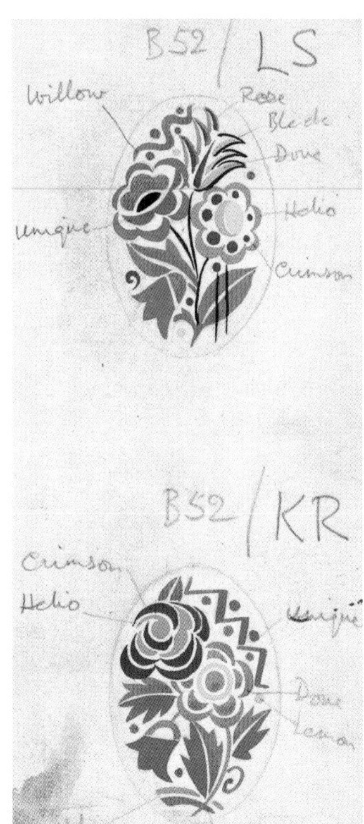

Table and Domestic Wares

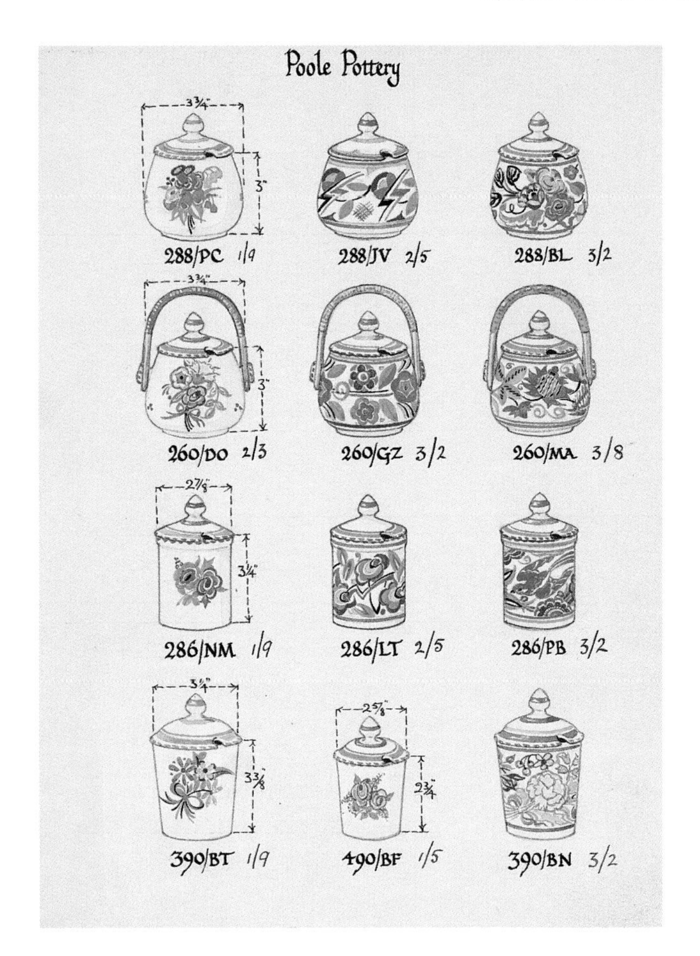

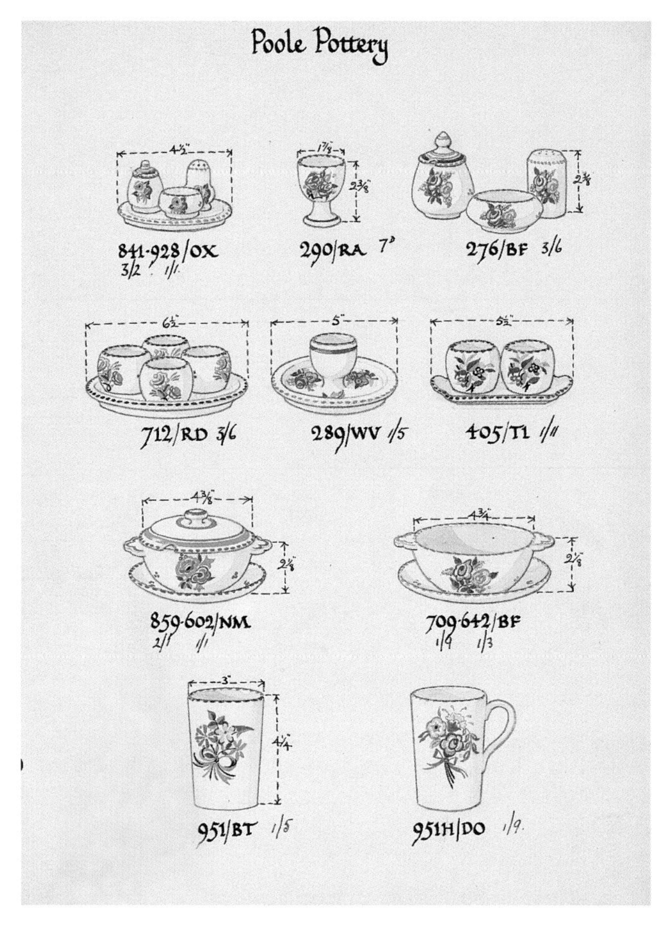

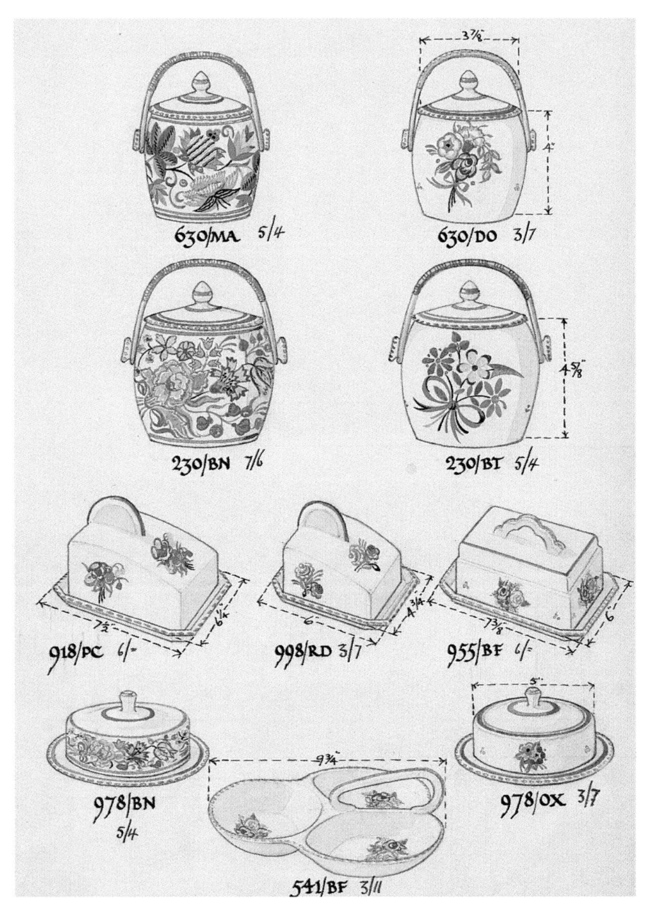

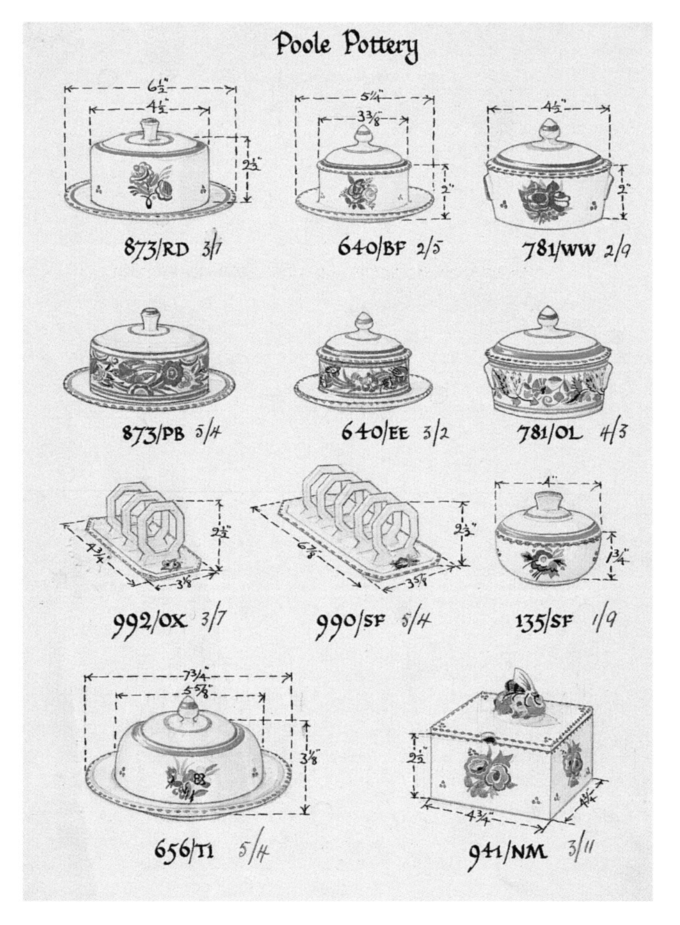

Above and facing page: factory pattern sheets of the late 1930s showing table and domestic ware ranges with traditional designs.

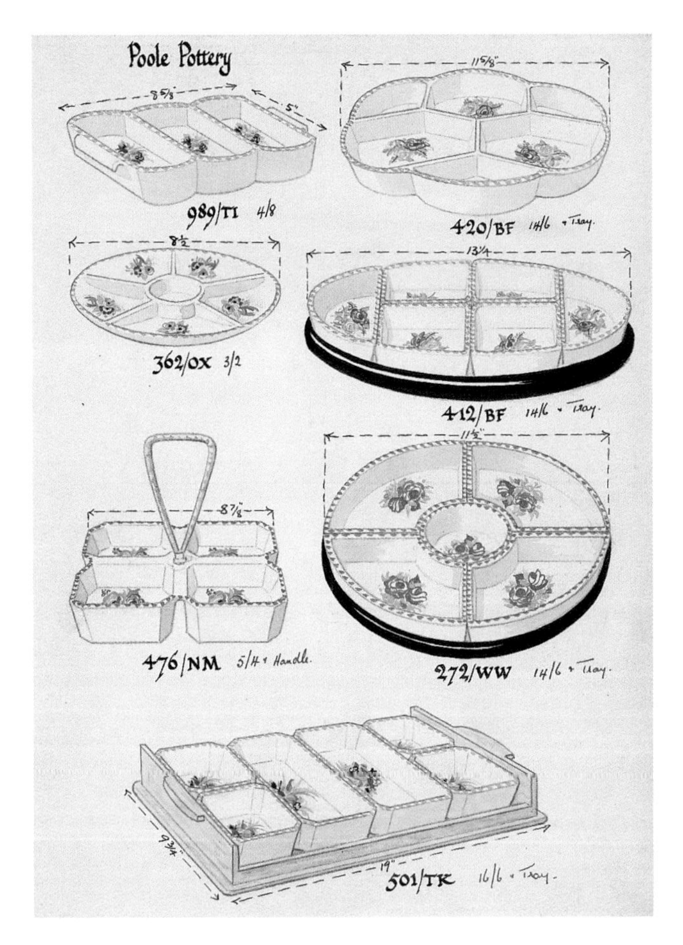
Poole Pottery
989/TI 4/8
420/BF 14/6 + Tray.
362/OX 3/2
412/BF 14/6 + Tray.
476/NM 5/4 + Handle.
272/WW 14/6 + Tray.
501/TK 16/6 + Tray.

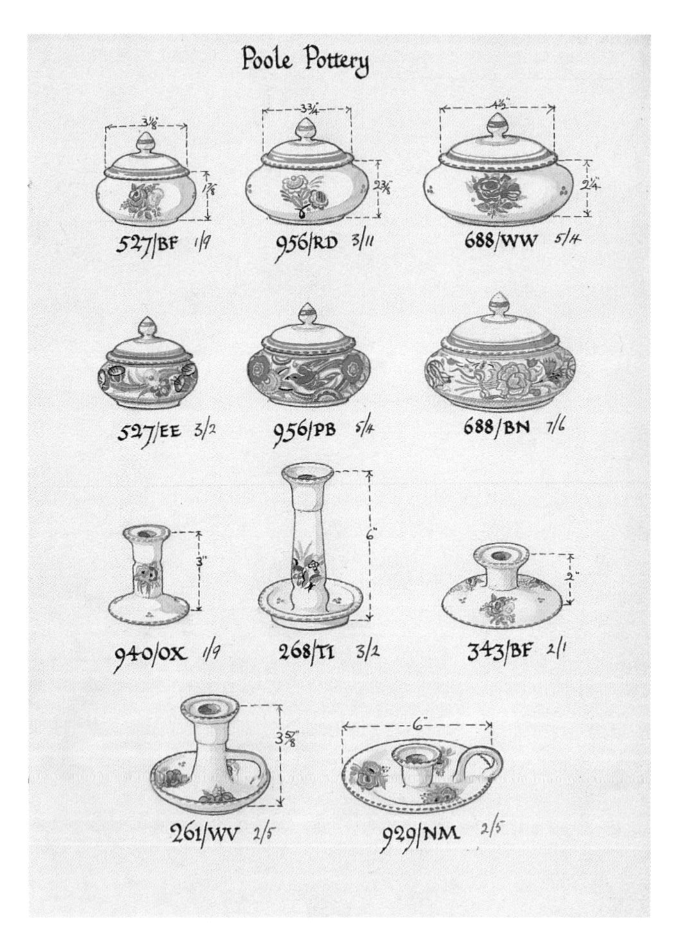
Poole Pottery
527/BF 1/9
956/RD 3/11
688/WW 5/4
527/EE 3/2
956/PB 5/4
688/BN 7/6
940/OX 1/9
268/TI 3/2
343/BF 2/1
261/WV 2/5
929/NM 2/5

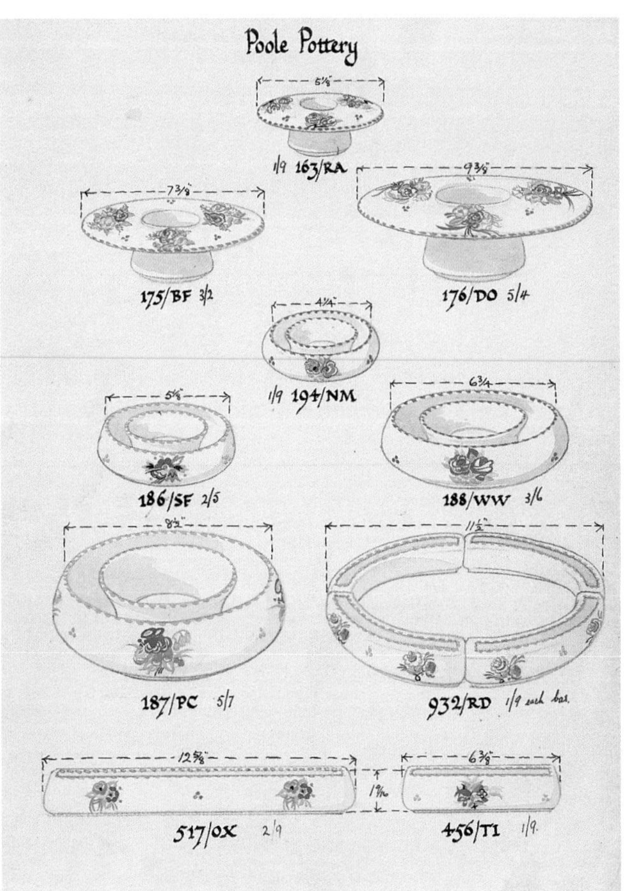
Poole Pottery
1/9 163/RA
175/BF 3/2
176/DO 5/4
1/9 194/NM
186/SF 2/5
188/WW 3/6
187/PC 5/7
932/RD 1/9 each box.
517/OX 2/9
456/TI 1/9.

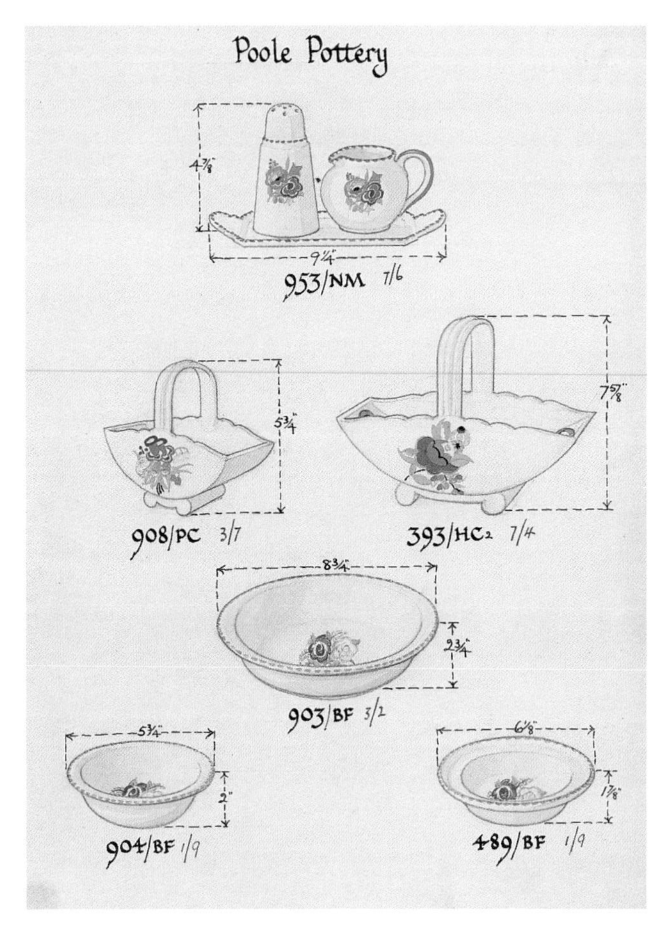
Poole Pottery
953/NM 7/6
908/PC 3/7
393/HC2 7/4
903/BF 3/2
904/BF 1/9
489/BF 1/9

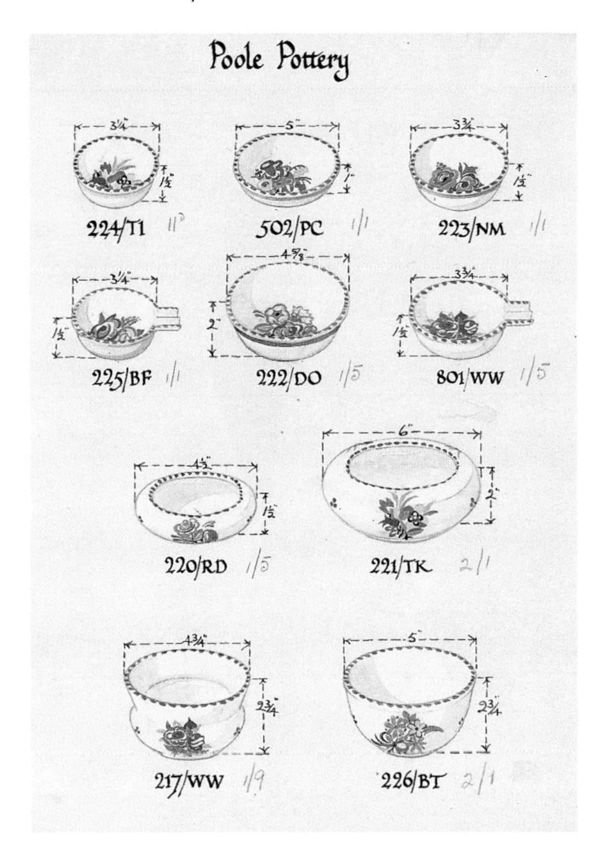

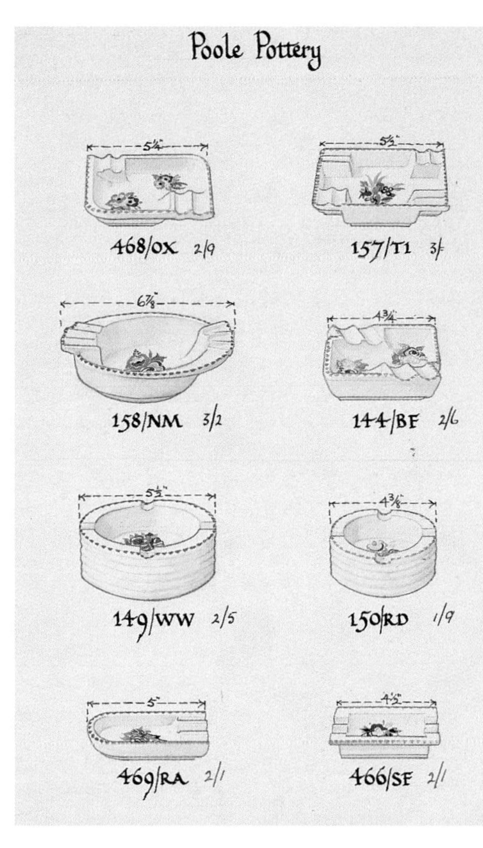

Left: factory pattern sheets of the late 1930s showing table and domestic ware ranges with traditional designs.

Red earthenware kitchen jars, hand painted on clear glaze over white slip, the lettering painted by Margaret Holder, 1927-1928, mark No.21. Height 5ins (12.5cm). Also made in white earthenware in two sizes, with lettering cut through blue slip to the white body beneath.

A selection of red earthenwares with patterns designed by Truda Adams, hand painted on clear glaze over white slip. Left to right: jam pot 287/JG, painted by Nellie Bishton, 1927-1932, mark No.21; cheese box 978/HR, painted by Myrtle Bond, 1927-1934, mark No.19; powder bowl 956/GF, painted by Gladys Brown, 1933-1934, mark No.21; vase 594/HI, painted by Myrtle Bond, 1927-1934, mark No.21; coffee cup 664/OR and coffee saucer 665/OR, painted by Ethel Barratt, 1925-1927, mark No.20; powder bowl 688/OR, painted by Lily Pedley, 1925-1932, mark No.21; egg stand 712/OR, painted by Lily Pedley, 1925-1928, mark No.20; egg cups 713/OR, painted by Myrtle Bond, 1927-1934, mark No.19; jam pot 390/TJ, painted by Hilda Hampton, 1927-1934, mark No.19; jam pot 286/FK, painted by Grace Burge, 1927-1929, mark No.19. Vase height 5ins (12.5cm).

A selection of white earthenwares, hand painted on white glaze with patterns designed by Truda Carter. Left to right: jug 505/PC, painted by Margaret West, 1951-1954, mark No.36; butter pot (excluding lid), 293/BW, painted by Hazel Allner, 1946-1949, mark No.19; egg cup 713/RD, painted by Mollie Skinner, 1937-1940, mark No.19; jug 657/TI, painted by Esther Meads, 1948-1949, mark No.19; flower block 121/OX, painted by Hilda Trim, 1937, mark No.19; jug 317/AX, painted by Winifred Rose, 1934-1937, mark No.19; butter pot 135/BF, painted by Freda Coward, 1940, mark No.19; perfume bottle 387/DO, painted by Winifred Rose, 1937-1938, mark No.19; jam pot (excluding lid) 490/RE, painted by Esther Turner, 1937-1942, mark No.19. Tallest jug height 3¼ins (8cm).

A selection of red earthenwares with geometric patterns in the James Radley Young tradition, designed by Truda Adams and hand painted on clear glaze over white slip. Left to right: candlestick 940/TQ, painted by Iris Skinner, 1928-1934, mark No.11; vase 585/VL, painted by Phyllis Way, 1928-1934, mark No.19; jug 559/EH, painted by Gertie Warren, 1925-1927, mark No.21; candlestick 931/VL, painted by Doris Marshall, 1927-1934, mark No.11; jug 294/XF, painted by Marian Heath, 1925-1934, mark No.21; bowl 409/QO, painted by Winifred Collett, 1925-1934, mark No.21; jam pot 288/SP, painted by Grace Burge, 1927-1929, mark No.21. Taller jug height 6ins (15cm).

A selection of table and other wares. The hand thrown white earthenware teapot 513/WW designed by John Adams, 1922, with pattern designed by Minnie McLeish, painted on white glaze by Hilda Trim, 1926-1930. The remaining red earthenwares painted on a clear glaze over white slip. Left to right: egg cup and stand 289/TL, pattern designed by Cissie Collett and painted by Marjorie Batt, 1925-1934, mark No.19; vase 583/BF, pattern designed by Truda Adams and painted by Marian Jones, 1930-1934, mark No.19; bowl 971/BF, pattern designed by Truda Adams and painted by Iris Skinner, 1928-1934, mark No.19; plant pot 529/PC, pattern designed by Truda Adams and painted by Lily Pedley, 1924-1932, mark No.19; tumbler 951/HA, pattern designed by Truda Adams and painted by Myrtle Bond, 1928-1934, mark No.21; tea cup 765/WW and tea saucer 602/WW, pattern designed by Minnie McLeish and painted by Hilda Trim, 1926-1930, tea cup mark No.19, tea saucer mark No.20; egg cup on stand 289/OX, pattern designed by Truda Adams and painted by Clarice Heath, 1929-1934, mark No.19. Plant pot height 4ins (10cm).

A selection of red earthenwares, hand painted on clear glaze over white slip with patterns designed by Truda Adams. Left to right: sugar sifter 300/TI, painted by Myrtle Bond, 1929-1934; powder bowl (excluding lid) 956/FA, mark No.21; coffee cup 664/CV and coffee saucer 665/CV, painted by Gertie Warren, 1925-1927, mark No.20; cheese dish 955/BF, painted by Clarice Heath, 1929-1934, mark No.11 and hexagon impressed; miniature pot 570/FJ, pattern designed by Cissie Collett and painted by Myrtle Bond, 1927-1934, mark No.21; vase 352/NK, painted by Rene Hayes, 1925-1934, mark No.21; candlestick 343/PC, painted by Phyllis Allen, 1930-1934, mark No.19. Vase height 4ins (10cm).

Fish and sandwich set 281S/UPG, the fish motifs in sea green and grey, designed by Truda Carter and painted on alpine white glaze by Gwen Haskins, 1952-1955, mark No.37. Length of serving tray 15ins (38cm). Alternative colour scheme UPP coral pink and grey. Also painted with crustacean motifs HJG (green) and HJP (pink). The fish motifs, designed in the late 1930s, were re-drawn and re-issued in the 1950s.

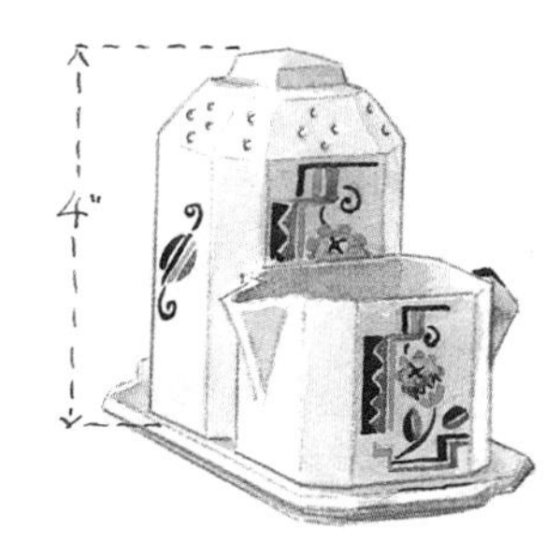

Sugar and cream set and cruet set in the celadon body shown on a factory pattern sheet, about 1930. Egg and preserve sets were also made in this range.

Honey boxes designed by Harold Brownsword, with bee knop designed by John Adams and patterns designed by Truda Adams. Left to right: red earthenware box 941/WL, painted on clear glaze over white slip by Ethel Barratt, 1927, mark No.11; white earthenware box 941/BN, painted on white glaze by Jean Cockram, 1945-1949, mark No.19; red earthenware box 941/CL, painted on clear glaze over white slip by Nellie Bishton, 1927-1932, mark No.11. Size 5ins (12.5cm) square. Lids with other shaped knops were also made.

White earthenware butter pot 135, the inscription designed by Truda Carter and painted on white glaze by Freda Coward, mark No.19. Height 3½ins (9cm).

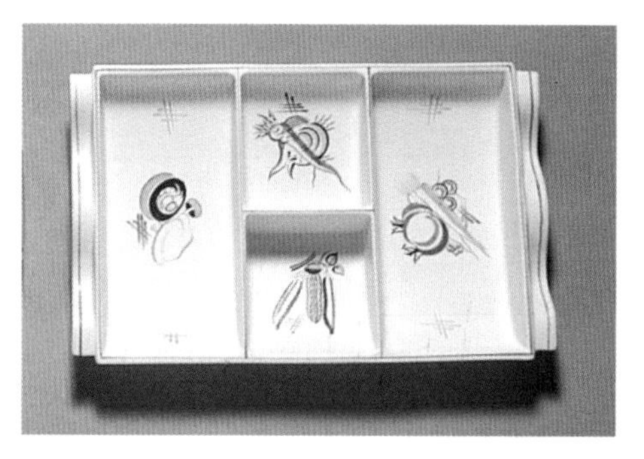

Hors D'oeuvres dishes with patterns designed by Truda Carter and hand painted on alpine white glaze. Dish 884/KUB, vegetable motifs painted by Josephine Smith, 1959-1962, mark No.41. Dish 245/KUA, fish and crustacean motifs painted by Gwen Haskins, 1959-1967, mark No.41. Larger dish width 13¼ins (33.5cm).

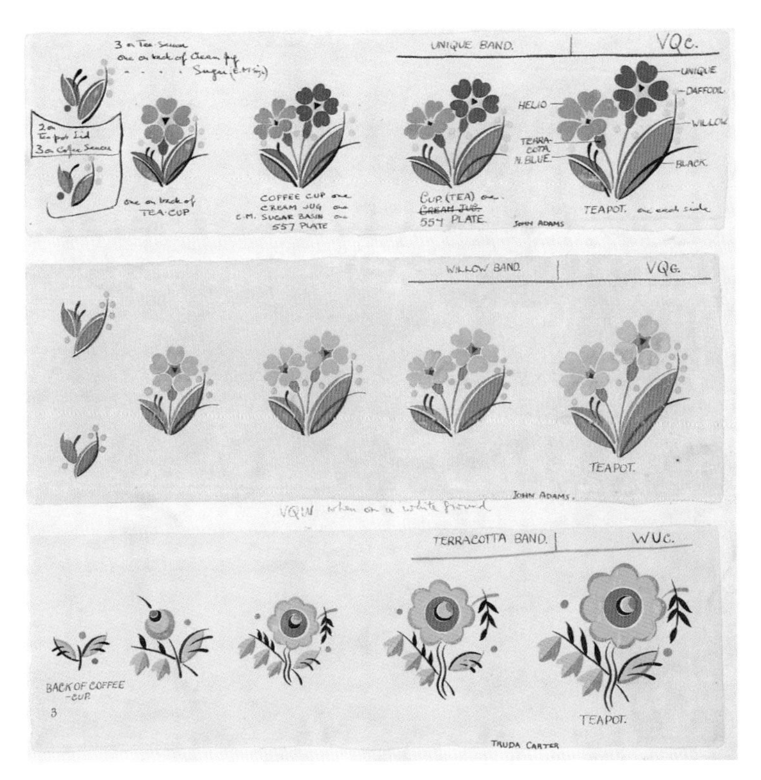

Factory pattern sheets showing tableware borders and motifs designed by John Adams and Truda Carter, c1935.

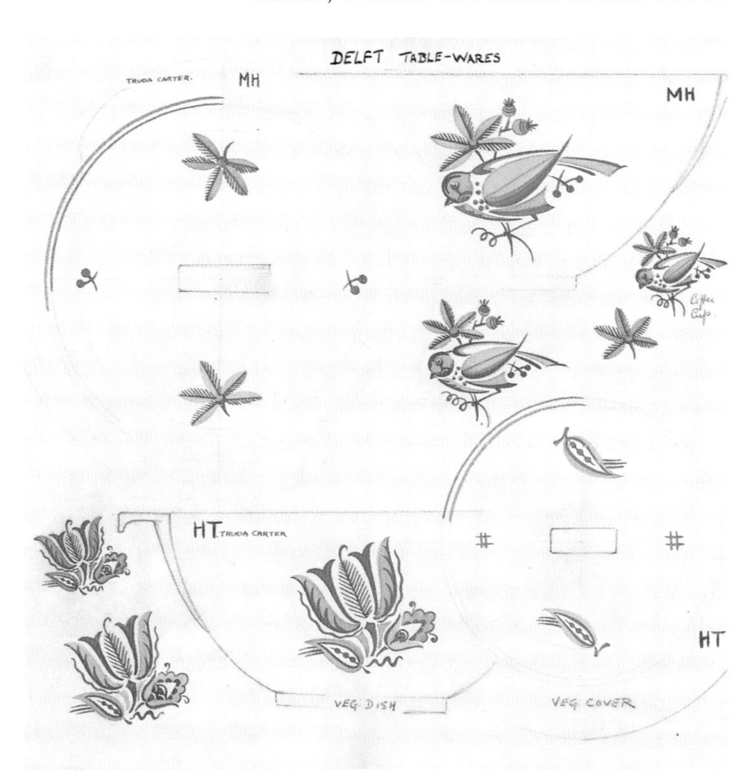

Factory pattern sheet showing tableware motifs for the Delftware range, designed by Truda Carter, c1935.

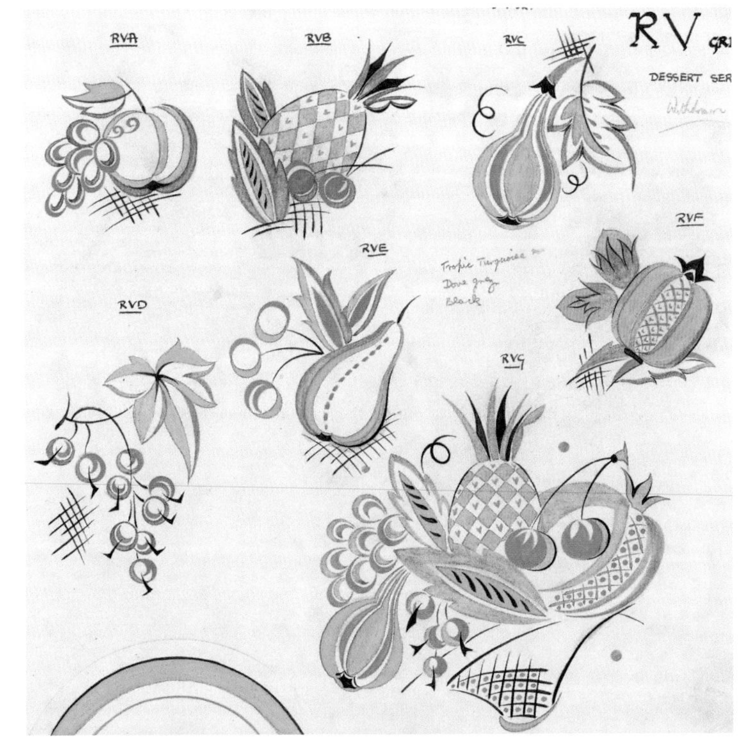

Factory pattern sheets showing dessert service fruit motifs designed by Truda Carter. Left, as re-drawn in the early 1950s, right as originally drawn in the late 1930s.

Everest tea wares illustrated in *The Studio Year Book*, 1932.

Advertisement for Picotee tablewares from *The Studio Year Book*, 1933.

A selection of streamline coffee cups and saucers in white earthenware, the shape designed by John Adams, 1935-1936 and sprayed in various two-colour glaze effects: Red Indian and magnolia glazes, 1950-1956, mark No.34, C95 and sprayer's mark stamped; sky blue and magnolia glazes, 1938-1950, mark No.34, C84 and sprayer's mark stamped; pink and seagull glazes, 1936-1941, mark No.34, C50 and sprayer's mark stamped; sepia and mushroom glazes, 1936-1950, mark No.34, C54 and sprayer's mark stamped. Height 2¼ins (5.5cm).

Streamline and Two-Colour

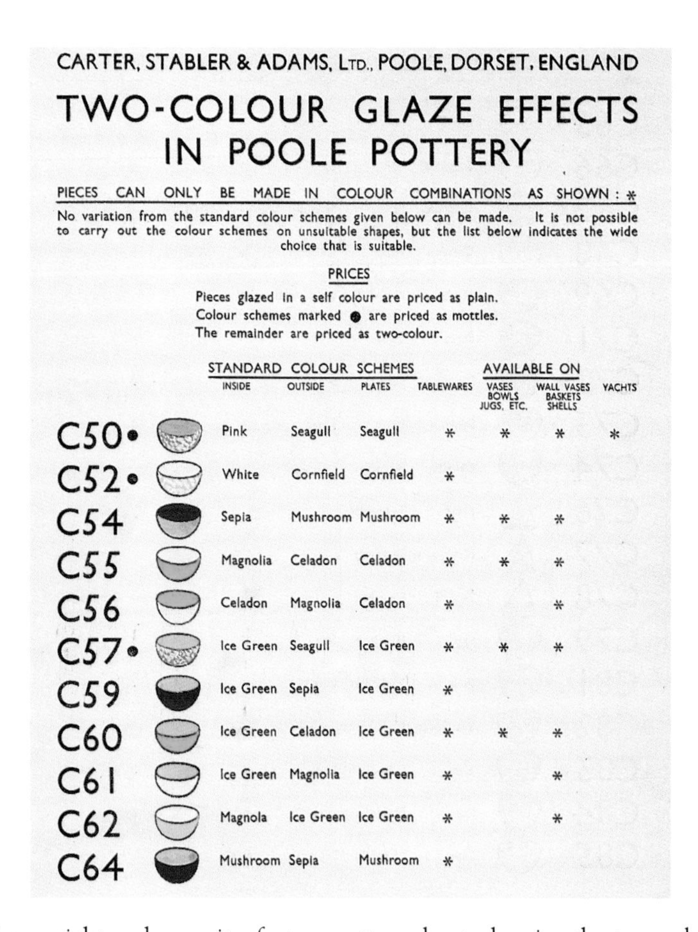

CARTER, STABLER & ADAMS, LTD., POOLE, DORSET, ENGLAND

TWO-COLOUR GLAZE EFFECTS IN POOLE POTTERY

PIECES CAN ONLY BE MADE IN COLOUR COMBINATIONS AS SHOWN : *

No variation from the standard colour schemes given below can be made. It is not possible to carry out the colour schemes on unsuitable shapes, but the list below indicates the wide choice that is suitable.

PRICES

Pieces glazed in a self colour are priced as plain.
Colour schemes marked ● are priced as mottles.
The remainder are priced as two-colour.

	STANDARD COLOUR SCHEMES			AVAILABLE ON			
	INSIDE	OUTSIDE	PLATES	TABLEWARES	VASES BOWLS JUGS, ETC.	WALL VASES BASKETS SHELLS	YACHTS
C50 ●	Pink	Seagull	Seagull	*	*	*	*
C52 ●	White	Cornfield	Cornfield	*			
C54	Sepia	Mushroom	Mushroom	*	*	*	
C55	Magnolia	Celadon	Celadon	*	*	*	
C56	Celadon	Magnolia	Celadon	*		*	
C57 ●	Ice Green	Seagull	Ice Green	*	*	*	
C59	Ice Green	Sepia	Ice Green	*			
C60	Ice Green	Celadon	Ice Green	*	*	*	
C61	Ice Green	Magnolia	Ice Green	*		*	
C62	Magnola	Ice Green	Ice Green	*		*	
C64	Mushroom	Sepia	Mushroom	*			

	STANDARD COLOUR SCHEMES			AVAILABLE ON			
	INSIDE	OUTSIDE	PLATES	TABLEWARES	VASES BOWLS JUGS, ETC.	WALL VASES BASKETS SHELLS	YACHTS
C65 ●	Magnolia	Shagreen	Shagreen	*		*	*
C66	Sunshine	Polar	Sunshine	*	*	*	
C67 ●	Celadon	Seagull	Seagull	*	*	*	
C68	Celadon	Polar	Celadon	*	*	*	
C69	Mushroom	Magnolia	Mushroom	*			
C71	Sepia	Zulu			*	*	
C72 ●	Sepia	Seagull	Seagull	*	*	*	*
C73	Sepia	Polar	Polar	*	*	*	
C74	Celadon	Magnolia			*		
C76	Polar	Turquoise					*
C77	Mushroom	Shagreen					*
C78	Seagull	Shagreen					*
C79	Sky	Hyacinth	Sky	*			
C81	Pink	Magnolia	Pink	*		*	
C82 ●	Sea Green	New Forest			*		
C83 ●	Sky	Seagull	~~Sky~~ Seagull	*	*	*	*
C84	Sky	Magnolia	Sky	*		*	*
C85	Sepia	Magnolia	Sepia	*		*	*

Above, right and opposite: factory pattern sheets showing the two-colour standard range, c1938. The colourways already withdrawn by this date include C51 Ice Green Polar, C53 Celadon Ice Green, C58 Shagreen Shagreen, C63 Magnolia Mushroom, C70 Nigger Polar, C75 Magnolia Shagreen and C80 Seagull Celadon. Post war additions to the range, then called Twintone, are on page 98.

Factory pattern sheet showing two-colour jugs, c1938.

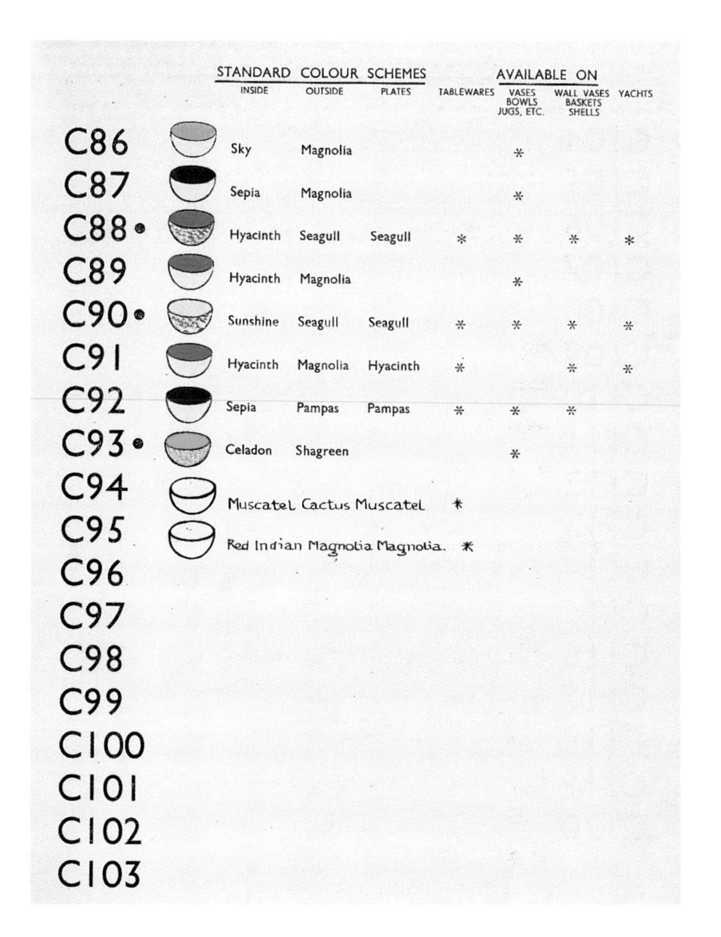

	STANDARD COLOUR SCHEMES INSIDE	OUTSIDE	PLATES	AVAILABLE ON TABLEWARES	VASES BOWLS JUGS, ETC.	WALL VASES BASKETS SHELLS	YACHTS
C86	Sky	Magnolia			*		
C87	Sepia	Magnolia			*		
C88 •	Hyacinth	Seagull	Seagull	*	*	*	*
C89	Hyacinth	Magnolia			*		
C90 •	Sunshine	Seagull	Seagull	*	*	*	*
C91	Hyacinth	Magnolia	Hyacinth	*		*	*
C92	Sepia	Pampas	Pampas	*	*	*	
C93 •	Celadon	Shagreen			*		
C94	Muscatel	Cactus	Muscatel	*			
C95	Red Indian	Magnolia	Magnolia	*			
C96							
C97							
C98							
C99							
C100							
C101							
C102							
C103							

EARLY MORNING SETS		PLAIN	TWO-COLOUR & MOTTLE
455	COMPLETE WITH POTTERY TRAY	8/11	9/10
482	COMPLETE WITH POTTERY TRAY	12/6	13/6
216		9/10	11/-

BREAKFAST-IN-BED-SET	PLAIN	TWO-COLOUR & MOTTLE	
1 TEAPOT 216 1 HOT WATER JUG 232 1 CUP & SAUCER 108 1 PLATE 367 1 PLATE 557 1 EGG-CUP 134 1 BUTTER DISH 497 1 CRUET SET 841 1 TOAST RACK 992 1 SUGAR BASIN 212 1 SLOP BASIN 109 1 HOT WATER PLATE 452 1 CREAM JUG 211	27/6	29/6	30/-

CARTER, STABLER & ADAMS LTD, POTTERS, POOLE, DORSET.

Factory pattern sheet showing Streamline breakfast and tea wares with two-colour glazes, c1938.

21 PIECE TEA SET:	PLAIN	TWO-COLOUR & MOTTLE
6 TEA-CUPS & SAUCERS 6 TEA-PLATES 1 BREAD & BUTTER PLATE 1 MILK JUG 1 SUGAR BASIN	25/-	27/6
40 PIECES.	45/3.	59/9.
TEA-POT 218 4 CUP	4/2	5/7
- - 125 6 CUP	6/-	7/4
- - 454	6/-	7/4
HOT WATER JUG 126	5/5	5/8.

29 PIECE BREAKFAST SET:	PLAIN	TWO-COLOUR & MOTTLE	
6 BREAKFAST CUPS & SAUCERS 6 BACON PLATES 2 BREAD & BUTTER PLATES 1 MILK JUG 1 SUGAR BASIN 1 SLOP - 6 EGG CUPS	38/-	41/-	
TOAST RACK 992 3 BAR	3/2	3/2	3/7
- - 990 5 BAR	4/8	4/8	5/4

COFFEE SET:	PLAIN	TWO-COLOUR & MOTTLE
6 CUPS & SAUCERS 1 SUGAR BASIN 1 HOT MILK 1 COFFEE POT	17/6	21/-

CARTER, STABLER & ADAMS LTD., POTTERS, POOLE, DORSET.

Factory pattern sheet showing Streamline tea and coffee sets with two-colour glazes, c1938.

Factory pattern sheet showing Streamline and Ariel dinner wares, c1938.

Factory pattern sheet showing butter dishes with two-colour and other glazes, 1940.

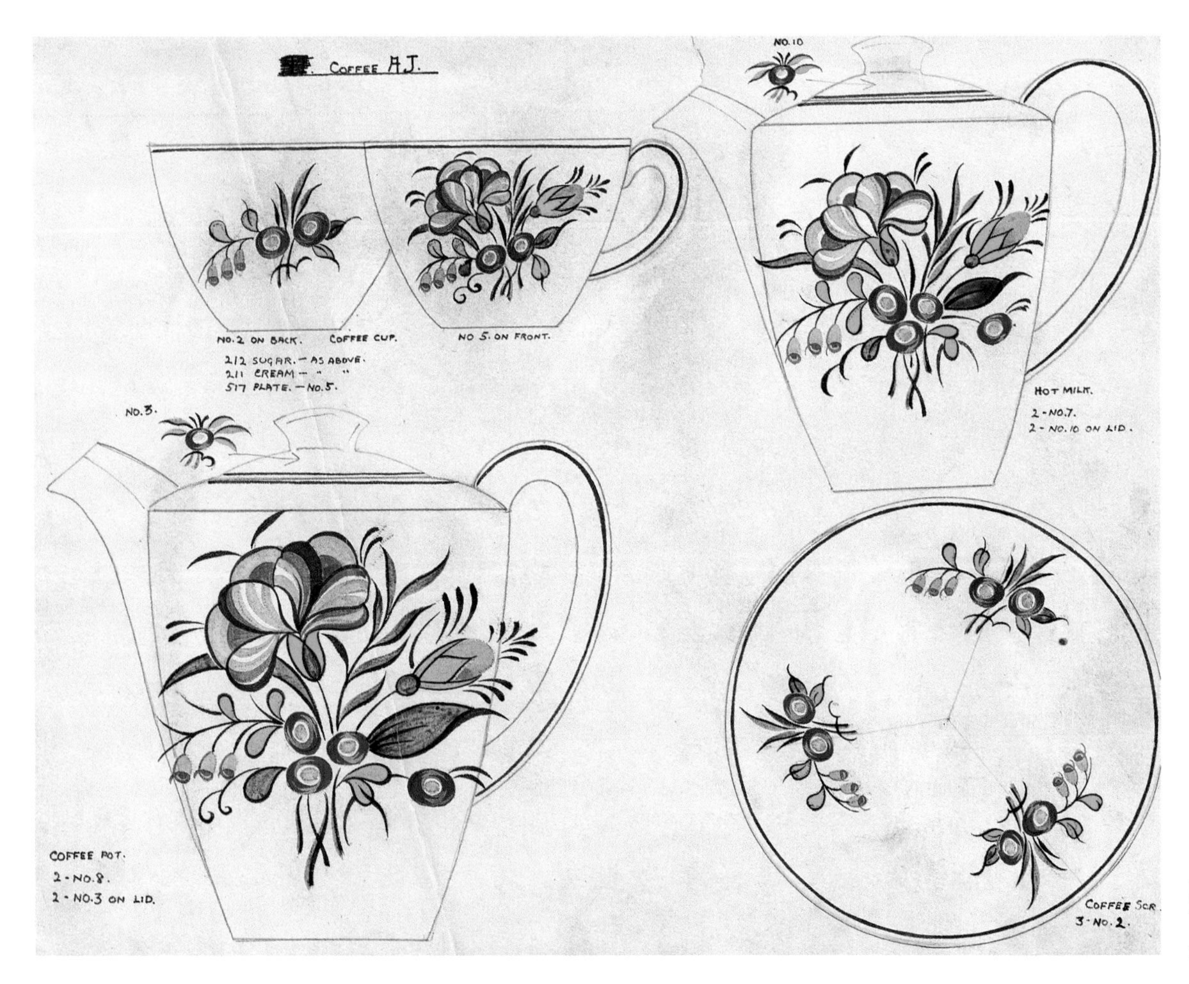

Factory design sheet showing Truda Carter flower sprays on the Streamline shape, c1938.

A selection of white earthenwares designed by John Adams, 1939-1948. Wimborne vegetable dish and cover in two-colour glaze effect mushroom and sepia, mark No.34, C54 and sprayer's mark stamped. Shown at the British Industries Fair, 1947 and illustrated in *The Studio Year Book*, 1943-1948; Streamline dinner plate with celadon green slip ground covered with clear crystal glaze. The pattern JYG Leaping Deer, renamed Spring, was designed by Truda Carter and painted on the biscuit by Jean Baker, 1951-1954, mark No.36; Sherborne covered sugar bowl in shell pink slip decoration contrasted with ivory white, clear crystal glaze, mark No.36; Wimborne coffee pot in two-colour glaze effect sepia and ice green, mark No.34, C59 and sprayer's mark printed in black ink. Shown in alternative colours at the British Industries Fair, 1947; Sherborne teapot in celadon green slip decoration contrasted with ivory white clear crystal glaze, mark No.36. Illustrated in *Designers in Britain* compiled by the Society of Industrial Artists, published 1949. Dish diameter 10ins (25.5cm).

A selection of white earthenwares: hot water plate 452, sprayed in celadon and seagull two-colour glaze effect, 1937-1941, mark No.19, C67 and sprayer's mark stamped; spill vase 408 sprayed in celadon glaze, 1937-1941, mark No.19, CELADON and sprayer's mark stamped; cigarette box 519 sprayed in ice green and mushroom (Twintone) glazes, 1952-1953, mark No.29 and C96 stamped. This combination of glazes was first used in 1952, by which time the cigarette box, made between 1947 and 1949 and held in biscuit stock, was no longer in the current range. A similar cigarette box was illustrated in *The Studio Year Book*, 1938 and shown at the British Industries Fair, 1947; embossed dessert plate 119 (first made 1937-1938) sprayed in ice green and seagull two colour glaze effect, 1947-1949, mark No.29 and C57 stamped; tea and hot water set designed by Harold Stabler and sprayed in mushroom and sepia two-colour glaze effect, 1937-1949, mark No.34, C54 and sprayer's mark stamped. A similar set was exhibited at the British Industries Fair, 1947, and illustrated in *Pottery & Glass*, November, 1947. The two pots closely resemble those designed by Harold Stabler for an Art Deco silver tea service made by Adie Brothers of Birmingham, 1935. Dessert plate diameter 7¾ins (19.5cm).

Part of a streamline coffee set consisting of a coffee pot, hot milk pot, and two coffee cups and saucers, in the two-colour glaze effect sepia and mushroom. The shape designed by John Adams, c1935. The glazes with a vellum semi matt finish developed by Ernest Baggaley, 1936, mark No.36 and C54 stamped. Coffee pot height 6ins (15cm).

Later Animal Models

A group of white earthenware figures decorated in various Picotee, vellum and Sylvan type glazes. Left to right: rabbit (made in two sizes) mark No.19 and No.3 incised, a similar figure exhibited at the British Industries Fair, 1935; lamb 828 designed and modelled by Marjorie Drawbell, 1947-1948, mark No.29, illustrated in *The Studio Year Book*, 1951-1952; Airedale 830 designed by John Adams, 1937-1938, mark No.19 with glaze trial number painted; rocking horses 825/1 and 825/2 designed by John Adams about 1934, mark No.19, illustrated in three sizes in *The Studio Year Book*, 1937; bear cub 846 designed and modelled by Marjorie Drawbell, 1948-1949, mark No.34; bird, probably designed by John Adams, 1935-1938, mark No.29; rabbit 827, designed and modelled by Marjorie Drawbell, 1947-1948, mark No.29, illustrated in *The Studio Year Book*, 1951-1952; gazelle 806/1 designed and modelled by Marjorie Drawbell, 1948, mark No.29, illustrated with the larger size gazelle 806/2 in *The Studio Year Book*, 1949, and in *Pottery & Glass*, October 1950. Height of tallest rabbit $6^1/_4$ins (16cm).

Bear cub 849 decorated in a brown glaze specially developed in 1951-1952.

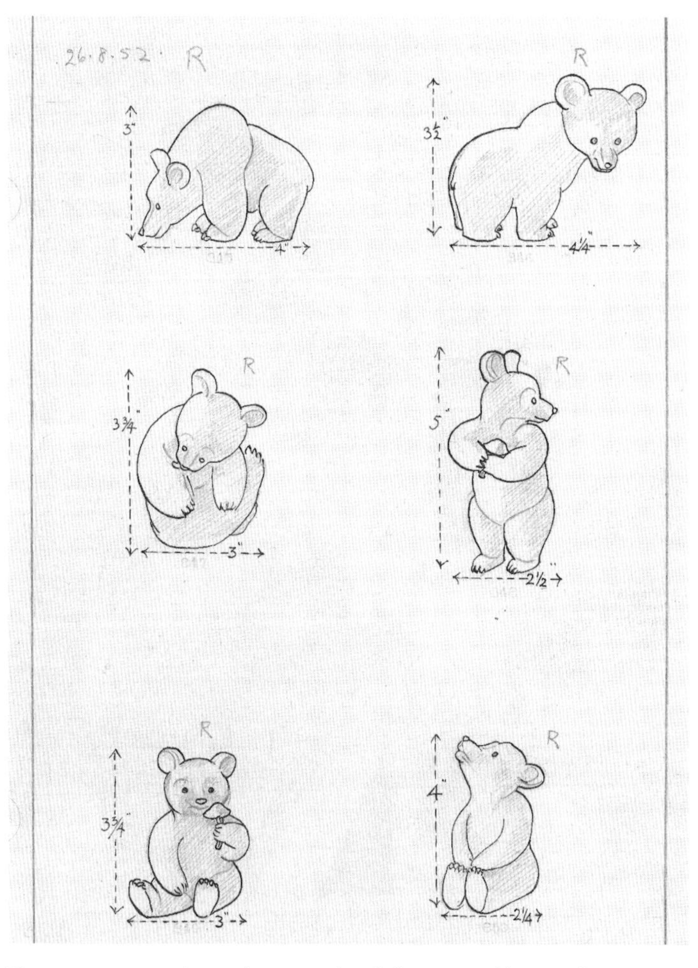

Factory pattern sheet showing the full range of bear cubs 1948-1949.

Chapter Seven

Carter, Stabler & Adams in the 1940s and 1950s

A reviewer at the British Industries Fair in 1939 commented: 'Poole Pottery is steadily widening its scope and at the same time increasing its power of appeal.' Company advertisements, still in the modernist style adopted in the early 1930s, underlined this by showing the wide range of wares from contemporary tablewares to traditional floral painting. With expanding sales, particularly in the export markets, the pottery seemed set fair for the future. However, the outbreak of war changed everything. Initially, production continued much as before but government restrictions soon began to change things. Decorative wares were still being advertised in the home market in 1940 but the pottery was already looking to the future by producing sets for butter rations. Government-imposed controls brought an end to the production of decorated pottery for the home market but by 1942 Poole, like so many other companies, were involved in the manufacture of the new Utility tablewares. In a letter written in December 1942, John Adams said: 'We now make only cheap, plain Utility ware at fixed prices, but I do think we are making some of the best in the country.' When the war came to an end, the restrictions did not, but Poole were already planning the next phase of its development. A new John Adams tableware shape, Wimborne, with fluid forms and two-colour finish made briefly before the war, was aimed initially at the export markets, which included Africa, North and South America, Australia, the West Indies, the Middle East, Europe and the Far East. This was followed by Sherborne, a slip decorated tableware range designed by Adams before the war and put into production in 1949. However, Streamline remained the standard tableware range, decorated either with Truda Carter's, and later Ruth Pavely's, simplified patterns or with the revised range of two-colour glazes that came to be known as Twintone. Many of the pre-war shapes continued in production, including vases and ornaments, domestic wares, animal and bird figures, shells and bookends, but new additions were turned banded wares and sgraffito decoration, along with models by Marjorie Drawbell and Lily Markus. The mainstay of the revived postwar production was the painted ware, the most characteristic Poole product. Advertisements and magazine illustrations featuring these wares began to appear from 1951, and in that year the painted patterns, to be known increasingly as traditional, were graded as elaborate, medium and simple, the first of a long series of rationalisations of the massive design legacy of Truda Carter, who had retired in 1950, although remaining nominally as a design consultant. Harold Stabler had died in 1945, and with the retirement of John Adams in 1950, Poole came to the end of an era. Cyril Carter, alone of those who had guided the pottery since the founding of Carter, Stabler & Adams in 1921, now stood at the head of another team as the company faced a new, and somewhat uncertain future.

Post War Traditional

Trade showroom at Poole Pottery 1950-1951.

Medium patterns.
A selection of white earthenwares with patterns designed by Truda Carter and hand painted on alpine white glaze. From left to right: cigarette box 301 M/NL, painted by Sheila Jenkins, 1952-1955, mark No.37; jug 303 M/LL, painted by Joan Shorto, 1952-1953, mark No.37; biscuit barrel 230 M/OC, painted by Sheila Jenkins, 1952-1955, mark No.37; dessert plate 219 M/AH, Strasbourg, painted by Jean Cockram, 1952-1955, mark No.37; bowl 221 M/JL, painted by Hazel Allner, 1952-1955, mark No.37; vase 695 M/MH, painted by Gwen Haskins, 1951-1952, mark No.29; jam pot 286 M/HT, painted by Jean Best, 1951, mark No.29. Vase height 8ins (20.5cm). The /AH pattern on plate 219 is one from a set of six individual patterns designed for the Strasbourg dessert set. This set, complete with a serving dish, shape number 920, was shown at the British Industries Fair, 1947.

Original and simplified sprig patterns.
A selection of hand painted floral sprig patterns on white earthenware. From left to right: ashtray 469 S/BF, with pattern designed by Truda Carter and painted on alpine white glaze by Josephine Smith, 1955, mark No.37; tea plate 109 S/NM, with pattern designed by Truda Carter and painted on alpine white glaze by Esther Meads, 1952, mark No.37; jam pot 286/KN, this Floriana sprig, designed by Ruth Pavely in 1956, is a simplified version of the WW pattern by Minnie McLeish, painted on alpine white glaze by Mary Stainer, 1956, mark No.39, and the letter A stamped; jam pot 288 S/KW, this Floriana sprig, designed by Ruth Pavely in 1956, is a simplified version of the BF pattern by Truda Carter, painted on alpine white glaze by Sylvia Penney, 1960, mark No.41; vase 112/KP, this Floriana sprig, designed by Ruth Pavely in 1956, is a simplified version of the RZ pattern by Truda Carter, painted on alpine white glaze by Ann Wiffen, 1956-1958, mark No.39; jam pot 288 S/KG, this Floriana sprig, designed by Ruth Pavely in 1956, is a simplified version of the NM pattern by Truda Carter, painted on alpine white glaze by Janet Goodhew, 1959-1960, mark No.41; ashtray 157/KW, this Floriana sprig, designed by Ruth Pavely in 1956, is a simplified version of the BF pattern by Truda Carter, painted on pearl grey glaze by Mary Lowman, 1962, mark No.41. Vase height 5ins (12.5cm).

Elaborate patterns.
A group of white earthenwares. From left to right: cheese dish 355/XA, the shape by Robert Jefferson with pattern designed by Ruth Pavely from an original by Truda Carter, painted on pearl grey glaze by Gwen Haskins, 1961-1962, mark No.41; trough vase 312/WL, an early free-form shape by Alfred Read, with pattern designed by Ruth Pavely from an original by Truda Carter, painted on pearl grey glaze by Jacqueline Way, 1961-1962, mark No.41 and 'Wessex Industries (Poole) Ld. Wrigley's Trucks' stamped; lamp base 658A E/SY,with pattern designed by Truda Carter and painted on alpine white glaze by Joan Shorto, 1951-1952, mark No.29. Designed by Roy Holland in 1951 to meet an unprecedented post war demand for table lamps when the throwing shop was working to capacity. Jollied in two halves using a slop basin mould, the two slightly thicker than normal basins were then joined rim to rim on the lathe by Jimmy Soper. Eight versions, number 652 to 659, were made, and all were designed with turned ridges as an additional decorative feature. On four lamps, the cut-away foot of the Sherborne tableware shape can be clearly identified. Vase 441/AP with pattern designed by Truda Carter and painted on alpine white glaze by Jean Cockram, 1947-1950, mark No.29; jam pot 288 E/QE, with pattern designed by Truda Carter and painted on alpine white glaze by Mollie Harman, 1951-1952, mark No.29. Vase height 6½ins (16.5cm).

Full and simplified versions of the elaborate BN pattern.
A group of white earthenwares, painted with pattern designed by Truda Carter: vase 969 E/BN, painted on alpine white glaze by Jean Cockram, 1952-1955, mark No.37; plate 120/BN, painted on pearl grey glaze by Jacqueline Way, 1961-1962, mark No.41; vase 84/BN, simplified pattern painted on alpine white glaze by Susan Allen, 1970-1973, mark No.48; vase 715/BN, the shape designed by Alfred Read and Guy Sydenham, 1952, the pattern painted on alpine white glaze by Pat Summers, 1963-1964, mark No.41 and A stamped. Tallest vase height 10ins (25.5cm).

Full and simplified versions of the elaborate LE pattern.
A group of white earthenwares painted with the LE pattern, designed by Truda Carter: jug 303 E/LE, painted on alpine white glaze by Betty Gooby, 1955-59, mark No.39; jug 549/LE, painted on alpine white glaze by Jacqueline Way, 1959-1964, mark No.41; vase 266 E/LE, painted on pearl grey glaze by Sylvia Davis, 1961-1962, mark No.41; plant pot 653/LE, simplified pattern painted on alpine white glaze by Gwen Haskins, 1967-1970, mark No.48; vase 83/LE, painted on alpine white glaze by Janice Wellman, 1975-1978, mark No.62. Taller jug height 7¼ins (18.5cm).

Full and simplified versions of the elaborate CS pattern.
A group of white earthenwares painted with the CS pattern, 1940-1967, designed by Truda Carter: vase 599/CS, painted on white glaze by Ruth Pavely, 1940, mark No.19 and W.T. L & S 1940 stencilled; biscuit barrel 230/CS, simplified pattern painted on alpine white glaze by Gwen Haskins, 1964-1967, mark No.41. Cane handle supplied by Stoke-on-Trent Workshops for the Blind. Vase 716/CS, the shape designed by Alfred Read and Guy Sydenham, 1957, the pattern painted on alpine white glaze by Gwen Haskins, 1959, mark No.41 and B stamped. Tallest vase height 8½ins (21.5cm).

Extra and full elaborate patterns.
A group of white earthenwares with patterns designed by Truda Carter: vase 660/SK, painted on alpine white glaze by Nellie Blackmore, 1959-1967, mark No.41; jug 484 E/YO, painted on alpine white glaze by Gwen Haskins 1964-1966, mark No.41; vase 337/TV, painted on pearl grey glaze by Iris Downton, 1961, mark No.41. Tallest vase height 13ins (33cm).

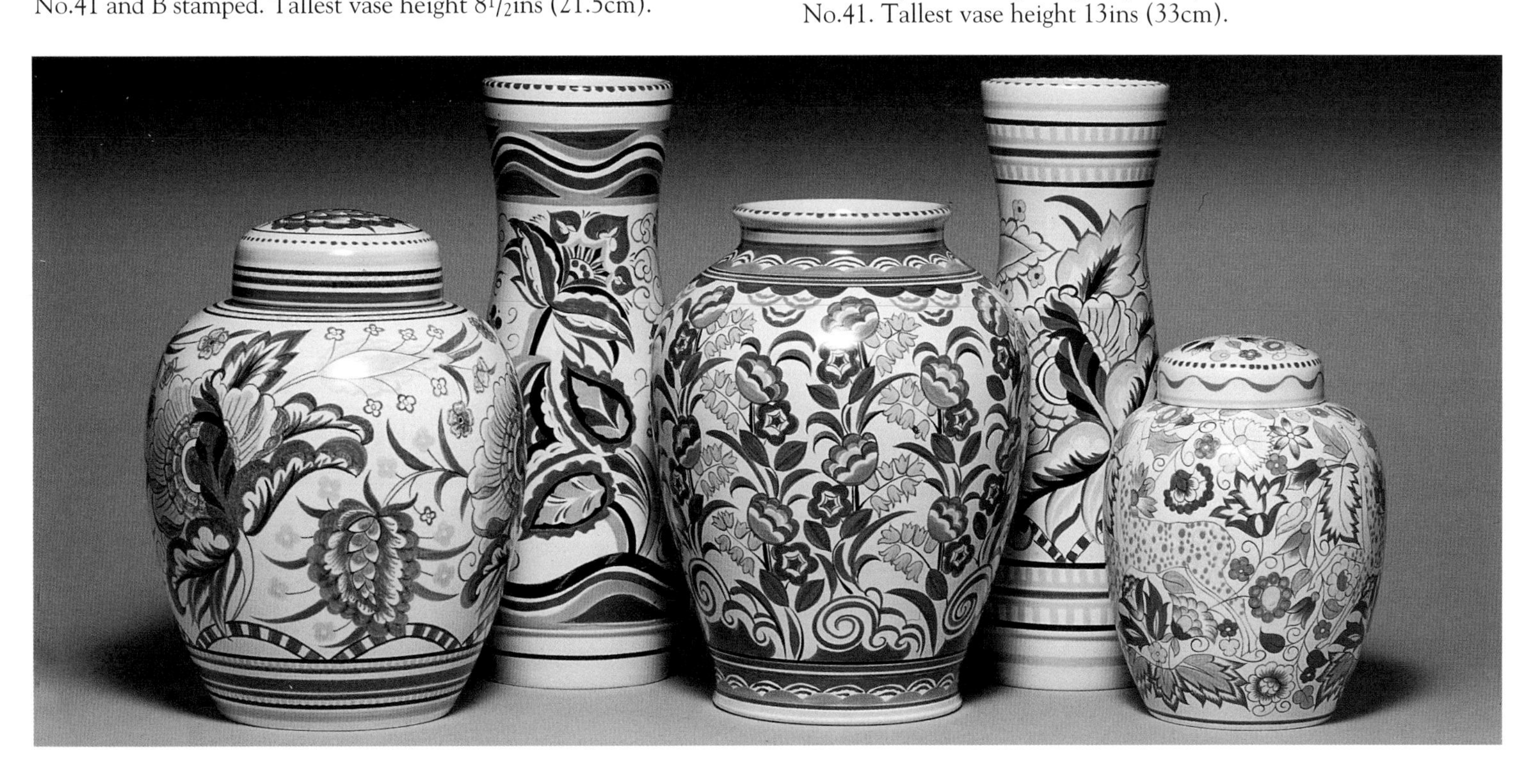

Full elaborate 'spot edged' patterns.
A selection of white earthenwares with patterns designed by Truda Carter and painted on Alpine white glaze. From left to right: covered ginger jar /YT, painted by Susan Russell, 1986, mark No.62; vase 85/EC, painted by Carolyn Davies, 1978, mark No.58; vase 660/BM, thrown by Alan White and painted by Karen Hickisson, 1978, mark No.64; vase 85/ZB, painted by Karen Hickisson, 1978, mark No.58; covered ginger jar /SK, painted by Carolyn Beckwith, 1986. Tallest vase height 16ins (40.5cm).

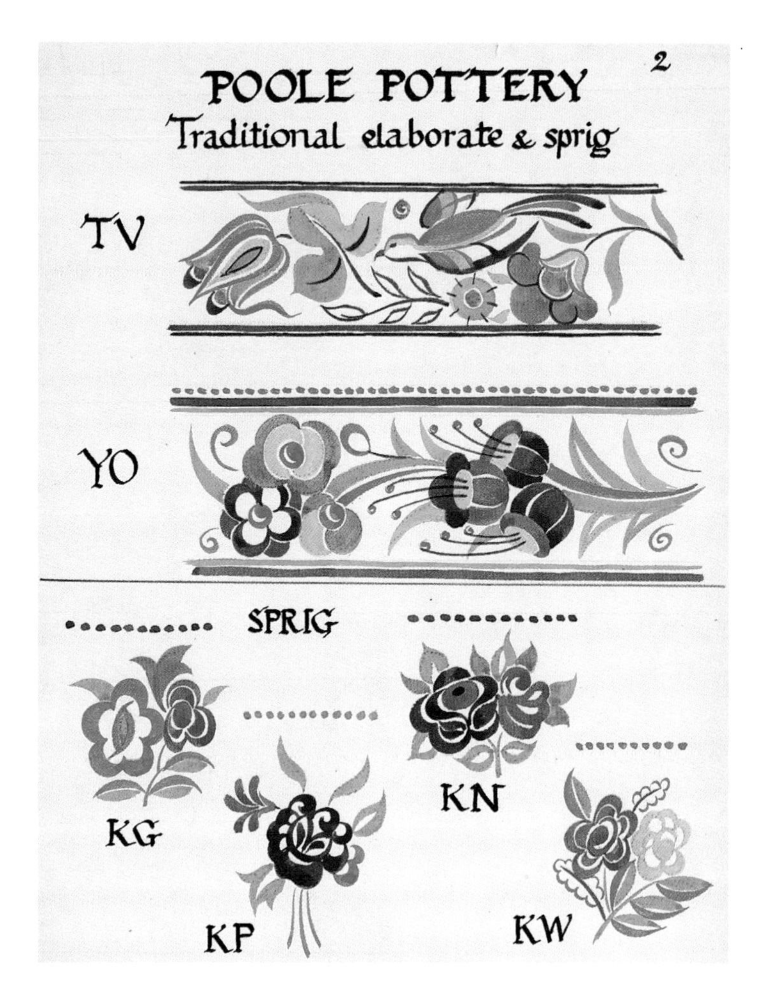

Above and below left: factory pattern sheets showing five elaborate designs as standardised in 1951, the revised and simplified 'Floriana' sprigs introduced in 1956 and the three elaborate designs simplified in 1963.

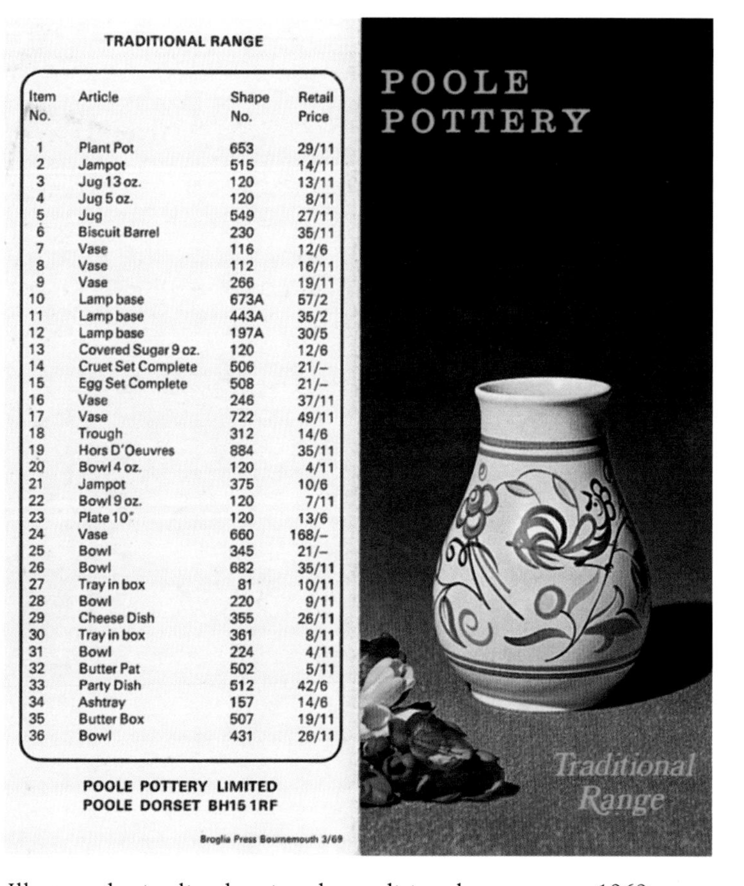
TRADITIONAL RANGE

Item No.	Article	Shape No.	Retail Price
1	Plant Pot	653	29/11
2	Jampot	515	14/11
3	Jug 13 oz.	120	13/11
4	Jug 5 oz.	120	8/11
5	Jug	549	27/11
6	Biscuit Barrel	230	35/11
7	Vase	116	12/6
8	Vase	112	16/11
9	Vase	266	19/11
10	Lamp base	673A	57/2
11	Lamp base	443A	35/2
12	Lamp base	197A	30/5
13	Covered Sugar 9 oz.	120	12/6
14	Cruet Set Complete	506	21/–
15	Egg Set Complete	508	21/–
16	Vase	246	37/11
17	Vase	722	49/11
18	Trough	312	14/6
19	Hors D'Oeuvres	884	35/11
20	Bowl 4 oz.	120	4/11
21	Jampot	375	10/6
22	Bowl 9 oz.	120	7/11
23	Plate 10"	120	13/6
24	Vase	660	168/–
25	Bowl	345	21/–
26	Bowl	682	35/11
27	Tray in box	81	10/11
28	Bowl	220	9/11
29	Cheese Dish	355	26/11
30	Tray in box	361	8/11
31	Bowl	224	4/11
32	Butter Pat	502	5/11
33	Party Dish	512	42/6
34	Ashtray	157	14/6
35	Butter Box	507	19/11
36	Bowl	431	26/11

POOLE POTTERY LIMITED
POOLE DORSET BH15 1RF

Broglia Press Bournemouth 3/69

POOLE POTTERY

Traditional Range

Illustrated price list showing the traditional ware range, 1969.

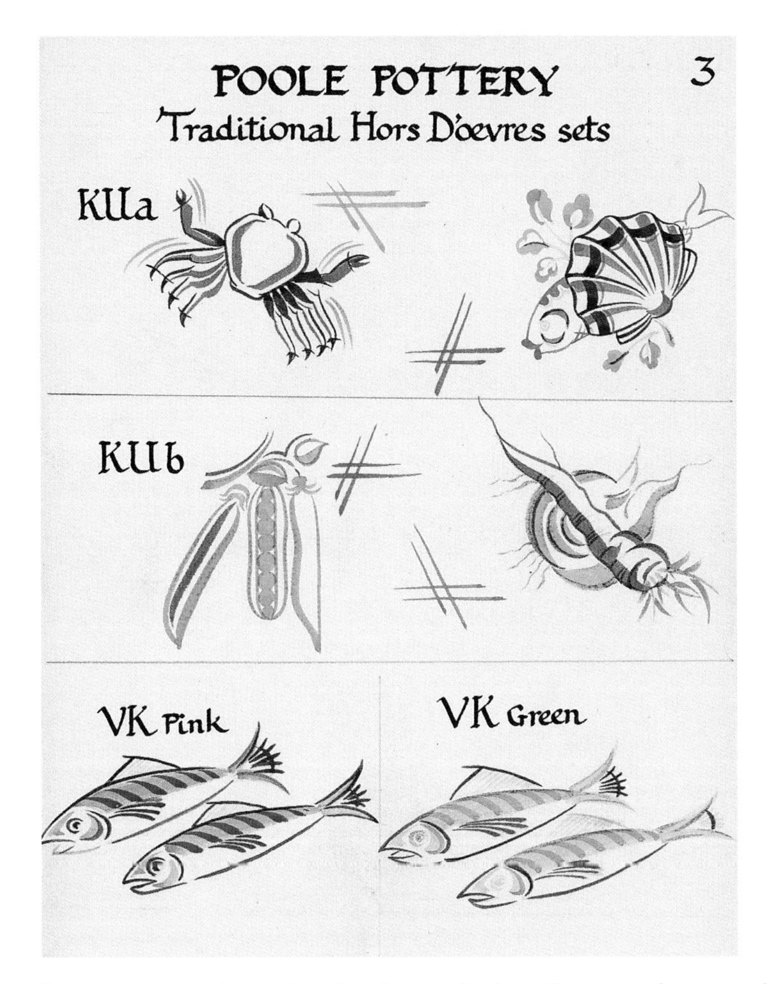

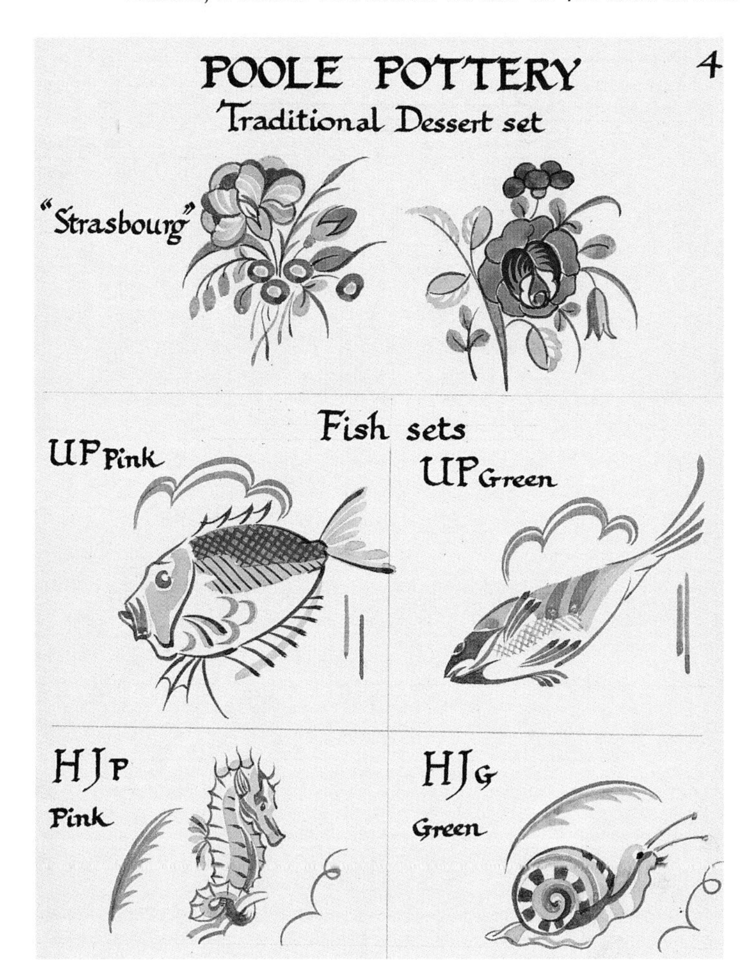

Factory pattern sheets showing designs for hors d'oeuvres dessert and fish sets re-drawn and simplified in the 1950s, see page 84.

TRADITIONAL RANGE

Item No.	Shape No.	Article	Retail Price £ s. d.	£p
1	34	Vase 11½"	42/–	2.10
2	15	Vase 9"	42/–	2.10
3 & 4	83	Vase 6"	29/–	1.45
5	31	Vase 3¾"	15/–	75
6	84	Vase 9"	79/–	3.95
7	506	Cruet Complete	27/3	1.36
8	197A	Lamp Base 4⅝"	37/–	1.85
9	443A	Lamp Base 6¾"	42/–	2.10
10	74	Plant Pot 5"	39/–	1.95
11	73	Plant Pot 4"	29/–	1.45
12	72	Plant Pot 3"	21/–	1.05
13	375	Jam Pot	13/–	65
14	32	Vase 4¼"	39/–	1.95
15		Jug 5 oz	11/–	55
16		Jug 13 oz	17/10	89
17		Jug 30 oz	29/–	1.45
18	77	Fruit Bowl 11"	59/–	2.95
19	76	Fruit Bowl 9"	39/–	1.95
20	75	Fruit Bowl 6"	21/–	1.05
21		Bowl 4 oz	6/5	32
22		Bowl 9 oz	9/5	47
23	508	Egg Set Complete	25/9	1.29
24	355	Cheese Dish	33/–	1.65
25	660	Vase 13"	210/–	10.50
26	82	Sweet Dish 17"	35/–	1.75
27	884	Hors d'Oeuvres	45/–	2.25
28	91	Dish 12"	31/–	1.55
29	85	Vase 16"	125/–	6.25
30	81	Sweet Dish 6" (Boxed)	19/–	95
31	361	Dish 7" (Boxed)	15/–	75
32	512	Party Dish	51/–	2.55
33	41	Pair of dishes 2½" ea. (Boxed)	15/–	75
34	42	Heptagonal Dish 6" (Boxed)	17/10	89
35	49	Dish 5"	9/5	47
36		Plate 10"	17/–	85
37	507	Butter Box	25/–	1.25

Factory catalogue page showing traditional ware range and price list, 1971. Many of the original painted shapes were replaced at this time by shapes designed for the Delphis decoration.

Paintresses at work in 1949. Left to right from the back: Nellie Blackmore, Jean Cockram, Barbara Meads, Gwen Haskins, Rene Hayes, Eileen Selby, Vera Morgan, Gwen Selby, Ruth Pavely (standing), Rachel Turner, Ann Ball, Hazel Allner, Gwyneth Flowers, Jean Best, Audrey Heckford.

Nellie Blackmore (née Bishton) giving a painting demonstration in Ipswich in 1968. She joined Poole in 1927 and with only a short break in the 1930s, became painting shop supervisor in 1950 and worked until 1976.

Visitors paint shop, 1941. Left to right: Gwen Eaves, Gwen Haskins, Audrey Miles, Pamela Ridout, Christine Lucas, Norah Preston.

Miscellaneous and Table Wares

Thrown white earthenwares with raised bands turned by Jimmy Soper. Left to right, vase 427, mushroom and sepia glazed 1938-1940, mark No.34 and C54 stamped; vase 818, ice green and mushroom glazed 1952, mark No.29 and C96 stamped; dish 971, ice green and mushroom glazed 1952, mark No.29 and C96 stamped; vase 419, alternate bands and border pattern painted on alpine white glaze (with mushroom glaze interior) 1951-1952, mark No.29; bowl 769, alternate bands and border pattern painted on alpine white glaze (with mushroom glaze interior) 1952, mark No.37; vase 409, alternate bands and border pattern painted on alpine white glaze (with mushroom glaze interior) by Gwendoline Selby, 1951. Dish diameter 12³/₄ins (32.5cm).

Thrown white earthenwares with sgraffito and applied relief decoration designed by John Adams and Truda Carter. Left to right: plant pot 665/111, 1952-1955, mark No.37; jam pot 288, about 1957, mark No.39, trial vase decorated by Margaret Holder, 1939-1940, mark No.19; vase 14/S19 from a range of sgraffito vases, bowls and jugs designed for Heal & Son, 1940, mark No.19. Tallest vase height 11¹/₂ins (29cm).

Thrown white earthenware vases covered with re-active glazes of Chinese type over a red terracotta slip ground, 1953. Also two items from a range of tableware accessories designed by Tony Morris and Guy Sydenham, 1967-1968. Left to right: vase 443, Chinese green glaze, mark No.37; storage jar 513/1, Blue Lace, mottled effect glaze, mark No.48; vase 607, Chinese blue glaze, mark No.37 and R painted; ashtray, Sea Crest, olive green and ice green glazes used in combination. Tallest vase height 8¹/₄ins (21cm). Chinese blue and green vases and bowls were shown in an exhibition of Poole fine earthenware at the Tea Centre, Regent Street, London in 1953.

Plaque 313. A slip cast pierced wall decoration in white earthenware, finished in shaded tones of Picotee green and autumn brown glazes with black oxide colour, applied with an air brush on to a hard magnolia base glaze, mark No.29. Height 12¹/₂ins (32cm). Designed by Lily Markus and illustrated in *The Studio Year Book*, 1951-1952.

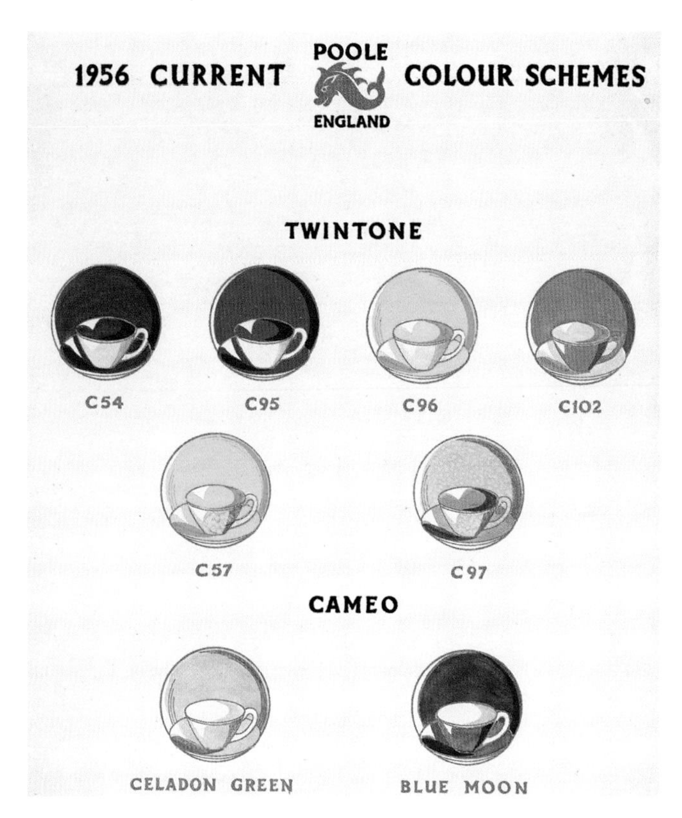

Factory catalogue sheet issued in 1956 showing also the current slip decorated Cameo colours.

POST-WAR ADDITIONS AND REVISIONS (TWINTONE)

	Inside	Outside	In Production From	To
C54	Sepia	Mushroom	Pre-war + 1946-50	1981
C57	Ice Green	Seagull	Pre-war + 1946-50	1981
C65	Magnolia	Shagreen	Pre-war + 1946-50	1950
C84	Sky Blue	Magnolia	Pre-war + 1946-50	1950
C95	Red Indian	Magnolia	1950	1956
C96	Ice Green	Mushroom	1952	1965
C97	Peach Bloom	Seagull	1953	1968
C98	Peach Bloom	Ice Green	1953	1954
C99	Ice Green	Peach Bloom	1953	1954
C100	Peach Bloom	Mist Blue	1953	1954
C101	Mushroom	Peach Bloom	1953	1954
C102	Lime Yellow	Moonstone Grey	1956	1957
C103	Lime Yellow	Seagull	1957	1966
C104	Sky Blue	Dove Grey	1958	1981
C105	Alpine White	Dove Grey (Grey Pebble)	1959	1961
C106	Alpine White	Black Panther (Black Pebble)	1959	1961
C107	Sweetcorn	Brazil	1965	1968
C108	Ice Green	Seagull (Seagull plates USA only)	1965	1967
C109	Sunshine Yellow	Seagull (Seagull plates USA only)	1965	1967

The complete post war range of Twintone glazes.

A selection of Streamline tableware in white earthenware, the basic shape designed by John Adams, 1935-1936, with updated circular knop to the lid, and coupe shaped rimless plates, designed by Alfred Read, 1953-1955. Left to right: teapot 109/DW, the pattern 'Trudiana' designed by Ruth Pavely and painted by Sheila Jenkins, 1955-1959, mark No.39. Trudiana was adapted from an original dessert set motif, designed by Truda Carter about 1938; coffee pot 229, sprayed in shiny hydrangea glaze, 1936-1937, mark No.19, HYDRANGEA stamped; mustard pot 130/KV4, a 'Watkinson' motif designed by Truda Carter and painted by Ruth Pavely, used on Dorset tableware supplied exclusively to Heal & Son, 1936-1940, mark No.19; plate 120/XL, the pattern Falling Leaves designed by Ruth Pavely and painted in mainly soluble colours by Josephine Smith, 1957-1958, mark No.39; coffee pot 109/FNP the Leaf pattern designed by Truda Carter, 1948-1949 and painted by Kathleen Riggs, 1950-1953, mark No.36; teapot 109/Utility, sprayed with a crystal glaze, 1946-1950, mark No.35; coffee pot 109/YU, the pattern Red Pippin designed by Ruth Pavely and painted in mainly soluble colours by Iris Downton, 1957-1958, mark No. 39. Plate diameter 6ins (15cm).

Factory promotional leaflet illustrating the Sherborne range in celadon green slip contrasting the white earthenware body and covered with a clear crystal glaze. Available also in shell-pink and white, the Sherborne shape was designed by John Adams and first made in the late 1930s. It was re-introduced in 1949 as an inexpensive alternative to Streamline tableware decorated with Twintone glazes containing costly tin and other metallic oxides.

Alfred Read and the 1950s

Design meeting 1954. Left to right: Alfred Read, Lucien Myers, and Roy Holland.

In 1950 Lucien Myers took over from John Adams as Managing Director. His experience as editor of the trade journal *Pottery and Glass* and in the wholesale and retail trades, helped considerably in establishing new market outlets for the pottery's expanding production. Adams had planned an extensive post war redevelopment of the pottery and its equipment and this was now well under way, under the control of Roy Holland, the newly appointed technical and works director. All that remained to be resolved was the appointment of a new design director. The first attempt was unsuccessful, with Claude Smale, a former Royal College of Art student, only staying for six months. His contribution, with Ruth Pavely, was the design of the range of commemorative wares planned for the Festival of Britain in 1951. The next proved to be a great success and marked a new stage in Poole's development. Alfred Burgess Read, R.D.I., an established industrial designer, was appointed head of the design unit set up to serve both the pottery and the tile works. Other members of the unit included design assistant Ruth Pavely and Guy Sydenham, the senior thrower, who had joined the pottery in 1931. Under Read's direction Poole embarked on a period of close co-operation between artists and technicians that resulted in a range of stylish and elegant wares whose unity of shape and decoration expressed totally the spirit of the 1950s. Working together, Read and Sydenham produced a new range of shapes in contemporary styles, designed for both hand-throwing and for casting. To decorate these, and the existing Streamline tablewares, Read and Pavely created an exciting range of new hand-painted and predominantly abstract patterns that, nonetheless, still relied on the traditional Delftware technique. These new wares were first shown, in an experimental form, at an exhibition at The Tea Centre, Regent Street, London early in 1953. At the same time as a celebration of Coronation Year, the Poole pottery was re-opened to the public. By the next year, the contemporary range was being widely displayed and advertised, and illustrated in publications such as *The Studio Year Book of Decorative Art*, placing Poole once again in the forefront of popular modernism. History was made, and traditionalism cast aside in 1955 when the Princess Royal visited Poole and was presented with a specially made vase in the new contemporary style, painted by Ruth Pavely. By 1956 the contemporary designs had been applied also to bowls, trays and posy ware, along with domestic tablewares such as butter dishes and cruet sets. Underlining the contemporary spirit was a group of freeform vases for flower arranging, designed by Read and Sydenham, and made both with painted patterns from the contemporary range and with monochrome glaze finishes, notably black panther and magnolia white. These were also made in the Twintone colours, and in solid colours with white interiors. The final development in this period was the expansion of the pattern range by Alfred Read's daughter Ann, whose bamboo design was particularly effective on tablewares. Having trained as a designer in fine arts at Chelsea School of Art, Ann also became responsible for a large series of painted plaques produced in limited editions, some on alpine white and some on black panther glazes introduced in 1956.

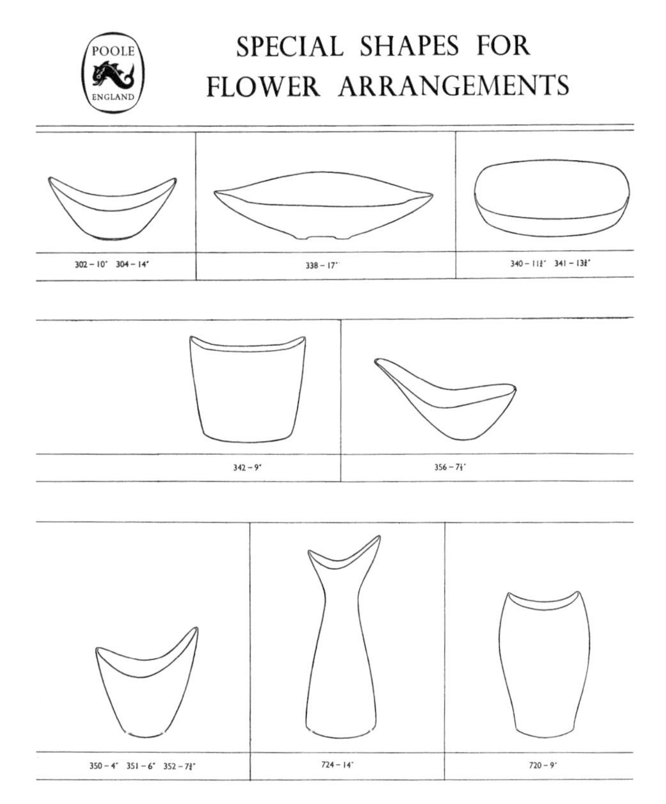

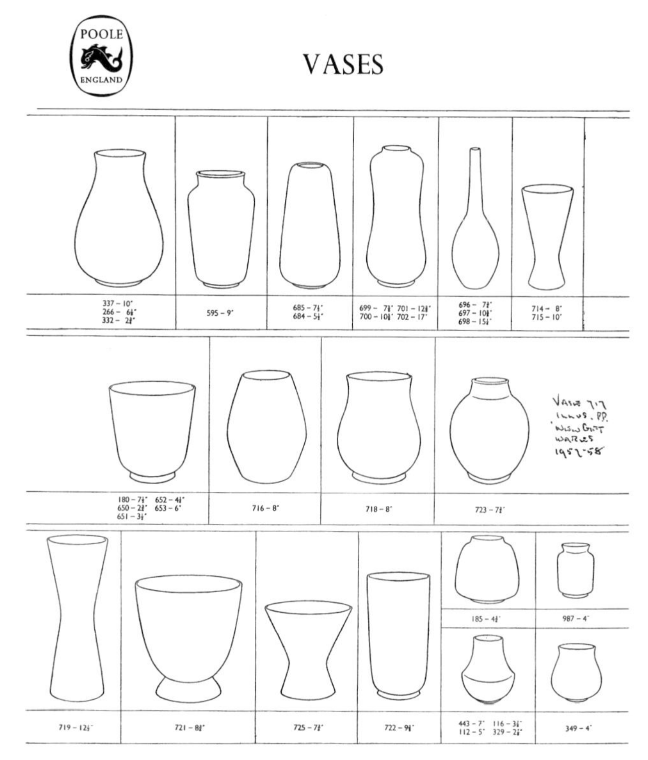

Factory pattern sheets showing contemporary and pre-war shapes for vases and for flower arranging.
Above: free form shapes designed for slip casting by Alfred Read and Guy Sydenham, 1956-1957.
Right: shapes designed for hand throwing by Alfred Read and Guy Sydenham 1953-1957, including marrow shaped vases 699-702, inspired by Lucien Myers and the following shapes from the 1920s and 1930s probably designed by John Adams: vases 112, 180, 185, 266, 332, 337, 349, 443, 595 and 987.

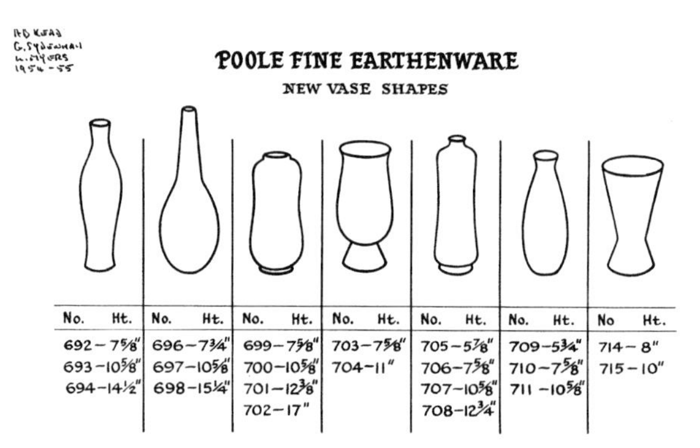

POOLE FINE EARTHENWARE

NEW VASE SHAPES

No. Ht.	No. Ht.	No. Ht.	No. Ht.	No. Ht.	No. Ht.	No Ht.
692 – 7⅝"	696 – 7¾"	699 – 7⅝"	703 – 7⅝"	705 – 5⅞"	709 – 5¾"	714 – 8"
693 – 10⅝"	697 – 10⅝"	700 – 10⅝"	704 – 11"	706 – 7⅝"	710 – 7⅝"	715 – 10"
694 – 14½"	698 – 15¼"	701 – 12⅜"		707 – 10⅝"	711 – 10⅝"	
		702 – 17"		708 – 12¾"		

ALL THE ABOVE ARE AVAILABLE IN THE CURRENT VASE GLAZE FINISHES AND IN ASSORTED HAND PAINTED DECORATIONS ON ALPINE MATT WHITE GLAZE, AS ILLUSTRATED.

Poole Pottery stand at the Tea Centre exhibition, Regent Street, London, January 1958.

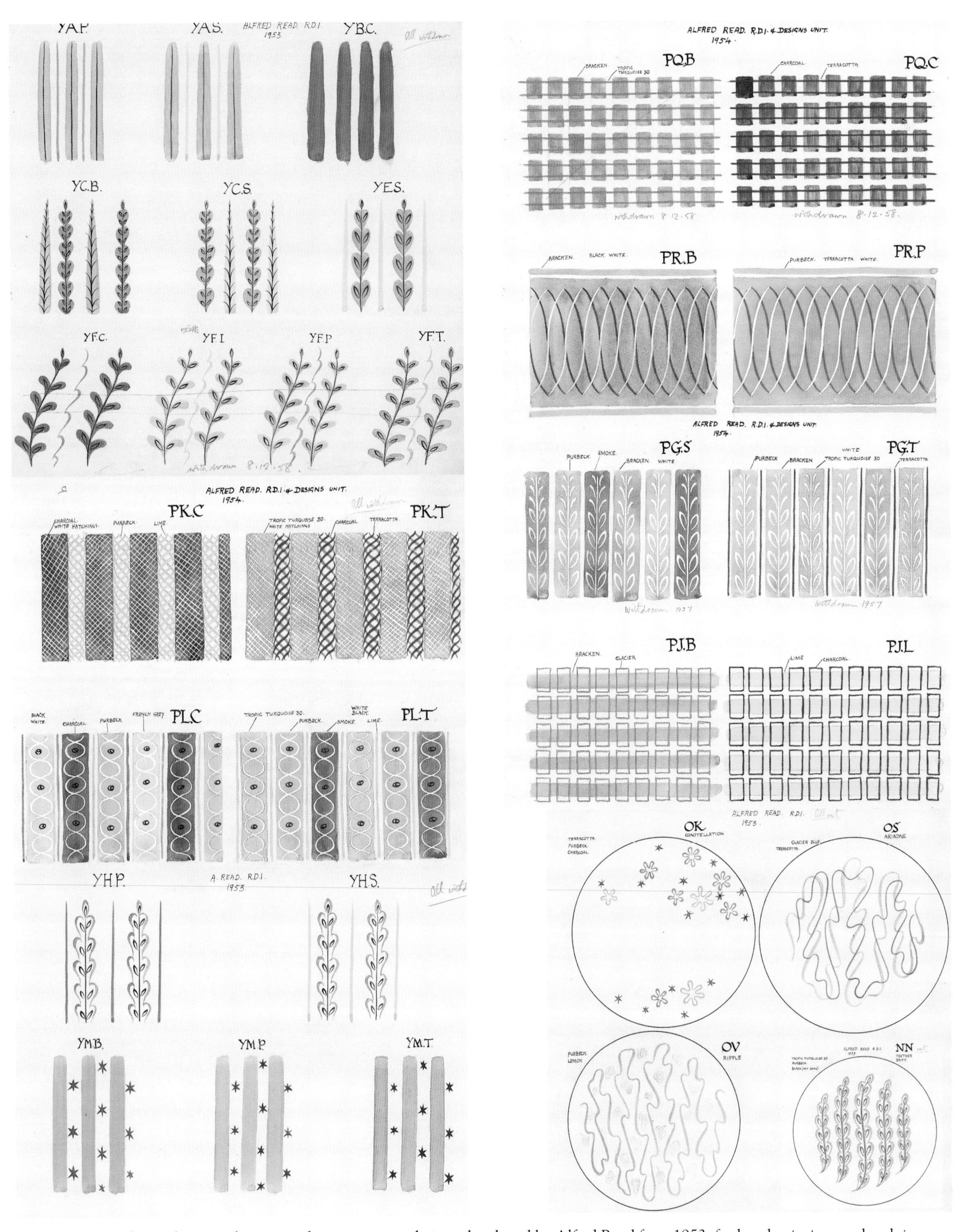

Factory pattern sheets showing the range of contemporary designs developed by Alfred Read from 1953, for hand painting on the alpine white glaze, on thrown shapes created by Alfred Read and Guy Sydenham and, from 1954, for hand painting on John Adams' Streamline tablewares.

A selection of hand thrown white earthenwares with contemporary patterns in mainly soluble colours designed by Alfred Read, 1953-1954, and hand painted on alpine white glaze. From left to right: vase 707 E/PGT, the shape designed by Alfred Read and Guy Sydenham, painted by Diane Holloway, 1955-1958, mark No.39; carafe 690 E/YAS, the shape designed by Claude Smale and Guy Sydenham, painted by Gwen Haskins, 1953-1955, mark No.37; dish 920 E/PRP, the shape probably designed by John Adams, 1936-1937, painted by Diane Holloway, 1955-1958, mark No.39; carafe 697/PRB, the shape designed by Alfred Read and Guy Sydenham, painted by Gwen Haskins, 1959-1962, mark No.41; vase 714/PRP, the shape designed by Alfred Read and Guy Sydenham, painted by Diane Holloway, 1955-1958, mark No.39; vase 266 E/YAS, the shape probably designed by John Adams, 1929-1930, painted by Gwen Haskins, 1953-1955, mark No.37. Dish diameter 13ins (33cm).

A selection of hand thrown white earthenwares with contemporary patterns in mainly soluble colours designed by Alfred Read in 1953-1954 and hand painted on alpine white glaze. From left to right: carafe 690 E/YCS, the shape designed by Claude Smale and Guy Sydenham, painted by Gwen Haskins, 1953-1955, mark No.37; vase 687 E/YFI, the shape designed by Claude Smale and Guy Sydenham, painted by Jean Cockram, 1953-1955, mark No.37; vase 686 E/YFT, the shape designed by Claude Smale and Guy Sydenham, painted by Jean Cockram, 1953-1955, mark No.37; vase 685 E/YHP, the shape designed by Claude Smale and Guy Sydenham, painted by Jean Cockram, 1953-1955, mark No.37; vase 337 E/YMP, the shape probably designed by John Adams, 1921-1926, painted by Gwen Haskins, 1955-1959, mark No.39; carafe 689 E/YFC, the shape designed by Claude Smale and Guy Sydenham, painted by Jean Cockram, 1953-1955, mark No. 37. Tallest vase height 10ins (25.5cm).

A selection of hand thrown, white earthenwares with contemporary patterns in mainly soluble colours, designed by Alfred Read in 1954 and hand painted on alpine white glaze. From left to right: vase 694/PKT, the shape designed by Alfred Read and Guy Sydenham, painted by Gwen Haskins, 1955-1959, mark No.39; vase 266 E/PKT, the shape probably designed by John Adams, 1929-1930, painted by Diane Holloway, 1955-1958, mark No.39; vase 715/PKT, the shape designed by Alfred Read and Guy Sydenham, painted by Pat Dightam, 1954-1955, mark No.37; dish 920/PKT, the shape probably designed by John Adams, 1936-1937, painted 1955-1959, mark No.39; vase 709/PKT, the shape designed by Alfred Read and Guy Sydenham, probably painted by Gwen Haskins, 1955-1959, mark No.39; vase 704/PKT, the shape designed by Alfred Read and Guy Sydenham, painted by Pat Dightam, 1954-1955, mark No.37; vase 711/PKT, the shape designed by Alfred Read and Guy Sydenham, painted by Gwen Haskins, 1955-1959, mark No.39. Tallest vase height 14½ins (37cm).

A selection of hand thrown white earthenwares with contemporary patterns in mainly soluble colours designed by Alfred Read in 1954 and hand painted on alpine white glaze. From left to right: carafe 698/PLT, the shape designed by Alfred Read and Guy Sydenham, painted by Gwen Haskins, 1959-1962, mark No. 41; vase 595/PLT, the shape probably designed by John Adams, 1930-1935, painted by Gwen Haskins, 1959-1962, mark No.41; vase 702/PLT, the shape designed by Lucien Myers and Guy Sydenham, painted by Gwen Haskins, 1959-1962, mark No.41; bowl 291/PJB, the shape probably designed by John Adams, 1929-1930, painted by Pat Dightam, 1955-1958; carafe 697/PJL, the shape designed by Alfred Read and Guy Sydenham, painted by Gwen Haskins, 1955-1959, mark No.39; vase 704/PQB, the shape designed by Alfred Read and Guy Sydenham, painted by Gwen Haskins, 1955-1959, mark No.39. Tallest vast height 17½ins (45cm). Vase 702/PLT and bowl 291/PJB were illustrated in *The Studio Year Book*, 1956-1957.

A selection of white earthenware tablewares and accessories with contemporary patterns in mainly soluble colours, hand painted on alpine white glaze. From left to right: cucumber dish 555/TNC the shape designed by John Adams about 1935, the pattern designed by Ruth Pavely 1954, and painted by Diane Holloway, 1955-1958, mark No.39; plate 120/, the shape and trial pattern designed by Alfred Read, 1953-1954, and painted by Gwen Haskins, 1955, mark No.39; coffee pot 42, cup and saucer 109/OV, the Streamline shape designed by John Adams, 1935-1936, modified and painted with the 'Ripple' pattern designed by Alfred Read 1953-1954; oval dish 120/OS, the shape and 'Ariadne' pattern designed by Alfred Read, 1953-1954; jam pot 286/NN, the shape probably designed by John Adams, 1921-1926, the 'Feather Drift' pattern designed by Alfred Read, 1953-1954; bowl 366/TNB, the shape probably designed by John Adams 1921-1922, the pattern designed by Ruth Pavely, 1954. Plate diamater 10ins (25.5cm).

A selection of white earthenware tablewares and accessories with contemporary patterns in mainly soluble colours, hand painted on alpine white or black panther glaze. From left to right: cream jug 505/OK, the shape probably designed by John Adams, 1935-1936, with the 'Constellation' pattern designed by Alfred Read, 1953-1954; teapot 36, 109/TUA, the Streamline shape designed by John Adams, 1935-1936, with shape modified and pattern designed by Alfred Read, 1954-1955, and painted by Jean Cockram; tea cup and saucer 109/NN, the Streamline shape designed by John Adams, 1935-1936; the 'Feather Drift' pattern designed by Alfred Read, 1953-1954; hors d'oeuvres 884 designed by John Adams about 1938, the trial pattern probably designed by Ruth Pavely, 1954; cucumber dish 555/ROL, the shape designed by John Adams about 1935, the pattern designed by Ruth Pavely, 1954. Hors d'oeuvres dish height 8¼ins (21cm).

Examples from a range of white earthenware vases, bowls and plant pots, designed by Alfred Read and Guy Sydenham, 1954-1957, and glazed in solid colours. Left to right: carafe 698/sky blue, mark No.41; carafe 696, black panther, mark No.41; plant pot 721/ lime yellow, mark No.41; freeform bowl 356, magnolia and red Indian, mark No.39; freeform vase 724/ ice green, mark No.41. Taller carafe height 15¼ins (39cm).

Ann Read

A selection of white earthenware plaques, the decorations designed by Ann Read, 1955-1956. With the exception of Yaffle Hill, this group is representative of a series of 52 plaques, each of which was produced in a limited edition, numbered or dated and signed by the artist. All were painted in glaze on alpine white, black panther, or other coloured grounds, and the series included five 7ins. plates, twenty-six 8ins. plates, two 12ins. round dishes, eleven 10ins. oval dishes, two 12ins. oval dishes and six 14ins. oval dishes. The retail prices ranged from three guineas to nine guineas each. Yaffle Hill, a view of Cyril Carter's house at Broadstone, painted by Ruth Pavely, is one of a set of four designed by Ann Read and presented to Cyril Carter on completing fifty years service with the Company. Inscribed 'C.S.A. Design Unit to C.C. Carter Esq. 1905-1955'; Stalking Cat, painted by Ann Read, the date 20.4.55 and artist's insignia painted on reverse; Lion, painted by Ann Read, 'Leo A-I and the artist's signature painted on reverse, mark No.38 excluding frame; Freya, painted by Nellie Blackmore, mark No.40. This plate is one of three Ann Read original designs incorporated into a range of twelve hand painted plates launched at the Tea Centre exhibition, Regent Street, London in 1958. The three plates, Freya, renamed VZ Poole Harbour, together with AW Reflections and UG Snow Goose, are illustrated with other plates in the 1958 range on page 106; Circus, painted by Ann Read, the date 27.5.55 and artist's insignia painted on reverse, mark No.37; Landscape, painted by Ann Read, 'The Peaks - 2' and the artist's insignia painted on reverse, mark No.38, excluding frame. Circus plaque length 16¼ins (41.5cm).

Ann Read painting a dish from her limited edition series, 1955-1956.

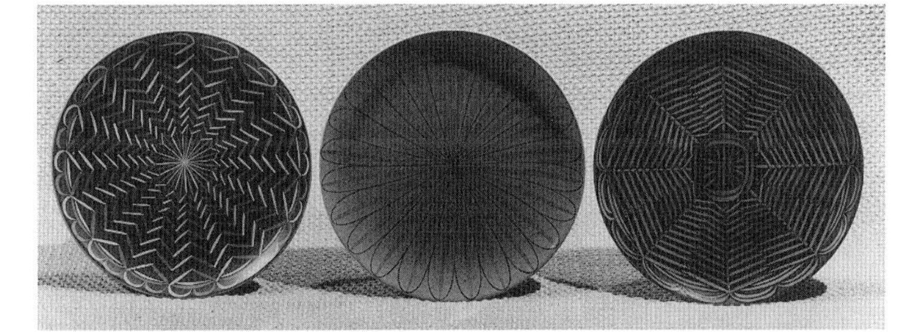

Selection of plates painted in various styles by Ann Read 1955-1956, including examples of her black ground range.

Left: Poole Pottery display plaque, designed and first painted by Ann Read in 1956, mark No.41. Length 14ins (35.5cm).

POOLE POTTERY

POOLE ENGLAND

New Giftwares

Above: Club Ash Tray No. 357. Suitable for desk, board room table, or the family circle. In Twintone colour schemes, and in a range of new handpainted decorations on Alpine matt white glaze with contrasting coloured glaze outside.

Below: A group of tableware accessory pieces from the new range, in Twintone finishes.

Top, left to right - Condiment Set No. 335.
Eggcup on stand No. 104.
Middle - - - T.V. Set No. 339.
Bottom, left to right Tray No. 360.
Tray No. 359.
Tray No. 364.

Also available in new handpainted decorations on Alpine matt white glaze with contrasting coloured glazes.

Above: Tableware accessory pieces in new handpainted decorations with contrasting coloured glazes on lids and stands, on the outsides of trays and the insides of the open hollow ware.

Top - - - Condiment Set No. 335.
Middle, left to right Small Tray No. 364.
Eggcup on stand No. 104.
Small Tray No. 360.
Front - - - Long Tray No. 365.
Small Tray No. 359.

Also available in current Twintone finishes.

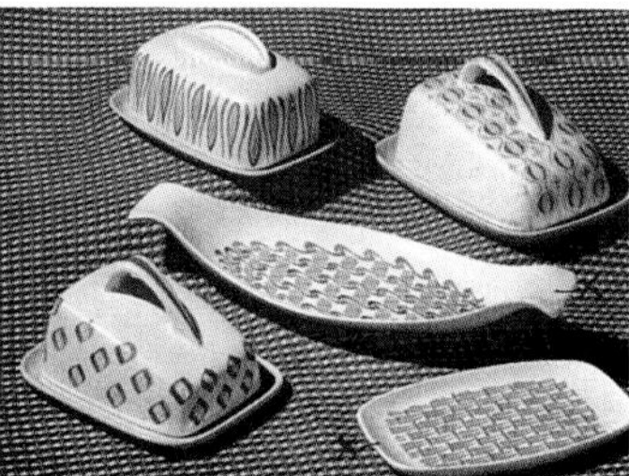

Right: More pieces from the new tableware fancies range in new handpainted decorations with contrasting coloured glazes.

Back, left to right - Butter Box No. 354.
Cheese Dish No. 355.
Middle - - - Tray No. 358.
Front - - - Cheese Dish No. 336.
Tray No. 361.

Also available in current Twintone finishes.

CARTER STABLER & ADAMS LTD.
POOLE · DORSET · ENGLAND

Bowls and Dishes

Right: A group of free form bowls from the new range. Handpainted patterns with Mushroom Pink inside — also in Black, and White, and solid colours.

Vase No. 352.
" No. 351.
" No. 350.
Bowl No. 356.

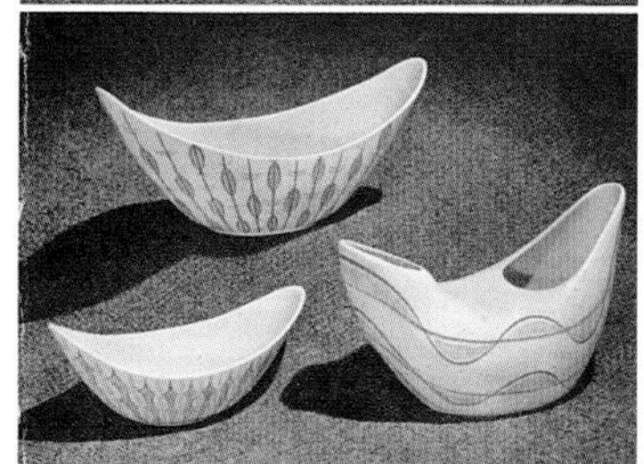

Right: Oval bowl in two sizes and two-hole vase.

Back - - Bowl No. 304.
Front, left - - Bowl No. 302.
Front, right - - Vase No. 343.

In new handpainted decorations, also available in solid colours.

Right: Dishes, available in a range of handpainted decorations on matt white glaze with contrasting Mushroom Pink glaze outside.

Planter Dish No. 341.
" " No. 340.
Dish No. 338.

Also available in Black, White, and in current Twintone finishes.

Left: Handpainted vases from the new range including hand-thrown and free form shapes, with handpainted decorations on Alpine matt white glaze with Mushroom Pink interiors, available also in Black Panther, White, and solid colours.

Back, left to right - Vase No. 720.
" No. 724.
" No. 342.
Front, left to right - Vase No. 716.
" No. 725.

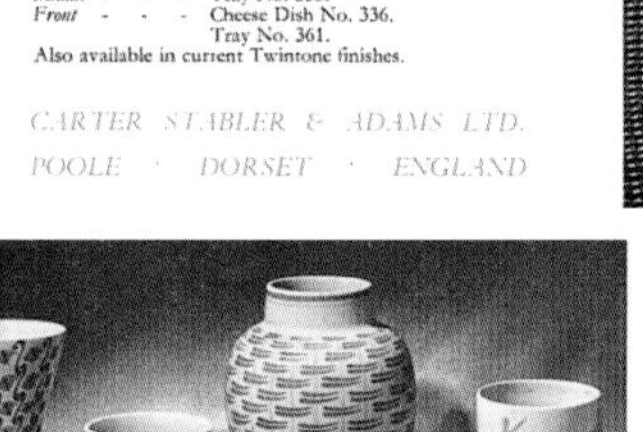

Above: Hand-thrown vases, part of the new range of shapes; handpainted decorations on Alpine matt white glaze with Mushroom Pink interiors.

Left to right - - Vase No. 719.
" No. 718.
" No. 717.
" No. 723.
" No. 722.

Also available in solid colour glazes with white inside.

Above: Plant pots in various sizes in handpainted decorations, also in solid colour glazes with white inside.

Back, left to right - Plant Pot No. 180.
" " No. 721.
" " No. 653.
Middle - - - Plant Pot No. 651.
" " No. 652.
Front - - - Plant Pot No. 650.

Vases, Plant Pots

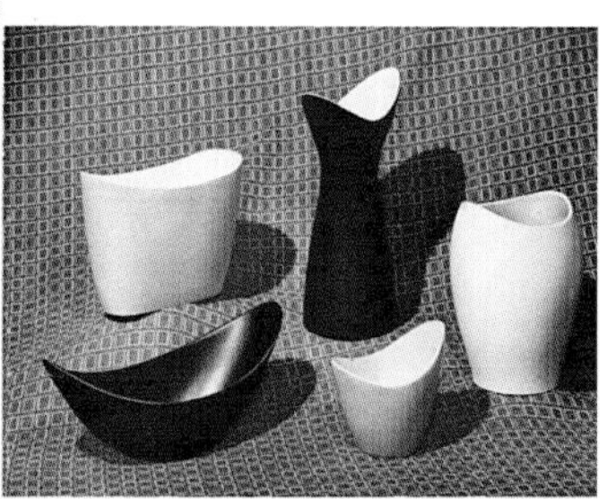

Above: A group of free form vases and bowls forming part of the new range. Finishes: Black Panther, Magnolia White glazes — also available in other solid colour glazes and with handpainted decorations.

Back, left to right - Vase No. 342.
" No. 724.
" No. 720.
Front, left to right - Bowl No. 304.
Vase No. 351.

Above: A further selection from the new vase shapes in various solid colour glazes with white interiors. The same shapes are also available with handpainted decorations.

Left to right - - Vase No. 719.
" No. 718.
" No. 717.
" No. 352.
" No. 725.

Handpainted Plates

each available in 3 sizes, 10", 12", 14" actual diameter

Left: Elaborate Traditional Poole decorations.
left to right:
Patterns CS, LE, TV.

Left: Elaborate Traditional Poole decorations.
left to right:
Pattern BN.
'Sugar' – CM.
'Persian Deer' – SK.

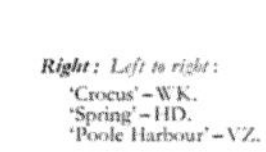

Right: *Left to right:*
'Crocus' – WK.
'Spring' – HD.
'Poole Harbour' – VZ.

Right: *Left to right:*
'Reflection' – AW.
'Snow Goose' – UG.
'Tropicana' – HF.

Printed in England by
J. Looker, Ltd., Poole, Dorset.

Pages of a promotional leaflet issued in 1958 showing contemporary giftwares, vases, bowls and plant pots, traditional wares, and Ann Read designs re-issued (not limited).

Ruth Pavely

Ruth Pavely, head of painting, 1955.

Guy Sydenham, senior thrower, 1953.

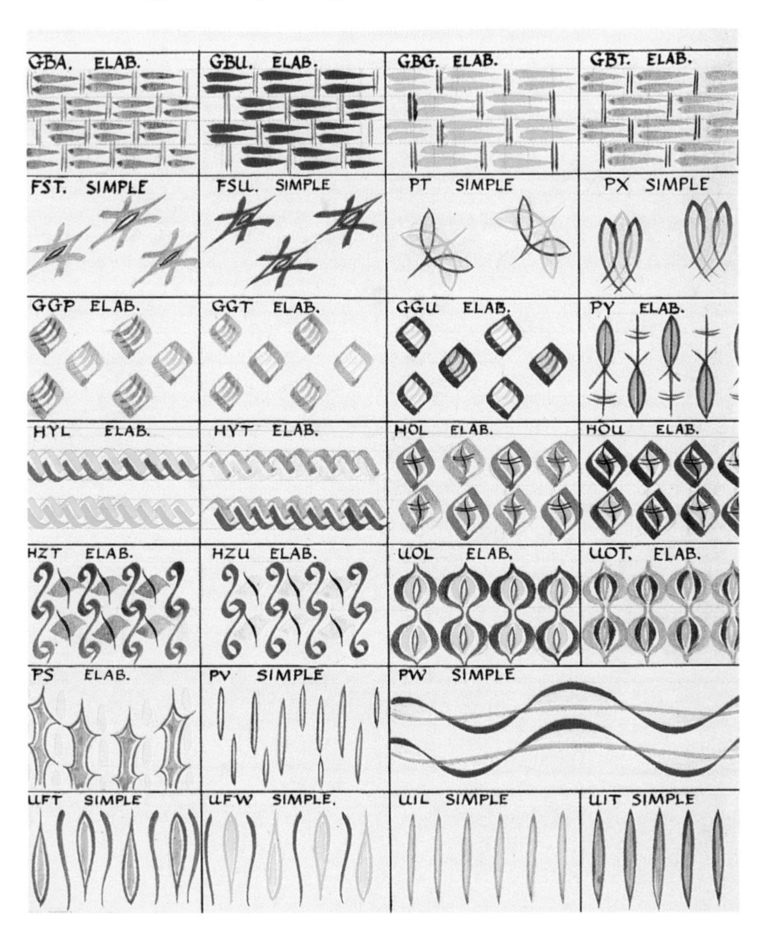

Contemporary pattern colour chart, showing the range of simple and elaborate designs in mainly soluble colours developed by Ruth Pavely and Ann Read (patterns GB and PS) for hand painting on shapes designed by Alfred Read and Guy Sydenham, 1956-1957.

A group of slip cast free form and hand thrown vases in white earthenware, designed by Alfred Read and Guy Sydenham, 1956-1957. Contemporary patterns in mainly soluble colours designed by Ruth Pavely and hand-painted on alpine white glaze. Left to right: free form vase 352/PW with a pattern of loops painted by June March, mark No.41; free form vase 724/PV, burst pattern painted by Gwen Haskins, mark No.39; free form vase 343/FSU, stars pattern painted by Gwen Haskins, mark No.39; vase 725/PT, butterflies pattern painted by Diane Holloway, mark No.39. Tallest vase height 14ins (35.5cm).

Hand thrown white earthenware vases designed by Alfred Read and Guy Sydenham, 1956-1957. Contemporary patterns in mainly soluble colours designed by Ruth Pavely (except where attributed to Ann Read) and hand painted on alpine white glaze. Left to right: vase 716/HYT, horizontal rope pattern, mark No. 39; vase 717/HYL, horizontal rope pattern painted by Gwen Haskins, mark No.39; vase 716/HOL, harlequin pattern painted by Gwen Haskins, mark No.41; vase 718/GBU, basket pattern designed by Ann Read and painted by Gwen Haskins, mark No.39. Tallest vase height 10ins (25.5cm).

Hand thrown and slip cast free form shapes in white earthenware designed by Alfred Read and Guy Sydenham, 1956-1957. Contemporary patterns in mainly soluble colours designed by Ruth Pavely (except where attributed to Ann Read) and hand painted on alpine white glaze. Left to right: free form vase 342/PS, bamboo pattern designed by Ann Read and painted by Diane Holloway, mark No.39; free form vase 720/PY, totem pattern painted by Gwen Haskins, mark No.39; plant pot 721/GGP, ravioli pattern painted by Gwen Haskins, mark No.39; free form vase 350/PS, bamboo pattern designed by Ann Read and painted by Gwen Haskins, mark No.39; vase 718/HZT, scroll pattern painted by Gwen Haskins, mark No.39. Tallest vase height 9¾ins (24.5cm).

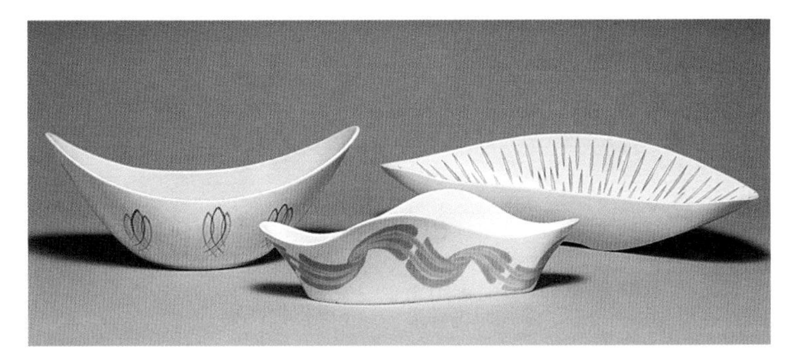

A group of slip cast free form shapes in white earthenware designed by Alfred Read, 1955-1957. Contemporary patterns in mainly soluble colours designed by Ruth Pavely and hand painted on alpine white glaze. From left to right: free form bowl 304/PX, tadpoles pattern painted by June March, mark No.41; free form flower trough 313/trial pattern, mark No.39; free form dish 338/PV, burst pattern painted by Gwen Haskins, mark No.39. Dish length 17½ins (45cm).

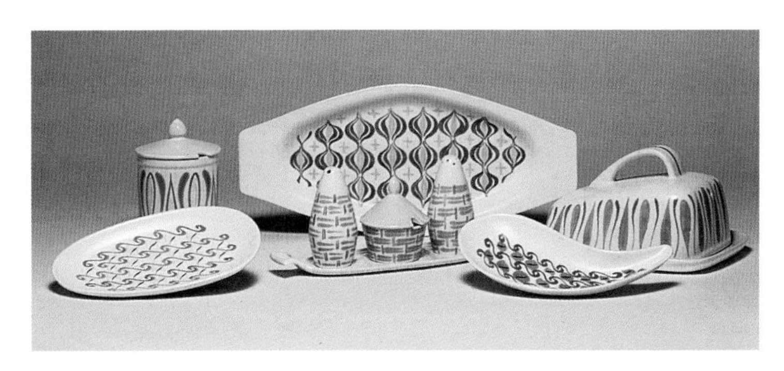

A group of white earthenware tableware accessories, the jam pot probably designed by John Adams, 1921-1926 and the remaining shapes designed by Alfred Read, 1957. Contemporary patterns in mainly soluble colours designed by Ruth Pavely and hand painted, 1958-1962. From left to right: oval tray 360/HZU, scroll pattern; jam pot 286/trial pattern; diamond tray 365/UOT, onions pattern; cruet set 335/GBG, basket pattern; tear-drop tray 359/HZT, scroll pattern; cheese dish 355/UFW, tears pattern. Longest tray height 5½ins (14cm).

A group of studio wares in white earthenware, thrown on the wheel by Guy Sydenham. From left to right: vase painted on alpine white glaze by Ruth Pavely, 1952-1954, mark No.37; vase painted on black panther glaze by Ruth Pavely about 1954, hexagon impressed, shown at the Tea Centre Exhibition, Regent Street, London 1958; glazed bowl, mark No.39 and M.M. Stent, 19.9.57 painted, signed G. Sydenham. Tallest vase height 15ins (38cm).

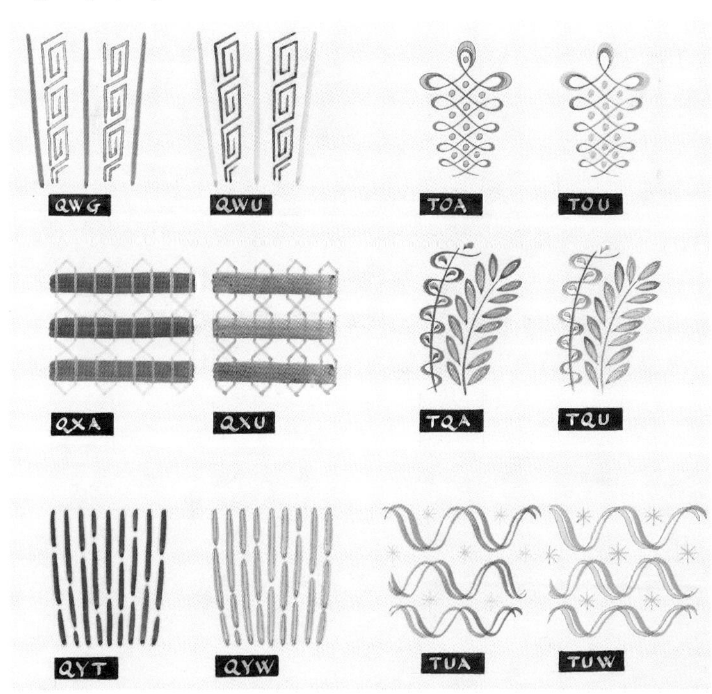

Factory pattern sheets showing contemporary tableware designs by Alfred Read for hand painting on black panther glaze 1954.

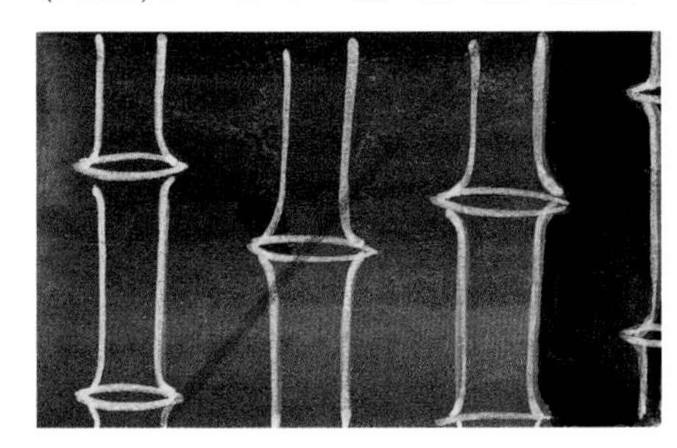

Above: bamboo pattern designed by Ann Read, 1955-1956, painted on black panther glaze.

Right: factory promotional photograph showing a bamboo table setting at Heal & Son, 1956.

Chapter Eight

Poole Pottery in the 1960s and 1970s

Despite the successes achieved by Alfred Read and the Design Unit, Poole began to look in new directions in the late 1950s. On 1st January 1958 Robert Jefferson became the new resident designer. Trained at the Royal College of Art, Jefferson had previously been a lecturer in ceramics at Stoke-on-Trent College of Art, with extensive experience in the pottery industry. Under his guidance, Poole's long association with modernism was maintained, with new styles taking the company firmly into the 1960s and the 1970s. Jefferson first made his mark on the domestic ranges, developing new oven-to-table wares whose elegant shapes were matched by stylish printed decoration. His first tableware shape, Contour, was along traditional Poole lines, and was used with both Twintone and Cameo colours and printed patterns. More contemporary was the stacking Compact shape of the mid 1960s. From the start, Jefferson was concerned with the need to bring new technology to Poole, particularly for tableware production. There was increasing use of printing and silk screen transfers and he introduced the Murray Curvex process of direct printing onto tableware, used for his Pebble designs introduced in 1959. His Bokhara range of jars linked Poole closely to the modern kitchen, and the needs of the burgeoning consumer market also inspired his new ranges of lamps and relief moulded trays and plaques. These, and other Jefferson designs, effectively gave Poole a new look and considerably raised the pottery's profile in both the consumer and the trade press. In 1962 Lucien Myers left, and Roy Holland, increasingly the natural successor to John Adams, took over as managing director, a change that gave more backing to the Jefferson approach. Even more significant was the great expansion of the Poole studio that took place under Jefferson. Part of his original design brief was to develop further the experimental approach to shapes and glazes which had been hinted at in the previous decade, with the ultimate aim of finding a modern hand-decorated range that could complement, or even replace, the traditional wares. Working with Guy Sydenham, Jefferson produced a series of individual pieces that relaunched the Poole Studio when they were first shown to the public at an exhibition at the Tea Centre, Regent Street, London, held in January 1961. Contemporary in shape and style, and decorated in largely abstract patterns in a variety of techniques, these expressed anew the Poole tradition of spanning the gulf between studio pottery and commercial production. From these there emerged a new series of shapes and, by experimenting with glazes and colours, drawn largely from those in standard use, a new range of decorative wares was produced. This was launched by Sir Gordon Russell at an exhibition at Heal's in 1963, and subsequently at stores throughout the country, as the Delphis Collection. The same year, Tony Morris, formerly a student at Newport School of Art, joined Poole and over the next two years he and Jefferson, working with selected paintresses, continued the experimental development of Delphis. From 1964 new, bought-in, glazes were increasingly used, and the distinctive Delphis style, with its dynamic and largely abstract designs in bright colours, was established. From 1965 it was marketed increasingly as a hand-painted range, with individual designs on a series of standard shapes, a pattern of development that culminated in the setting up of the new Craft Section in May 1966 as a production unit for both the standard Delphis range and the individual specials. The success of Delphis on both British and overseas markets took Poole by surprise and production was steadily increased through the late 1960s, with the emphasis on the bright colours and patterns, and with increasing numbers of paintresses making their individual mark. From 1971, the palette was simplified to red, orange, yellow and green, the most popular colours. Delphis remained a major part of Poole's output until its final withdrawal in 1980. Robert Jefferson left in 1966, but his influence remained in the wide range of individual and studio-inspired wares that maintained the Poole tradition for modernism in design. Next came the Aegean range, with its varied decorating techniques developed by Leslie Elsden and its dark colour palette. Introduced in 1970 on twenty-two standard shapes and designed initially as a replacement for Delphis, Aegean remained in production until 1980. Others included Atlantis, the name given from 1969 to pieces individually made by Guy Sydenham in the Craft Section from stoneware and other bodies, and Ionian, a more elaborate variation of the Aegean range. The influence of the Craft Section ranges was also reflected by tablewares designed in the late 1960s by Guy Sydenham and Tony Morris.

Robert Jefferson in the design studio at Poole, 1960-1961.

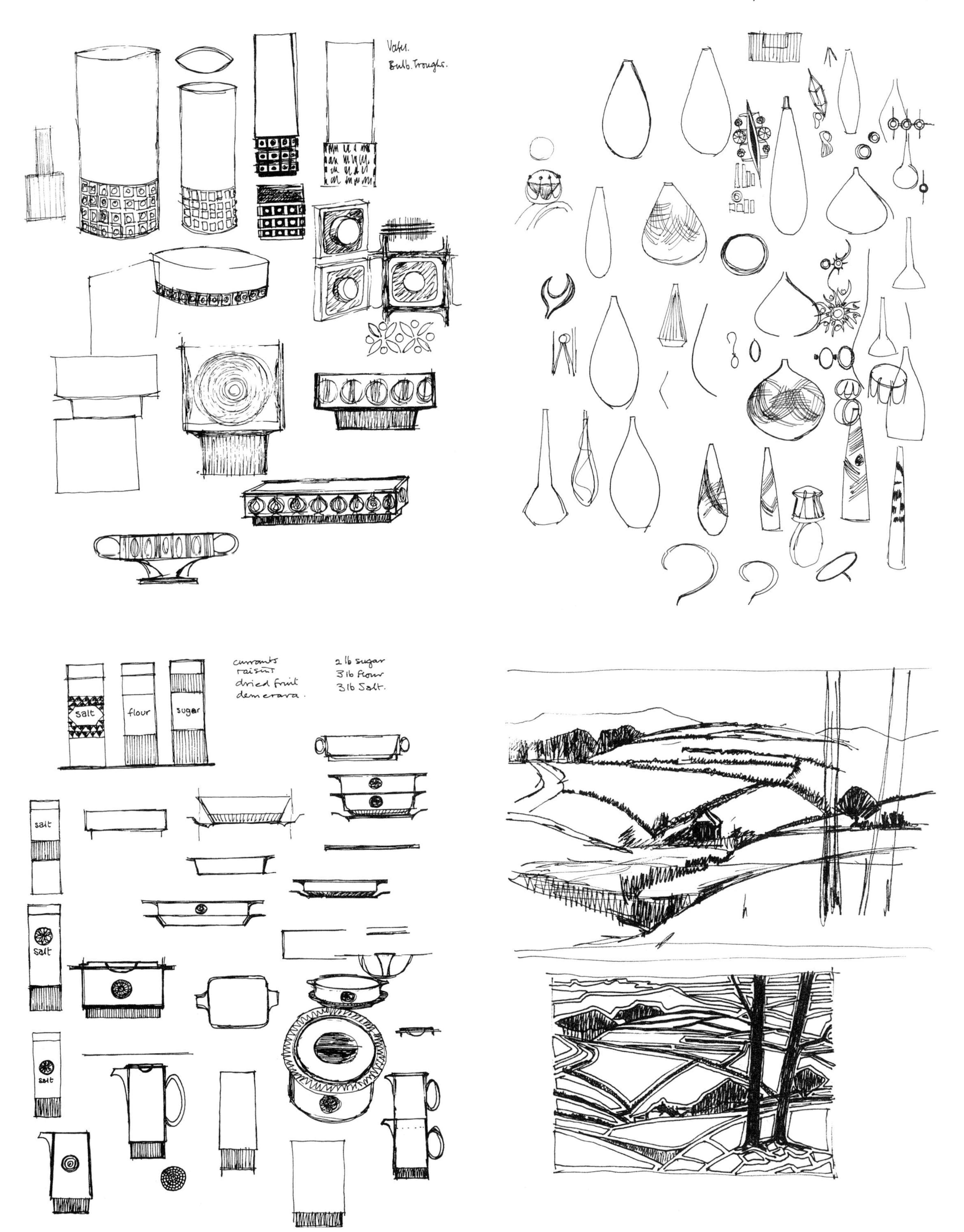

Drawings from Robert Jefferson's sketch book of the early 1960s showing sketches for table lamps, studio vases, the Compact tableware range and stylised landscapes of the kind used on studio wares.

POOLE

oven-to-table ware

Designed by Robert Jefferson, Des.R.C.A.

The new Poole oven-to-table ware is light-weight and elegant, heat resistant and guaranteed against oven breakage. It is available in the Cameo finish, solid colour with white contrast, in three beautiful colours, the popular Blue Moon and Celadon Green together with the exciting new Heather Rose. There are 15 oven pieces all designed to bring onto the table, with over sixty matching tableware pieces for luncheon, tea, dinner and all occasions. The oven-to-table pieces are all individually carton-packed and are ideal for presentation.

Right : The three round casseroles in Blue Moon finish, 1 pint, 2 pint and 5 pint, are designed to nest and need occupy no more cupboard space than the largest size alone. In this shape also, the middle size can be supplied with a heater stand if desired. Available also in Celadon Green and Heather Rose.

The Poole oven-to-table range designed by Robert Jefferson in 1960, and launched in 1961. It was made in three colours, Blue Moon, Celadon Green and Heather Rose.

Factory promotional photograph showing the Lucullus range of decorative oven-to-table wares designed by Robert Jefferson in 1961, and launched in 1962.

Factory promotional photograph showing contour tableware designed by Robert Jefferson, 1963-1964, with underglaze printed patterns, above: Desert Song designed by Pat Summers and, below: Morocco designed by Tony Morris, 1969.

Factory promotional leaflet showing the Herb Garden pattern for decorated oven ware designed by Robert Jefferson in 1961 and launched in 1963.

A selection of white earthenware tablewares and accessories by Robert Jefferson. Left to right: Style salt pot with the Country Lane pattern, 1980, mark No.79; Style teapot with the Springtime pattern designed by Elaine Williamson, 1978, mark No.73; Contour dinner plate with the Arabesque pattern designed for the Canadian market, 1963, mark No.41; spice jar, green diamond pattern from a set of six spices and four storage jars, 1963, mark No.41; Compact teapot with chestnut and snow white glazes, 1965, mark No.48; Compact tea cup and saucer modelled by Tony Morris, 1967, mark No.48; Bokhara kitchen jar 659/2 JB with sapphire blue and black scratched glaze decoration, 1964, mark No.41; Bokhara preserve jar 655/OBA, 1964, mark No.41. Plate diameter 10ins (25.5cm).

Factory promotional photograph showing the grey pebble printed tableware pattern designed by Robert Jefferson, 1959.

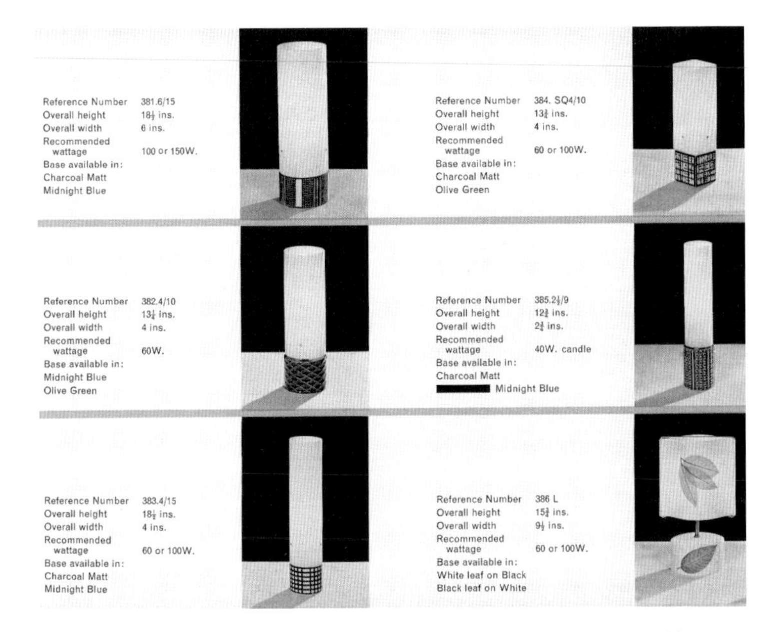

Reference Number 381.6/15
Overall height 18½ ins.
Overall width 6 ins.
Recommended wattage 100 or 150W.
Base available in:
Charcoal Matt
Midnight Blue

Reference Number 384. SQ4/10
Overall height 13¾ ins.
Overall width 4 ins.
Recommended wattage 60 or 100W.
Base available in:
Charcoal Matt
Olive Green

Reference Number 382.4/10
Overall height 13¼ ins.
Overall width 4 ins.
Recommended wattage 60W.
Base available in:
Midnight Blue
Olive Green

Reference Number 385.2½/9
Overall height 12¾ ins.
Overall width 2¾ ins.
Recommended wattage 40W. candle
Base available in:
Charcoal Matt
Midnight Blue

Reference Number 383.4/15
Overall height 18½ ins.
Overall width 4 ins.
Recommended wattage 60 or 100W.
Base available in:
Charcoal Matt
Midnight Blue

Reference Number 386 L
Overall height 15¾ ins.
Overall width 9½ ins.
Recommended wattage 60 or 100W.
Base available in:
White leaf on Black
Black leaf on White

Factory catalogue page showing Helios table lamps designed by Robert Jefferson, 1964.

A selection of tablewares including the black pebble pattern and Contour shape designed by Robert Jefferson. Left to right: Contour teapot with C104 sky blue and dove grey glazes, 1963, mark No.48; Streamline black pebble dinner plate, 1959, mark No.41 modified; Contour tea cup and saucer with royal blue and crystal glazes and Morocco pattern, 1969, mark No.49; Contour coffee pot with golden buff and crystal glazes and Desert Song pattern, 1969, mark No.49; Streamline black pebble coffee pot, 1959, mark No.41, modified. Plate diameter 10ins (25.5cm).

Factory promotional photograph showing Robert Jefferson's Compact tableware in chestnut and snow white glazes, 1965.

PLATE 10"	8/5	42p	CASSEROLE 3 pint	39/-	£1.95p	MEAT DISH 13½"	22/-	£1.10p
PLATE 8½"	7/-	35p	CASSEROLE 1½ pint	31/-	1.55p			
PLATE 7"	5/5	27p						
TEA POT 35 oz	27/-	£1.35p	COFFEE POT 45 oz	35/-	£1.75p	JUG 25 oz	15/-	75p
„ „ 25 oz	23/-	£1.15p				JUG 10 oz	10/5	52p
JUG/SAUCE BOAT 15 oz	13/-	65p	STEW POT 2½ pint	33/-	£1.65p	INDIVIDUAL COVERED DISH 18 oz	23/-	£1.15p
TEA CUP/MUG 10 oz	7/5	37p	SUGAR BOWL 10 oz	7/5	37p	SALT SHAKER 4"	9/-	45p
SAUCER 6"	3/10	19p				PEPPER POT 4"	9/-	45p
TEA CUP 7 oz	7/-	35p						
SAUCER 5¾"	3/5	17p						
SOUP/CEREAL/FRUIT BOWL 15 oz	11/5	57p	EGG CUP	3/-	15p	OATMEAL BOWL 6"	8/5	42p

These illustrations are not to scale

Factory catalogue page showing Robert Jefferson's Compact tableware range, 1965, with lids remodelled by Tony Morris in 1969.

654 Preserve Jar
5 ins × 4 ins
OAA Sepia & Lilac
OAB Peacock, Lavender & Black
JB Sapphire Blue & Black
OAA OAB JB

655 Preserve Jar
4 ins × 4 ins
OBA Sepia, Orange & Black
OBB Quaker Grey, Salmon & Black
JB Sapphire Blue & Black
OBA OBB JB

656 Preserve Jar
4½ ins × 3½ ins
OEA Lavender & Plum
OEB Sepia & Chinese Blue
JB Sapphire Blue & Black
OEA OEB JB

657 Preserve Jar
4 ins × 4 ins
OGA Sepia, Orange & Black
OGB Old Gold, Lemon & Sepia
JB Sapphire Blue & Black
OGA OGB JB

658 Butter Box
3½ ins × 4½ ins
OHA Old Gold & Sepia
OHB Quaker Grey & Chinese Blue
JB Sapphire Blue & Black
OHA OHB JB

659 Kitchen Jar
659/1 4 ins × 2½ ins
659/2 4¼ ins × 3 ins
659/3 5½ ins × 3¾ ins
659/4 6½ ins × 4 ins
JC Black & White
JB Sapphire Blue & Black
JC JB

674 Vase
674/1 6½ ins × 3½ ins
674/2 8 ins × 4½ ins
JB Sapphire Blue & Black
JB

675 Vase
675/1 6 ins × 3 ins
675/2 8 ins × 4 ins
JB Sapphire Blue & Black
JB

676 Vase
676/1 6 ins × 2½ ins
676/2 8 ins × 3½ ins
JB Sapphire Blue & Black
JB

Factory catalogue page showing the Bokhara range of hand thrown jars and vases designed by Robert Jefferson, 1964.

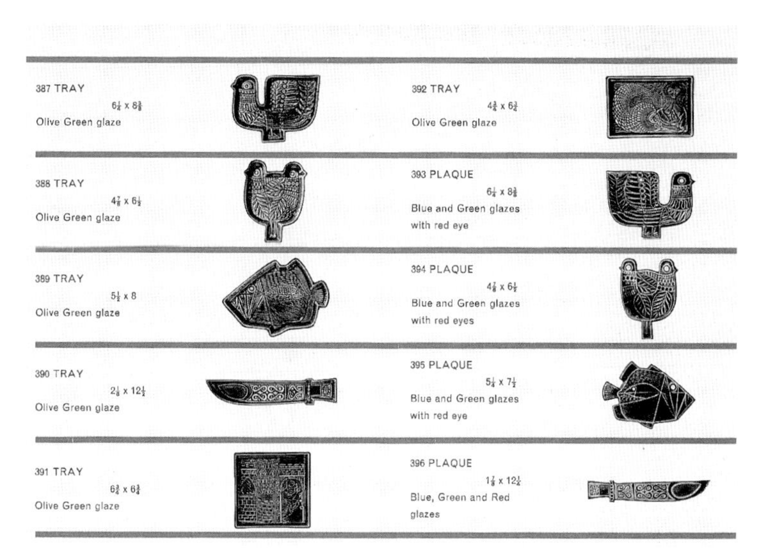

387 TRAY
6¼ x 8⅜
Olive Green glaze

392 TRAY
4¾ x 6¾
Olive Green glaze

388 TRAY
4⅞ x 6½
Olive Green glaze

393 PLAQUE
6¼ x 8⅜
Blue and Green glazes
with red eye

389 TRAY
5½ x 8
Olive Green glaze

394 PLAQUE
4⅞ x 6½
Blue and Green glazes
with red eyes

390 TRAY
2⅛ x 12½
Olive Green glaze

395 PLAQUE
5¼ x 7½
Blue and Green glazes
with red eye

391 TRAY
6¾ x 6¾
Olive Green glaze

396 PLAQUE
1⅞ x 12¼
Blue, Green and Red
glazes

Factory catalogue page showing the range of Robert Jefferson trays and wall plaques, 1964, including Delphis studio ware shapes 38-42.

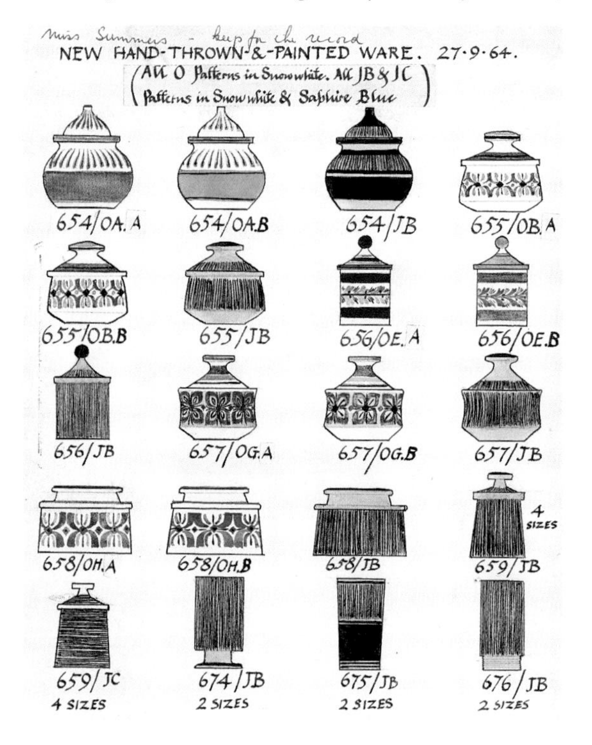

Miss Summers - keep for the record
NEW HAND-THROWN-&-PAINTED WARE. 27·9·64.
(All O Patterns in Snowwhite. All JB & JC
Patterns in Snow white & Saphire Blue)

654/OA.A 654/OA.B 654/JB 655/OB.A
655/OB.B 655/JB 656/OE.A 656/OE.B
656/JB 657/OG.A 657/OG.B 657/JB
658/OH.A 658/OH.B 658/JB 659/JB 4 SIZES
659/JC 4 SIZES 674/JB 2 SIZES 675/JB 2 SIZES 676/JB 2 SIZES

Factory pattern sheet showing shapes and colourways for the Bokhara range, 1964.

Wall plaques and trays with moulded, raised line decoration designed by Robert Jefferson and included in the 1964 Spring Collection. Fulfilling one of the principal aims of the Poole Studio, this range, made initially as a studio line, was transferred to the production departments when greater output was required. All the plaques and trays illustrated are stamped with mark No.41, except the dagger plaque 396 on which studio mark No.43 appears. Length of dagger tray 390, 13ins (33cm). Tray 391 in Cameo celeste, has been glazed in a non-standard colour.

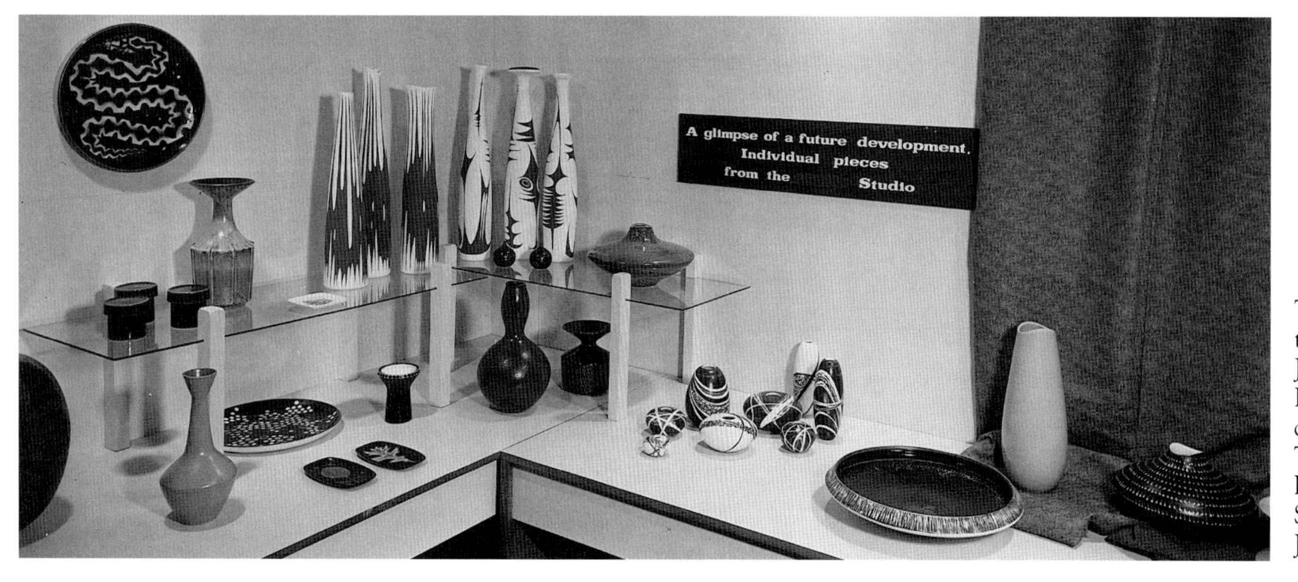

The first productions of Robert Jefferson and the Poole Studio, displayed at the Tea Centre Exhibition, Regent Street, London, January 1961.

Delphis Studio Wares by Robert Jefferson and Tony Morris 1963-1966

A representative range of Studio shapes designed by Robert Jefferson, 1961-1963. These became known as The Delphis Collection when launched as a standard repeatable range in October 1963. Thrown in white earthenware by Guy Sydenham and decorated initially by Robert Jefferson and Tony Morris, other artists including Elizabeth Hayne and Christine Tate were also involved in the early studio productions of 1964-1965. From left to right: vase shape 37 (short version), mark No.43 and triangle impressed; shape 16, mark No.43; shape 10, mark No.45; shape 50, mark No.46; shape 1, mark No.43; bowl shape 21, mark No.43 and triangle impressed; vase shape 34, mark No.46; shape 24, mark No.43 and shape 8, mark No.46. Tallest vase shape 50, height 15½ins (39.5cm).

A group of studio dishes with decorations designed and painted by Robert Jefferson, 1962-1963. Mark No.43 appears on three dishes with designer's monogram and Poole Studio painted. Length 16ins (40.5cm).

Studio dish with decoration designed and painted by Robert Jefferson, 1962-1964, mark No.43. Studio bowl shape 5, with decoration designed and painted by Tony Morris, 1964-1966, mark No.46. Dish length 16¼ins (41.5cm).

The Poole Pottery section at Rackhams Department Store, Birmingham, 1965.

Window display at Eaden Lilly's shop, Cambridge, for the launch of the Delphis collection, October 1963.

Elizabeth Hayne, Poole School of Art trained decorator of studio and other wares, 1963.

Studio wares with decorations designed and painted by Tony Morris, 1963-1966, bowls and dish mark No.43; pebble vase sprayed with re-active glazes, mark No.46. Largest bowl shape 5, diameter 14ins (35.5cm). Tony Morris trained as a designer in fine arts at Newport School of Art.

Studio dish shape 43 with Sun Face decoration designed and painted by Tony Morris, 1963-1964, mark No.43. Diameter 16½ins (42cm).

Studio bowls with decorations designed and painted by Tony Morris, 1963-1964, mark No.43. Largest bowl shape 2, diameter 15ins (38cm).

Tile panel with Sun Face decoration designed and painted by Tony Morris, 1964-1965. Length 30ins (76cm).

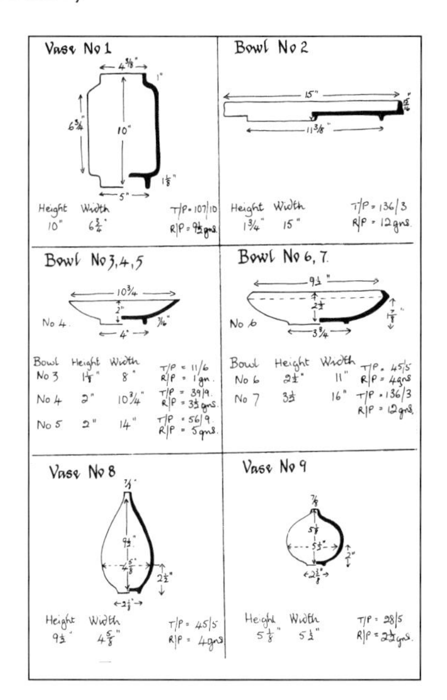

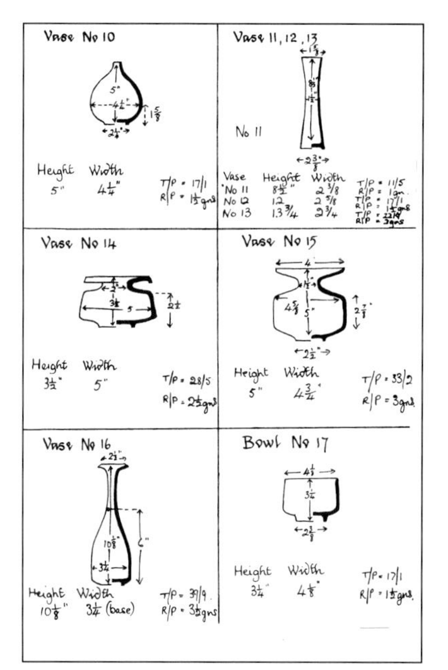

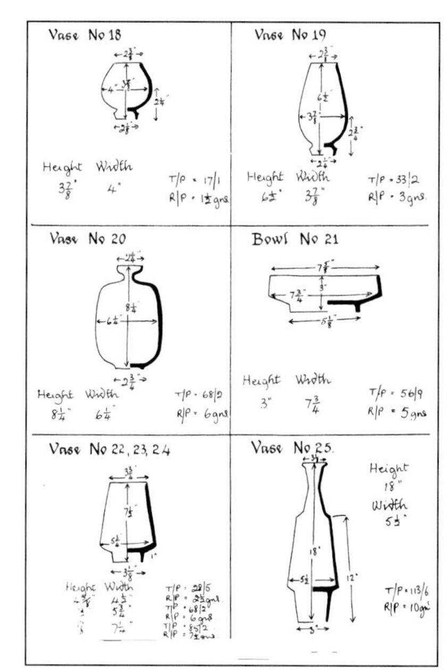

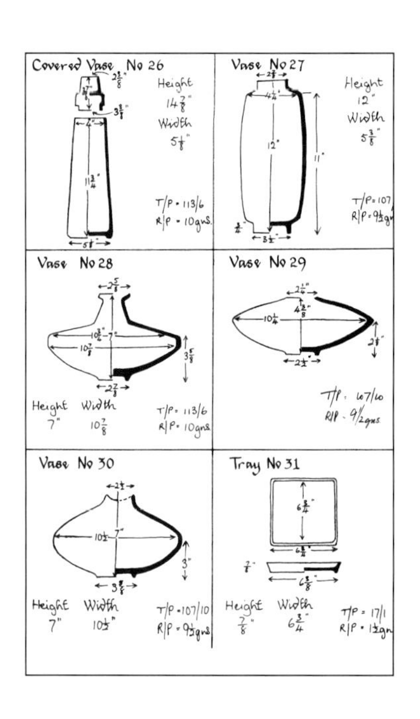

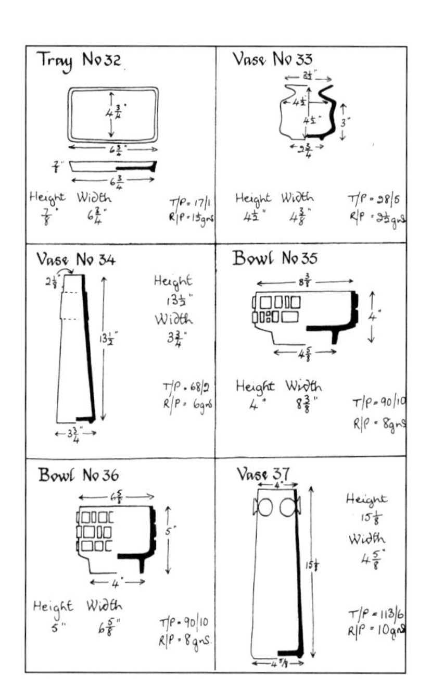

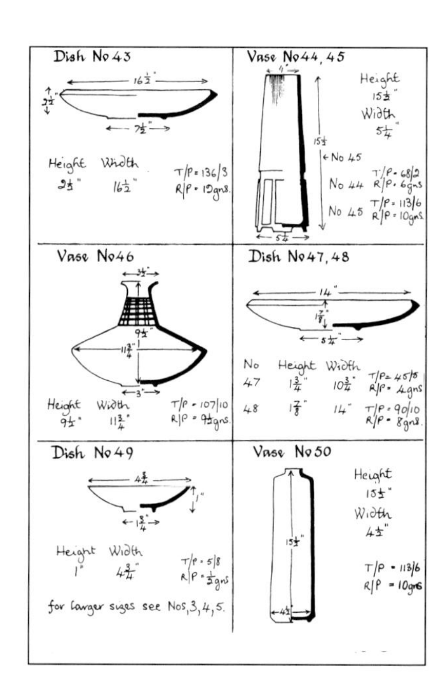

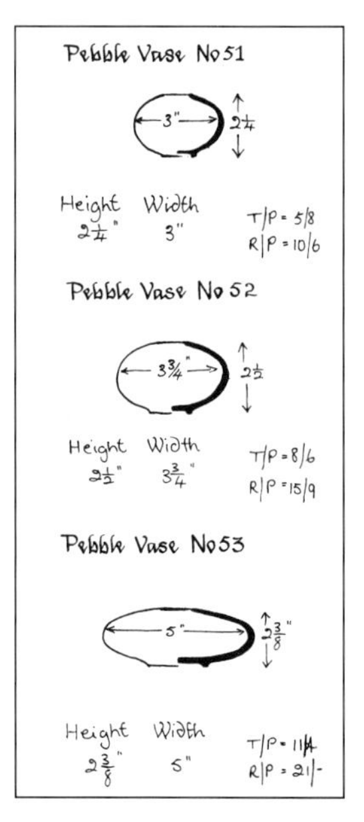

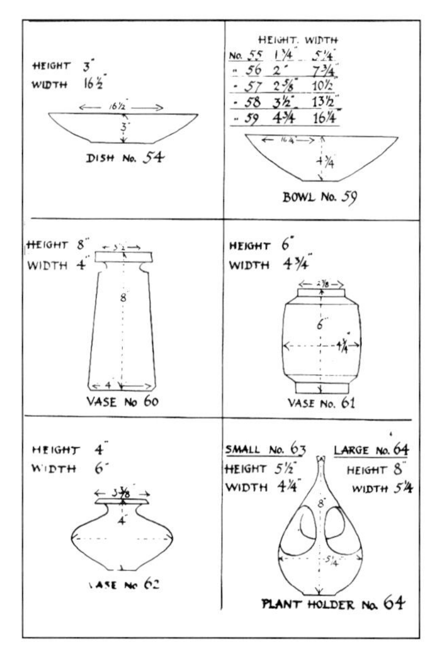

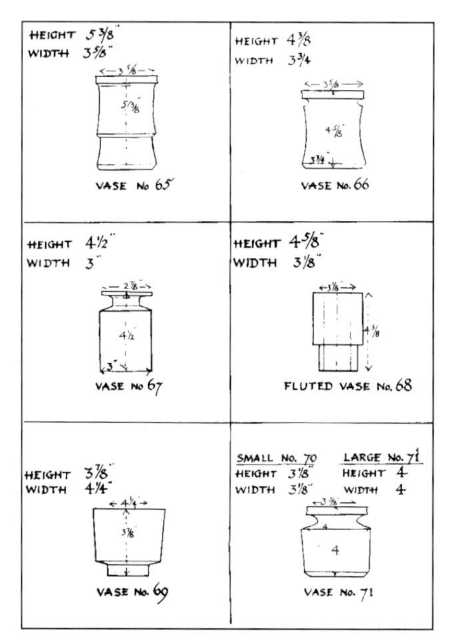

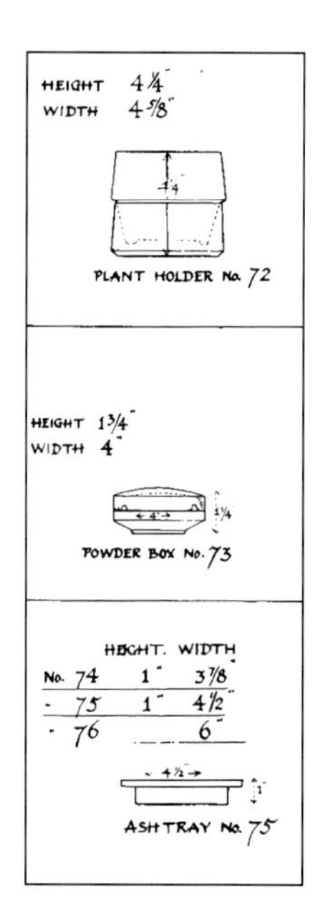

Factory pattern sheets showing the shapes, and their sizes, developed for the Delphis studio range from 1963.

Delphis Range – The Products of the Craft Section 1966-1979

Celebration of the opening of the Craft Section at Poole Pottery, 26th May 1966. Left to right: Roy Holland, Carole Holden, Linda Elliott, Margaret Anderson, Thelma Bush, Patricia O'Meara.

Delphis paintresses, May 1966.

A selection of Delphis studio and Delphis range dishes and a bowl with decorations designed and painted by Christine Tate, 1964-1968. Tiger's head and owl dishes, mark No.43; John Dory fish and Wrestler dishes, mark No.46; Delphis range bowl and dish, mark No.47. The No.54 dish (centre right) is one of about fifty dishes commissioned by Ricemans of Canterbury in 1970 to commemorate the 800th anniversary of the martyrdom of Thomas Becket. The decoration by Christine Tate is based upon a window in the cathedral and the back of the dish bears the inscription 'Thomas Becket Centenary 1170-1970', mark No.41 (used out of date) and the monogram of the artist. The dish is the first example of the use of a glaze decorating technique which became known as stained glass window, and was further developed by Tony Morris in his designs for calendar and cathedral plates, 1971-1975, see pages 148-149. Largest dish shape 54, diameter 16ins (40.5cm). Christine Tate trained as a graphic designer at Bournemouth and Poole College of Art.

Delphis studio and Delphis range dishes, 1964-1966, mark No.46 and No.47. Largest dish shape 54, diameter 16ins (40.5cm). A number of well designed and painted pieces from the Studio and early Delphis ranges were produced without paintresses insignia.

Delphis studio and Delphis range bowl and vases painted by Jennifer Wiles, 1965-1966. From left to right: vase shape 10, mark No.43; bowl shape 3, mark No.43; vase shape 62, mark No.47. Diameter of bowl 8ins (20.5cm).

Delphis studio and Delphis range bowls and dishes painted by Margaret Anderson, 1966-1967. Left to right, top row: bowl shape 56, mark No.47; dish shape 54, mark No.47; bowl shape 3, mark No.46. Bottom row: dish shape 4, mark No.47; dish shape 49, mark No.47; sweet dish shape 82, mark No.47. Diameter of dish shape 54, 16ins (40.5cm).

Delphis studio and Delphis range dishes painted by Betty Bantten, 1965-1967, mostly after designs by Christine Tate. Top row: dish shape 5, mark No.47; round chop dish, mark No.46. Bottom row: dish shape 3, mark No.47; dish shape 4, mark No.47; sweet dish shape 81, mark No.47. Diameter of dish shape 5, 14ins (35.5cm).

Delphis range dishes painted by Shirley Campbell, 1966-1969, mostly after designs by Christine Tate, mark No.47. Largest dish diameter 16ins (40.5cm).

A group of Delphis range dishes painted by Carole Holden, 1966-1969, mark No.47. The hovering seagull dish has a magnolia glazed back, indicating that this was an early piece painted before the introduction of crystal glazed backs in late 1966. Delphis dishes with carved decoration are also represented in this group. Largest dish shape 54, diameter 16ins (40.5cm). Carole Holden trained as a graphic designer at Bournemouth and Poole College of Art.

A selection of Delphis range bowls and dishes painted by Jean Millership, 1966-1969, mark No.47. Length of sweet dish shape 82, 17ins (43cm). Jean Millership trained at Wakefield College of Art, where life classes were included in her foundation and commercial art courses.

Delphis range dishes. Top row: dish shape 4, painted by Christine Phillips, 1969-1970; dish shape 4 painted by Thelma Bush, 1966. Bottom row: sweet dish shape 82 painted by Christine Phillips, 1969-1970. Right: two sweet dishes shape 82 painted by Thelma Bush, 1966. All mark No.47. Length of sweet dish shape 82, 17ins (43cm). Thelma Bush trained at Bournemouth and Poole College of Art.

Delphis range dishes painted 1966-1967, numerous dishes and vases were unsigned by the paintresses as these examples of early Studio dishes, mark No.47. Largest dish shape 5, diameter 14ins (35.5cm).

Delphis range dishes painted by Josephine Wall, 1967-1968, mark No.47. Diameter of centre dish shape 5, 14ins (35.5cm). Josephine Wall trained in fine arts at Bournemouth and Poole College of Art. The fascination of this paintress with insects and animals, butterflies in particular, was much in evidence while working at Poole Pottery. In 1968 she modelled, carved and glazed a number of insect and animal figures in a new stoneware body and these were first shown in a London exhibition at the Carlton Towers Hotel and subsequently in a display at Harrods. An African horned chameleon sculptured by this artist was illustrated in *The Gift Buyer International*, August 1968.

Delphis range bowl and dishes painted by Irene Kerton, mark No.47. Largest dish shape 5, diameter 14ins (35.5cm). Irene Kerton trained as a sculptor at Bournemouth and Poole College of Art, 1968-1969.

A selection of Delphis range carved and painted wares. From left to right, back row: vase shape 85 by Angela Wyburgh, 1968-1969, mark No.47; vase shape 85 by Margaret Anderson, 1966-1967, mark No.47; vase shape 85 by Christine Tate, 1966-1969, mark No.47; vase shape 85 by Sally Murch, 1969, mark No.47. Centre row: vase shape 84, 1966-1969, mark No.47; vase shape 84 by Ann Godfrey, 1966-1969, mark No.47; vase shape 84, 1966-1969, mark No.47. Front row: vase shape 83, 1966-1969, mark No.47; plant pot shape 79, 1966-1968, mark No.47. Tallest vase height 16ins (40.5cm).

Delphis range dishes painted by Angela Wyburgh, 1968-1973, mark No.47. Length of sweet dish shape 82, bottom right, 17ins. (43cm). Angela Wyburgh trained at Bournemouth and Poole College of Art.

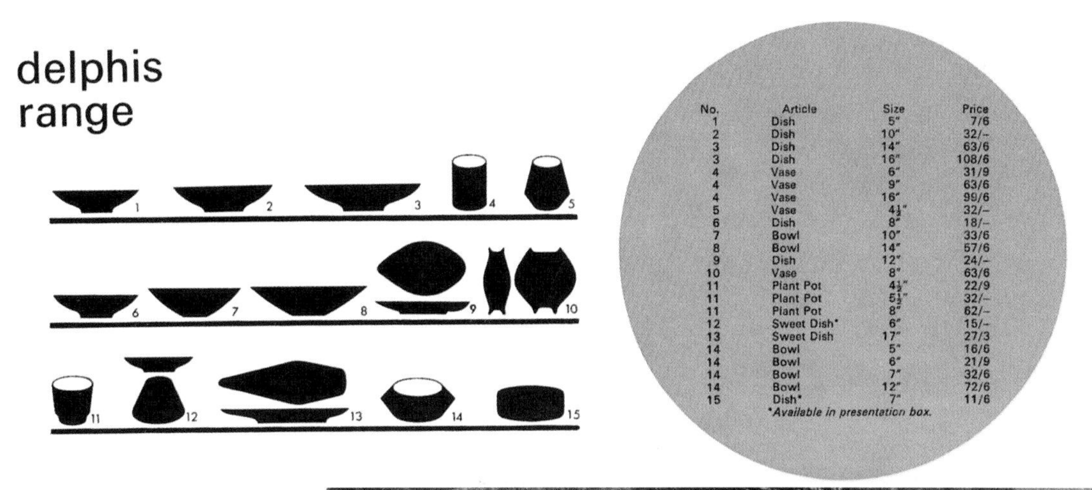

No.	Article	Size	Price
1	Dish	5"	7/6
2	Dish	10"	32/-
3	Dish	14"	63/6
3	Dish	16"	108/6
4	Vase	6"	31/9
4	Vase	9"	63/6
4	Vase	16"	99/6
5	Vase	4½"	32/-
6	Dish	8"	18/-
7	Bowl	10"	33/6
8	Bowl	14"	57/6
9	Dish	12"	24/-
10	Vase	8"	63/6
11	Plant Pot	4½"	22/9
11	Plant Pot	5½"	32/-
11	Plant Pot	8"	62/-
12	Sweet Dish*	6"	15/-
13	Sweet Dish	17"	27/3
14	Bowl	5"	16/6
14	Bowl	6"	21/9
14	Bowl	7"	32/6
14	Bowl	12"	72/6
15	Dish*	7"	11/6

**Available in presentation box.*

This range of ornamental ware has been developed to provide a unique series of pieces, each of which is produced by hand. No two pieces are alike; the colours and decorations have been developed to offer the customer the opportunity of purchasing a range which is absolutely unique.
Illustrated on the right are several of the individual shapes available. The decorations illustrated cannot be reproduced.

A factory promotional leaflet for the Delphis range, showing shapes and prices, 1968.

A selection of Delphis range dishes and a bowl. Left to right, top row: dish shape 91 painted by Gillian Taylor, 1971-1972, mark No.47; dish shape 91 painted by Judi Evans, 1974-1976, mark No.47; dish shape 91 painted by Sarah Worrel about 1970, mark No.47; dish shape 49 painted by Gillian Taylor, 1971-1972, mark No.47; dish shape 3 painted by Wendy Smith, 1975-1977, mark No.47. Bottom row: dish shape 3 painted by Sarah Worrel about 1970, mark No.47; bowl shape 57 painted by Judi Evans, 1974-1976, mark No.47; dish shape 91 painted by Gillian Taylor, 1971-1972, mark No.47; dish shape 3A painted by Wendy Smith, 1975-1977, mark No.47. Dish shape 91, length 12ins (30.5cm). Gillian Taylor trained at Bournemouth and Poole College of Art, Wendy Smith trained at Ashton-under-Lyme College of Art and Judi Evans trained as a tile painter at Carter Tiles Ltd.

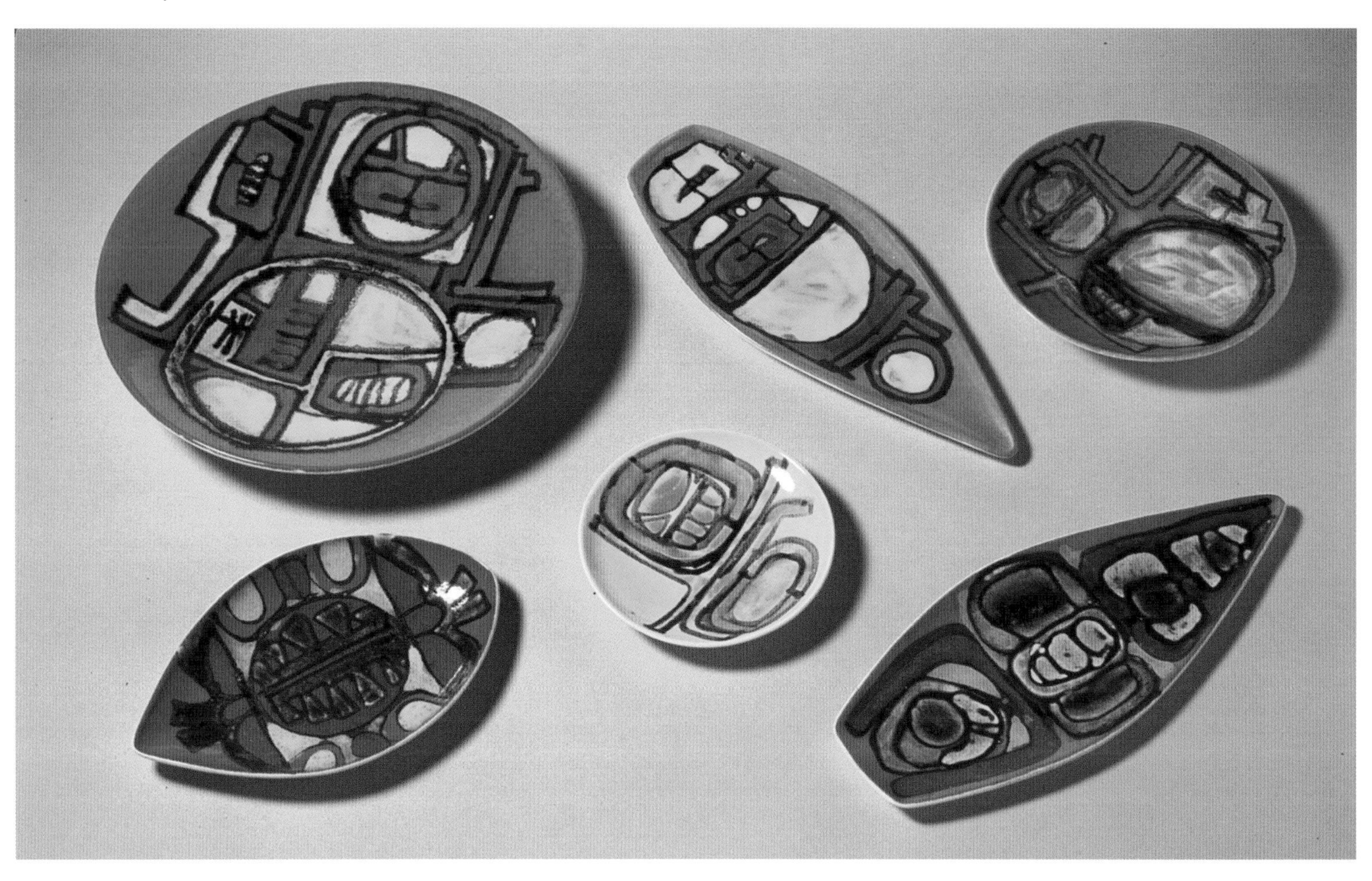

A group of Delphis range bowls and dishes painted by Carol Cutler, 1969-1976, mark No.47. Length of sweet dish shape 82, bottom right, 17ins (43cm). Carol Cutler trained as a graphic designer at Salisbury College of Art.

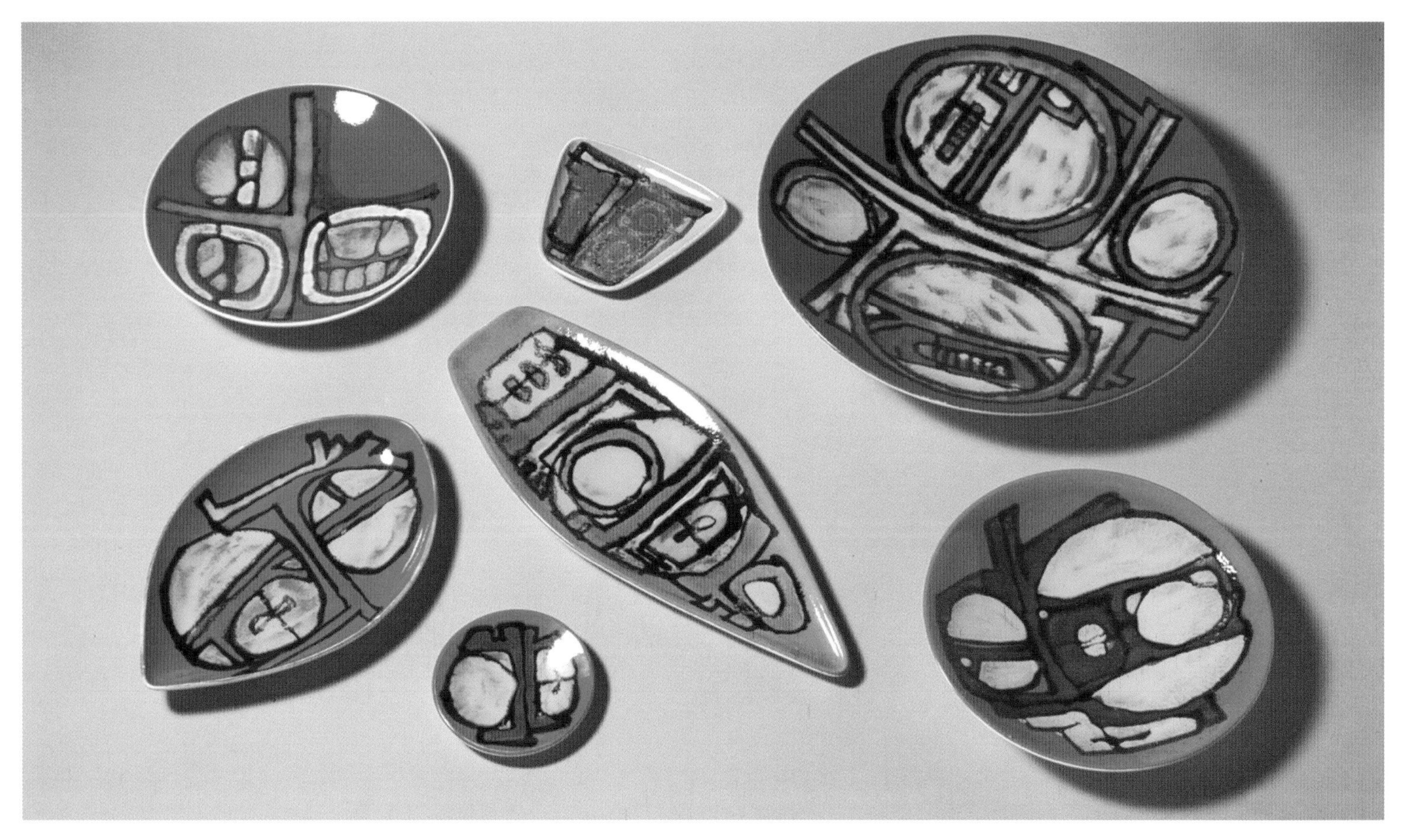

A selection of Delphis range bowls and dishes painted by Carol Cutler, 1969-1976, mark No.47. Length of sweet dish shape 82, centre, 17ins (43cm).

A selection of Delphis range vases and a plant pot. Left to right: vase shape 84 painted by Ann Lloyd, 1969-1970, mark No.47. Three vases painted by Carol Cutler: shape 85, 1969-1971, mark No.47; shape 93, 1973-1976, mark No.47; shape 85, 1971-1976, mark No.47. Plant pot shape 80 painted by Shirley Campbell, 1966-1968, mark No.47. Tallest vase height 16ins (40.5cm).

A group of Delphis range dishes and a vase painted by Loretta Leigh, about 1970, mark No.47. Length of sweet dish shape 82, bottom row, 17ins (43cm).

A selection of Delphis range vases. From left to right, back row: vase shape 85 painted by Janet Laird, 1971-1974, mark No.47; vase shape 85 painted by Jean Millership, 1966-1969, mark No.47; vase shape 85 painted by Christine Tate, 1966-1970, mark No.47. Front row: vase shape 90 painted by Angela Wyburgh, 1968, mark No.47; vase shape 83 painted by Janet Laird, 1971-1974, mark No.47; vase shape 84 painted about 1975, mark No.47; vase shape 90 painted by Jean Millership, 1967-1968, mark No.47; vase shape 83 painted by Angela Wyburgh, 1971-1973, mark No.47. Tallest vase height 16ins (40.5cm).

A selection of Delphis range vases. Left to right: shape 31 painted by Lynn Gregory, 1971-1974, mark No.47; shape 85 painted 1970-1971, mark No.47; shape 84 thrown by Carol Kellett and painted by Cynthia Bennett, 1976-1977, mark No.58; shape 85 thrown by Alan White and painted by Judi Evans, 1974-1976, mark No.58; shape 83, painted by Valerie Pullen, 1974-1975, mark No.47; shape 85 painted by Lynn Gregory, 1971-1974, mark No.47; shape 31 painted by Rosina St. Clayre, 1971-1972, mark No.47; shape 36 painted by Cynthia Bennett, 1975, mark No.47. Tallest vase height 16ins (40.5cm).

A group of Delphis range dishes, vase and a bowl painted by Andrée Fontana, 1973-1977, mark No.47. During 1976-1977 floral patterns were a speciality of this paintress. Diameter of largest dish shape 54, 16ins (40.5cm). Andrée Fontana trained in graphic design at Poole Technical College as part of a structured training course within the Pottery.

Delphis range dishes, shape 5, painted by Janet Laird, 1969-1970, mark No.47. Dish diameter 16ins (40.5cm). Janet Laird trained as a graphic designer at Bournemouth and Poole College of Art.

A group of Delphis range dishes painted by Ros Sommerfelt, 1970-1971, floral patterned dish shape 4 (top right), painted about 1976, mark No.47. Length of sweet dish shape 82, bottom left, 17ins (43cm). Ros Sommerfelt trained at Plymouth College of Art and as a designer in ceramics at Loughborough College of Art and Design.

Irene Kerton painting a Delphis range bowl, 1968.

Delphis wares hot from the kiln, 1975.

Left: Angela Wyburgh modelling a John Dory fish in a 'free time' period about 1970.

Right: factory promotional leaflet for the Delphis range, with shapes and prices, 1973.

Delphis Range

An individual hand-painted technique – each piece different – using special bright coloured glazes. Bold reds – orange – yellows – greens being the predominant colours. Some new shapes now being included in the 1972 range.

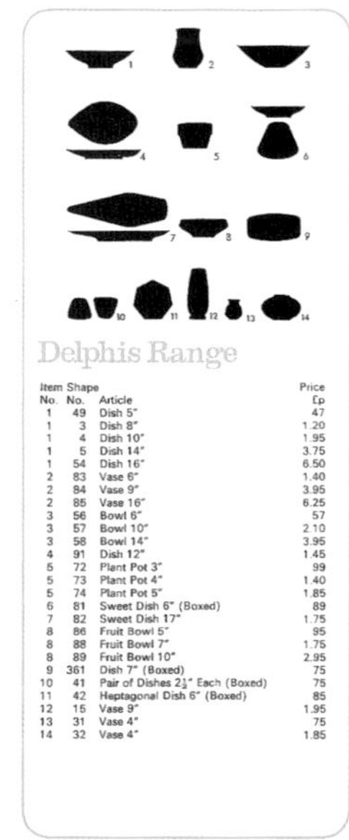

Delphis Range

Item No.	Shape No.	Article	Price £p
1	49	Dish 5"	47
1	3	Dish 8"	1.20
1	4	Dish 10"	1.95
1	5	Dish 14"	3.75
1	54	Dish 16"	6.50
2	83	Vase 6"	1.40
2	84	Vase 9"	3.95
2	85	Vase 16"	6.25
3	56	Bowl 6"	57
3	57	Bowl 10"	2.10
3	58	Bowl 14"	3.95
4	91	Dish 12"	1.45
5	72	Plant Pot 3"	99
5	73	Plant Pot 4"	1.40
5	74	Plant Pot 5"	1.85
6	81	Sweet Dish 6" (Boxed)	89
7	82	Sweet Dish 17"	1.75
8	86	Fruit Bowl 5"	95
8	88	Fruit Bowl 7"	1.75
8	89	Fruit Bowl 10"	2.95
9	361	Dish 7" (Boxed)	75
10	41	Pair of Dishes 2½" Each (Boxed)	75
11	42	Heptagonal Dish 6" (Boxed)	85
12	15	Vase 9"	1.95
13	31	Vase 4"	75
14	32	Vase 4"	1.85

A group of Delphis range dishes painted by Pamela Bevans, 1970-1971, mark No.47. Diameter of dish shape 54, centre, 16ins (40.5cm). Pamela Bevans trained in ceramics and glass at Birmingham College of Art.

A group of Delphis range dishes painted by Rosina St. Clayre, 1971-1973, mark No.47. Length of sweet dish shape 82, bottom left, 17ins (43cm). Rosina St. Clayre trained in fabric design at Stourbridge College of Art.

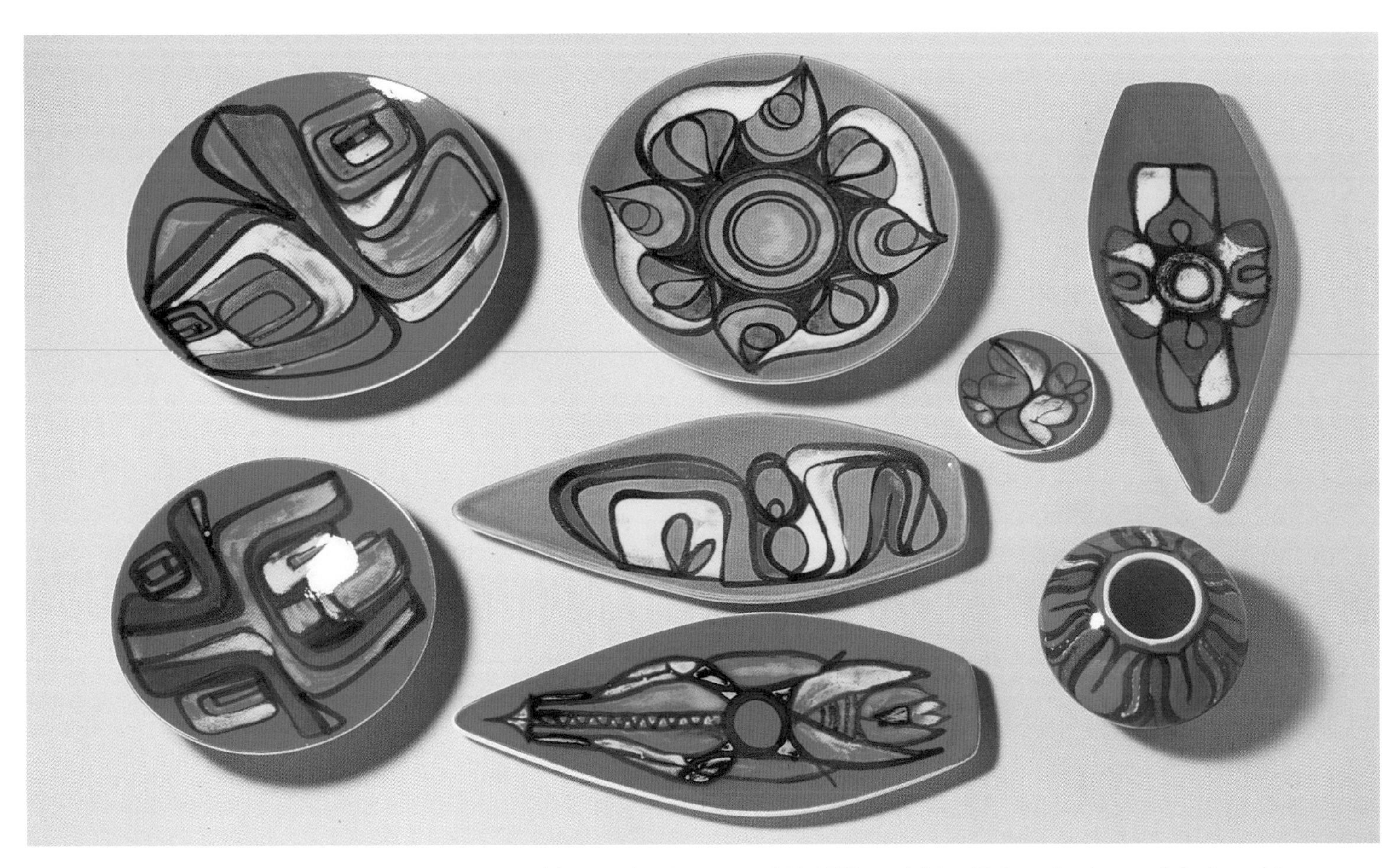

A Delphis range vase and a selection of dishes painted by Cynthia Bennett, 1971-1977, mark No. 47. Length of sweet dish shape 82, centre, 17ins (43cm). Cynthia Bennett trained in painting and lithography at Doncaster School of Art and as a teacher at Manchester College of Art.

A Delphis range bowl and a selection of dishes. Left to right, top: bowl shape 57 and dish shape 5 painted by Mary Albon, 1972-1974; dish shape 3 painted by Valerie Pullen, 1974-1975. Centre: sweet dish shape 82 painted by Mary Albon, 1972-1974; dish shape 49 painted by Beverley Mantel, 1974-1975; dish shape 361 painted by Valerie Pullen, 1974-1975. Bottom: dish shape 4 painted by Mary Albon, 1972-1974; dish shape 4 painted by Ingrid Hammond, 1971-1973; dish shape 3 painted by Beverley Mantel, 1974-1975. All mark No.47. Length of sweet dish shape 82, 17ins (43cm).

A selection of dishes painted by Lynn Gregory, 1971-1974, mark No.47. Largest dish diameter 16ins (40.5cm). Lynn Gregory subsequently trained in technical illustration at Bournemouth and Poole College of Art.

Aegean

A range of Aegean dishes with fish patterns. Left to right, top: dish shape 4, designed and decorated in the silhouette technique by Andrée Fontana, 1973-1979; dish shape 5, designed by Christine Tate and decorated in the sgraffito technique, 1969-1979; dish shape 4, decorated in the sgraffito and silhouette techniques, 1969-1979. Centre: dish shape 3, designed and decorated in the sgraffito and silhouette techniques by Carolyn Wills, 1972-1979. Bottom: sweet dish shape 82, decorated in the sgraffito technique, 1969-1974; dish shape 361, decorated in the sgraffito and silhouette techniques, 1969-1979; dish shape 4, decorated in the silhouette technique, 1969-1979; dish shape 91, designed and decorated in the sgraffito technique by Carole Holden, 1970-1974. All mark No.47 and No.51.

Factory promotional phototograph for the Aegean range, 1972.

Leslie Elsden masterminded the Aegean range, the culmination of a career at Poole that spanned fifty years.

A range of Aegean dishes and plaques in special finishes. Top: dish shape 54, designed and decorated in the carved clay technique by Carole Holden, 1970-1974, mark No.47; dish shape 54 designed by Carole Holden, decorated in the sgraffito and silhouette techniques by Karen Ryall, 1978-1979, mark No.47 and No.51. Centre: dish shape 54 designed and decorated in the sgraffito technique by Carole Holden, 1970-1974, mark No.47 and No.51; dish shape 5, designed by Leslie Elsden and decorated in the sgraffito and silhouette techniques by Diana Foreman, 1978-1979, mark No.51. Bottom: plaque shape 6 designed by Carole Holden, decorated in the sgraffito and silhouette techniques by Diana Davis, 1973-1977, mark No.47 and No.51; plaque shape 6 designed by Carole Holden, decorated in the sgraffito and silhouette techniques by Louise Lazarowicz, 1979, mark No.47 and No.51. Largest dish diameter 16ins (40.5cm).

A selection of bowls and dishes decorated by Leslie Elsden to his own designs, and including the 'Harry Paye' designed by Tony Morris. Top: bowl decorated in the sgraffito and silhouette techniques, 1969-1979; dish shape 54, decorated in the silhouette technique, 1969-1979. Centre: dish shape 54 'Harry Paye' decorated in the silhouette technique, 1969-1979; oval dish, decorated in the sgraffito technique, 1969-1979. Centre: bowl shape 57, decorated in the flowline technique, 1969-1979. Bottom: dish shape 4, decorated in the Mosaic technique, 1969-1979; sweet dish shape 82, decorated in the sgraffito technique, 1969-1974. All mark No.47 and No.51. Length of sweet dish shape 82, bottom right, 17ins (43cm).

Aegean dishes in special finishes. Top: dish shape 54 designed by Carole Holden, decorated in the sgraffito technique by Carolyn Wills, 1972-1979, mark No.47 and No.51; dish shape 54 designed by Carole Holden, decorated in the sgraffito and silhouette techniques by Diana Davis, 1973-1978, mark No.47 and No.51. Centre: dish shape 54 decorated in the carved clay technique by Carolyn Wills, 1973, mark No.59; oval dish decorated in the sgraffito and silhouette techniques, 1972-1975, mark No.47 and No.51. Bottom: dish shape 5, decorated in the sgraffito and silhouette techniques by Laura Wills, 1977-1978; dish shape 5 decorated in the sgraffito and silhouette techniques by Diana Davis, 1973-1974, mark No.57. Largest dish diameter 16ins (40.5cm).

A selection of dishes designed and decorated by Ros Sommerfelt, 1972-1977. Top: two dishes shape 5, with the sgraffito technique; dish shape 5, with the silhouette technique. Centre: dish shape 3, with the silhouette technique, sweet dish shape 81, with the sgraffito technique. Bottom: two sweet dishes shape 82, with the silhouette technique. All mark No.47 and No.51. Length of sweet dish,shape 82, 17ins (43cm).

A collection of wares, designers and paintresses unattributed, decorated 1969-1979. Top: dish shape 4, with the silhouette technique; vase shape 32, with sgraffito technique. Centre: large dish shape 5, with the silhouette technique; dish shape 3, with sgraffito and silhouette techniques; dish shape 91, with sgraffito technique. Bottom: two sweet dishes shape 82, with silhouette technique. All mark No.47 and No.51. Length of sweet dish shape 82, 17ins (43cm).

A selection of dishes with patterns of Yachts designed by Leslie Elsden. Top: dish shape 4, decorated in the sgraffito and silhouette techniques, 1969-1979; dish shape 4A decorated in the sgraffito technique by Carole Holden, 1970-1974; dish shape 5, decorated in the silhouette technique, 1969-1979. Bottom: sweet dish shape 81, decorated in the sgraffito technique by Jane Brewer, 1972-1975; dish shape 91, decorated in the silhouette technique by Carole Holden, 1970-1974; dish shape 3, decorated in the sgraffito technique by Leslie Elsden, 1969-1979; dish shape 3, decorated in the silhouette technique by Andrée Fontana, 1973-1979. All mark No.47 and No.51. Largest dish diameter 14ins (35.5cm).

Carole Holden carving a plant pot, shape 80, in the leather hard clay state prior to biscuit firing.

Drawings from Carole Holden's sketch pad showing Delphis designs and a preliminary design for a series of dishes in the Aegean range entitled 'Signs of the Zodiac'.

Dishes and a bowl with leaf patterns designed by Leslie Elsden and decorated using the sgraffito and silhouette techniques. Top: sweet dish shape 81, decorated by Carole Holden, 1970-1974; bowl shape 58, decorated by Andrée Fontana, 1973-1979. Bottom: dish shape 91, decorated by Carole Holden, 1970-1974; dish shape 4A, decorated 1969-1979. All mark No.47 and No.51. Diameter of bowl shape 58, 14ins (35.5cm).

Dishes with early patterns designed and developed using the sgraffito technique: sweet dish shape 82, mermaid pattern designed by Carole Holden and decorated by Leslie Elsden, 1970-1974; sweet dish shape 82, wild deer pattern designed by Leslie Elsden and decorated 1969-1974; dish shape 91, water bird pattern designed by Leslie Elsden and decorated by Jane Brewer, 1972-1975; dish shape 3, Corfe Castle pattern designed by Carole Holden and decorated by Leslie Elsden, 1970-1974. All mark No.47 and No.51. Length of sweet dish shape 82, 17ins (43cm).

A collection of vases and a bowl decorated by Diana Davis. Left to right: vase shape 93, thrown by Chris White and decorated in the silhouette technique, 1975-1978, mark No.28; vase shape 84, thrown by Jenny Haigh and decorated in the sgraffito and silhouette techniques, 1973-1976, mark No.28; vase shape 93, decorated in the sgraffito and silhouette techniques, 1973-1978, mark No.47 and No.51; vase shape 84, thrown by Alan White and decorated in the silhouette technique, 1973-1978, mark No.28; bowl shape 57, decorated in the silhouette technique, 1973-1978, mark No.47 and No.51. Tallest vase height 12½ins (32cm). Diana Davis trained in Arts and Crafts and as a teacher at Hereford College.

Bowl shape 7, a Royal Lancastrian Pottery shape decorated at Poole in the silhouette technique by Carolyn Wills, 1975-1976; vase shape 85, thrown by Jenny Haigh and decorated in the sgraffito and silhouette techniques by Carolyn Wills, 1974-1976, mark No.64; vase shape 93, thrown by Chris White and decorated in the sgraffito and silhouette techniques by Lindsay Loader, 1978-1979, mark No.64; tray shape 361, decorated in the silhouette technique by Donna Brogan, 1977-1979, mark No.47 and No.51; dish shape 3A, decorated in the silhouette technique, 1976-1978, mark No.47 and No.51; tray shape 361, decorated in the silhouette technique by Andrée Fontana, 1973-1979, mark No.47 and No.51. Tallest vase height 16ins (40.5cm).

Deborah McCutchion, thrower at the Poole Craft Section, 1976-1979.

The Aegean section, 1976. Left to right, standing: Diana Davis, Jacqueline Mackenzie, Ros Sommerfelt, Julie Wills; seated, Carolyn Wills, Leslie Elsden.

Factory pattern sheet showing designs for Aegean dishes. Harry Paye, top right, by Tony Morris, the remainder unattributed.

Ionian and Atlantis

A range of Ionian ware. Top row: plaque shape 6, pattern designed and glaze decorated by Carolyn Wills, 1974-1975, mark No.29 and No.61; bowl shape 57, pattern carved in clay and decorated 1974, mark No.47 and No.61; plaque shape 6, pattern designed and decorated by Susan Allen, 1974-1975, mark No.29 and No.61. Bottom row: plaque shape 6, pattern designed and decorated by Carolyn Wills, 1974-1975, mark No. 29 and No. 61; plaque shape 6, pattern designed and decorated by Julie Wills, 1974-1975, mark No.29 and No.61; plaque shape 6, diameter 12½ins (32cm), pattern designed by Carole Holden and decorated by Susan Allen, 1974-1975, mark No.29 and No.61.

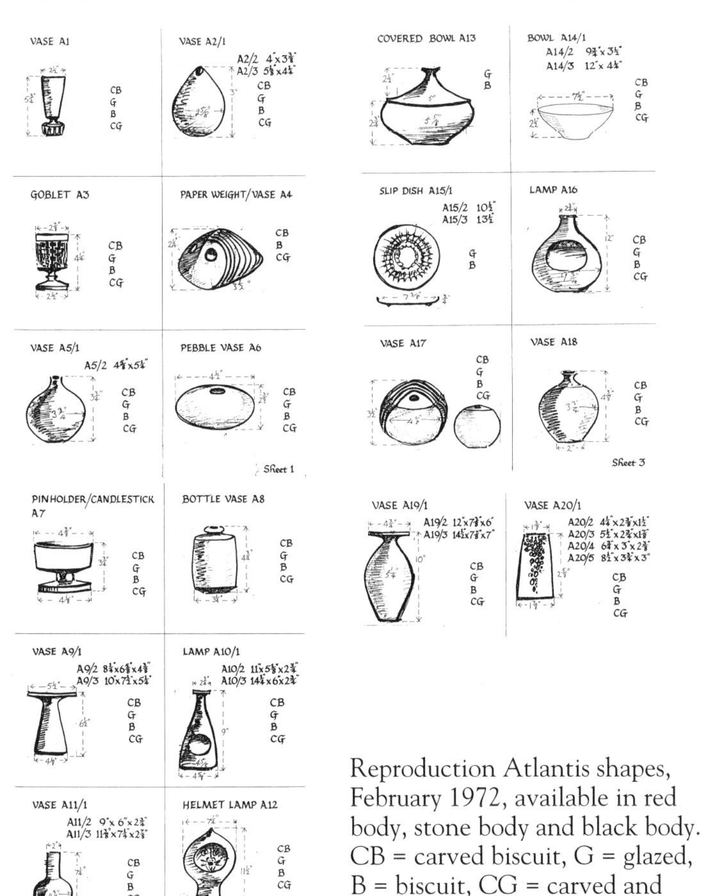

Reproduction Atlantis shapes, February 1972, available in red body, stone body and black body. CB = carved biscuit, G = glazed, B = biscuit, CG = carved and glazed.

White earthenware studio vase with applied reliefs, thrown and glazed by Guy Sydenham, 1966, mark No.28. Height 14½ins (37cm). Shown at the Trade Exhibition, Carlton Towers Hotel, London, 1966.

Factory promotional photograph showing a selection of wares, including slip trailed dishes from the Atlantis range, 1972-1977. Variously coloured slips, magnolia, olive green and crystal glazes and a copper/iron oxide wash were used on this range of once fired and vitrified products designed by Guy Sydenham.

Chess set (part) in grey stoneware and red earthenware, thrown and shaped by Guy Sydenham, carved, glazed and detailed with oxides by Beatrice Bolton, 1972-1974, mark No.29. Height of queen 4$^{1}/_{2}$ins (11.5cm).

A group of red earthenware lamps, thrown, carved and glazed by Guy Sydenham, 1972-1977. Left to right: helmet lamp A12, lamp A16, helmet lamp A12. All mark No.29. Height of lamp A16, 12$^{1}/_{4}$ins (31cm).

A group of red earthenware vases, from left to right: vase A19/2, thrown, carved and glazed by Jenny Haigh, 1973-1976, mark No.29; vase A9/2, thrown, carved and glazed by Guy Sydenham and Susan Dipple, 1972-1975, mark No.29; vase A19/2, thrown, carved and glazed by Jenny Haigh, 1973-1976, mark No.29; vase A20/5, thrown, carved and glazed by Guy Sydenham, 1972-1977, mark No.29; vase A19/1, thrown, carved and glazed by Jenny Haigh, 1973-1976, mark No.29. Tallest vase height, 12¼ins (31cm).

Left to right: two red earthenware vases A20/3, thrown and carved by Beatric Bolton, 1972-1974; grey stoneware vase A11/1, thrown, carved and glazed by Guy Sydenham and Susan Dipple, 1972-1975, mark No.29; red eathenware vase A5/2, thrown, carved and glazed by Guy Sydenham, 1972-1977, mark No.29; grey stoneware vase A11/1, thrown, carved and glazed by Guy Sydenham and Susan Dipple, 1972-1975, mark No.29. Tallest vase height 7¼ins (18.5cm).

Back: Large black stoneware vase, thrown, carved and glazed by Guy Sydenham, mark No.29. Front, left to right: red earthenware pebble vase A6, thrown and carved by Guy Sydenham, 1972-1977, mark No.29; red earthenware pebble vase A6, thrown, carved and glazed by Guy Sydenham, 1972-1977, mark No.29; red earthenware vase A2/1, thrown, carved and glazed by Beatrice Bolton, 1972-1974, mark No.29; red earthenware vase A2/2, thrown, carved and glazed by Guy Sydenham, 1972-1977, mark No.29; red earthenware vase A2/3, thrown, carved and glazed by Guy Sydenham and Susan Dipple, 1972-1975, mark No.29. Largest vase height 7½ins (19cm).

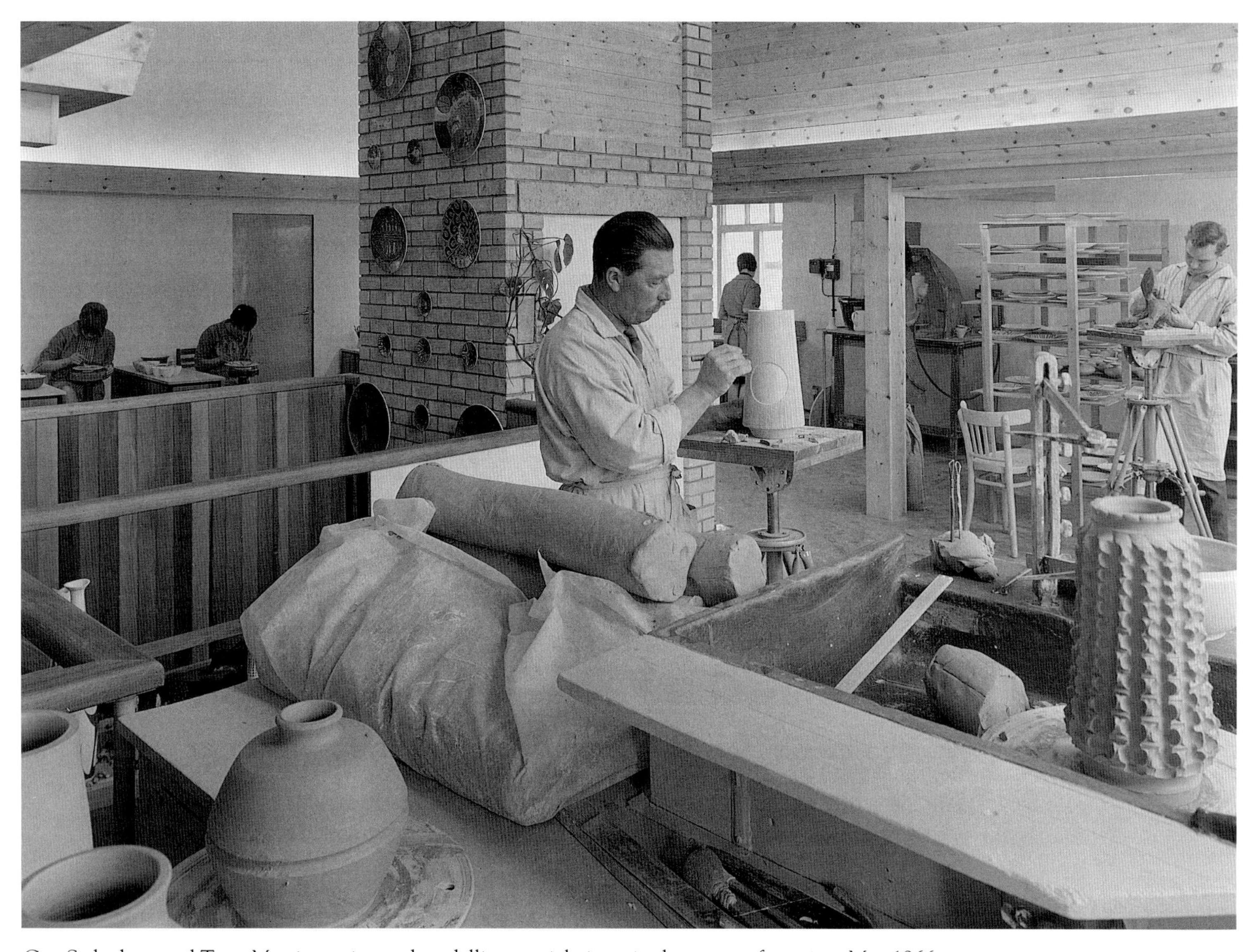

Guy Sydenham and Tony Morris carving and modelling special pieces in the new craft section, May 1966.

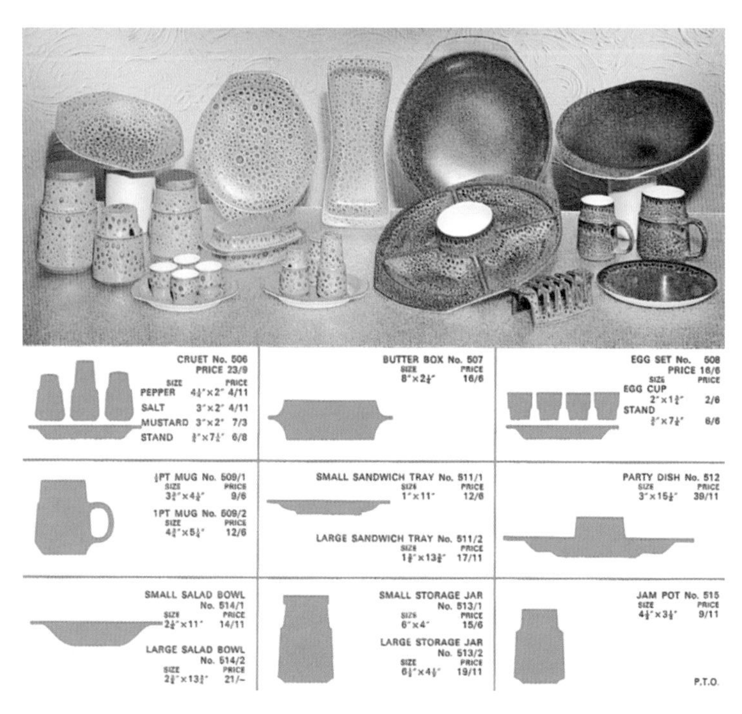

CRUET No. 506
PRICE 23/9

	SIZE	PRICE
PEPPER	4½"×2"	4/11
SALT	3"×2"	4/11
MUSTARD	3"×2"	7/3
STAND	⅜"×7½"	6/8

BUTTER BOX No. 507

SIZE	PRICE
8"×2½"	16/6

EGG SET No. 508
PRICE 16/6

	SIZE	PRICE
EGG CUP	2"×1¾"	2/6
STAND	⅜"×7½"	6/6

½PT MUG No. 509/1

SIZE	PRICE
3¾"×4½"	9/6

1PT MUG No. 509/2

SIZE	PRICE
4¾"×5¼"	12/6

SMALL SANDWICH TRAY No. 511/1

SIZE	PRICE
1"×11"	12/6

LARGE SANDWICH TRAY No. 511/2

SIZE	PRICE
1⅜"×13⅜"	17/11

PARTY DISH No. 512

SIZE	PRICE
3"×15½"	39/11

SMALL SALAD BOWL No. 514/1

SIZE	PRICE
2½"×11"	14/11

LARGE SALAD BOWL No. 514/2

SIZE	PRICE
2¾"×13¾"	21/–

SMALL STORAGE JAR No. 513/1

SIZE	PRICE
6"×4"	15/6

LARGE STORAGE JAR No. 513/2

SIZE	PRICE
6½"×4½"	19/11

JAM POT No. 515

SIZE	PRICE
4½"×3½"	9/11

P.T.O.

Catalogue page showing Poole Pottery shapes and price list for Sea Crest and Blue Lace tableware accessories designed by Tony Morris and Guy Sydenham, 1967-1968.

Catalogue page showing the New Stoneware coffee set in Pampas and Serpentine. Designed by Guy Sydenham, thrown, carved and glazed by Alan White and Angela Wyburgh, 1967.

Chapter Nine

Poole Pottery in the 1970s and 1980s

As the 1970s drew to a close, the distinctive productions of the Craft Section that had characterised Poole's links with contemporary design were mostly withdrawn. In 1973 the company had celebrated its centenary, and in 1979 the factory had been honoured by a visit from Her Majesty the Queen and the Duke of Edinburgh, the fitting climax to several decades of ceramic individuality. From this point on, and now under the direction of Trevor Wright who had taken over as Managing Director when Roy Holland retired at the end of 1976, Poole's output was marked by a new spirit of diversity. The revived traditional wares took over the mantle of hand painting from the Craft Section, initially pushing the pottery back towards its roots. At the same time, the needs of the table and giftware markets were becoming increasingly dominant. Robert Jefferson's Compact range was in production throughout the period, along with Style, a new tableware shape designed by him for Poole in 1979. Printed patterns were now standard, generally following the fashions of each period. Typical were the Parkstone and Broadstone glazes used with the re-active lithographs on tablewares that reflected both the craft styles popular in the late 1970s, and the new demands made by modern kitchen equipment such as freezers and, later, microwaves. During the 1980s Poole's design policy was to become much more broadly based with increasing use of independent and external designers, but initially the distinctive Poole style was maintained by the series of map plates, developed from an idea by Robert Jefferson, and by Tony Morris's Cathedral and Calendar plates with their medieval stained glass inspiration, the latter made between 1972 and 1975. Another introduction of the 1970s that maintained the Poole tradition was the series of stoneware wildlife sculptures, plates and related wares designed by Barbara Linley Adams, an internationally recognised sculptor and ceramic modeller who had been trained at the Slade and Central Schools of Art. Aimed at a newly emerging collector market, the series was launched in 1972 when Adams first came to work at Poole. The first model was the Wren on Branch, and this was followed by over a hundred different animals and birds designed up to 1983, when she retired. From 1979 some models were reproduced in earthenware, and from 1985 a bone china body was also used. This period was marked by an expansion from 1967 in the making of wildlife figures generally at Poole, finished mainly in the dolphin blue glaze. Some subjects were also issued as low relief trays, designed by Tony Morris in 1974. The late 1970s were characterised by the production of a surprisingly diverse range of decorative wares, some featuring hand throwing and hand painting. These included Contrast and Sienna, with their re-active glaze effects, Olympus with stylised patterns by Ros Sommerfelt, the black and white Domino wares and Calypso, a revival by Leslie Elsden of the 1930s Picotee wares. All were marketed as clearly defined ranges, with a series of specially designed shapes. More directly derived from Delphis was the Dorset Collection, with leaf designs in strong colours by Ros Sommerfelt, introduced in 1977, and later expanded by her and other designers. From this came a variety of cache pots in various styles, a direct response to current market fashions. Ros Sommerfelt made her mark during this period as an imaginative designer. She contributed to the Camelot plate series in 1977 and was responsible for the development of the Beardsley Collection of 1979, a dramatic printed range that reflected current enthusiasms for Art Nouveau. This fin de siècle style was also the inspiration for Sommerfelt's Fleurie range of gift wares, another new departure for Poole prompted by the consumer market of the late 1970s and early 1980s. A selection of jewellery and other ranges include Bow Bells, Country Lane, Kandy and Wild Garden, the last named the creation of Elaine Williamson, who headed the Poole design unit in the early 1980s. Apart from gift wares, Williamson also designed the Concert tableware shape in 1985. The requirement of the gift ware market took Poole into Fine Bone China, and this traditional Staffordshire material was used for a number of ranges, including animal and bird figures. Other developments were the ranges of earthenware mugs and the scenic plates, the latter decorated with open stock patterns from 1983. Throughout the 1980s Poole relied both on their own staff designers and on outsiders to supply their increasingly diverse needs, with contributions from sources as varied as Mary Jones Design, John Bromley and Robert Welch. The latter's Campden tableware range was introduced from 1989. However, the most important design contribution during this period came from the Queensberry Hunt Partnership. Their relationship started in 1983 with the Flair tableware range. This was followed in 1989 by Astral tableware, but in between were an exciting group of modern decorative wares that featured both new shapes and glaze effects. First came Calypso, introduced in 1984 initially with pastel colours and then with more varied finishes, then the fluted Corinthian range. These were followed in 1990 by Cello with its distinctive marbled finish.

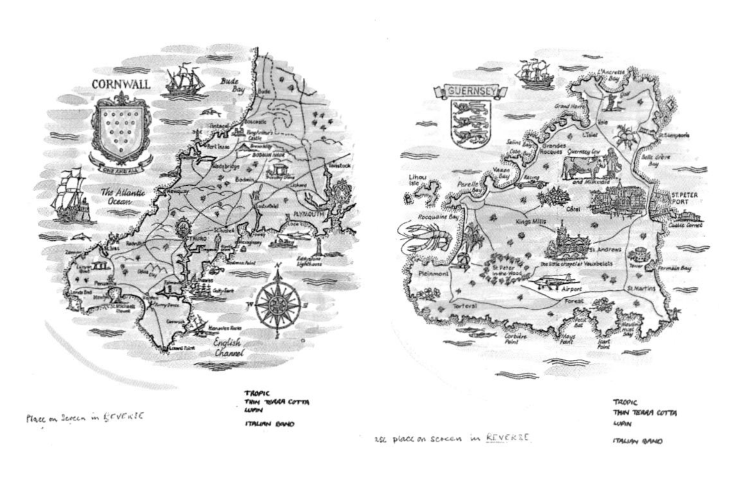

Designs by Tony Morris for the map plate series, showing Cornwall and Guernsey.

Map Plates and Calendar Plates

White earthenware with an alpine glazed ground, the black outline of the design applied with a silk screen transfer and painted with mainly soluble colours. Poole Harbour, the first in the series, was drawn by Robert Jefferson about 1963. The Beaulieu design is from a drawing by Norman Thelwell, commissioned by Lord Montagu and used as a poster from 1968-1970 to attract visitors to his ancestral home and famous motor museum. With the exception of the Isle of Purbeck, drawn by Ros Sommerfelt, the remainder, including the enlarged map of Poole Harbour, were drawn by Tony Morris, 1963-1978. Above left: Poole Harbour, Hampshire, Jersey, Isle of Wight, Poole Harbour (enlarged), Dorset, all mark No.62. Above right: Norfolk Federation of Women's Institutes Golden Jubilee, 1918-1968, mark No.47, Beaulieu, mark No.47, Isle of Purbeck, mark No.62, Bournemouth (Oakmead School), mark No.59, Devon, mark No.41. Beaulieu plate, diameter 10ins (25cm).

Above left: A group of five dishes, shape 361, selected from a range of similar pieces, screen printed on alpine glazed white earthenware, 1965-1975. Left: Hardy's Birthplace, painted in soluble colours, mark No.48 and THOMAS HARDY, BORN 1840 AT HIGHER BOCKHAMPTON, PRODUCED BY POOLE POTTERY FOR THE HARDY FESTIVAL 1968 screen printed on reverse; Haven House Inn, Mudeford Quay, painted in soluble colours, mark No.62. Centre: Thomas Becket, mark No.41 and THOMAS BECKET CENTENARY 1170-1970 CANTERBURY stamped. Right: Matapan, painted in soluble colours, mark No.48 and SPRING PROMOTION MAY 1968 stamped; Salisbury Cathedral, painted in soluble colours, mark No.62. Above right: A group of wares screen printed and painted on alpine glazed white earthenware after drawings by Tony Morris, 1965-1975. Left: plate shape 120, Brownsea Castle, mark No.41 and Brownsea Castle stamped; centre: dish shape 81, Guildford Cathedral, mark No.62; right: dish shape 81, moulded portrait of Thomas Hardy, covered with a chestnut transparent glaze, mark No.48. Plate diameter 8ins (20.5cm).

Cathedral plates designed by Tony Morris in the stained glass window technique. Limited to 1,000 of each edition, the plates, shape 6, were individually numbered and supplied in a presentation box with a signed certificate. Left to right: ADORATION OF THE MAGI, design 523, issued in 1975, based on a thirteenth century bible window in the north aisle of the choir in Canterbury Cathedral. The infant Christ is depicted on Mary's knee, adored by the shepherds and the Magi bearing gifts beneath the stars. Painted by Susan Pottinger, mark No.29 and No.55. CHRIST ON THE CROSS, design 479, issued in 1973, based on the twelth century lancet window in the Cathedral of Notre Dame at Chartres in France. The whole window depicts the Passion of Christ in fourteen medallions. Painted by Julie Wills, mark No.29 and No.55. FLIGHT INTO EGYPT, design 522, issued in 1975, based on a thirteenth century window in the south aisle of the choir in Canterbury Cathedral, Mary, Joseph and the Holy Child are seen fleeing from Herod into Egypt, painted by Susan Pottinger, mark No.29 and No.55.

Medieval calendar plates, designed by Tony Morris, shape 6, all mark No.54, diameter 12½ins (32cm). Limited to 1,000 of each edition, the individually numbered plates were supplied in a presentation box with a signed certificate. From left to right: JANUARY, drinking wine by the fire, design 949, painted by Susan Allen, issued 1972; FEBRUARY, chopping wood, design 919, painted by Tina Trapp, issued 1972; MARCH, digging in the fields and setting seeds, design 833, painted by Julie Wills, issued 1973.

APRIL, carrying a flowering branch, design 807, painted by Jacqueline Mackenzie, issued 1973; MAY, hawking, design 880, painted by Tina Trapp, issued 1974; JUNE, mowing the hay, design 698, painted by Julie Wills, issued 1974.

JULY, cutting corn with a sickle, design 920, painted by Julie Wills, issued 1975; AUGUST, threshing with a flail, design 648, painted by Susan Pottinger, issued 1975; SEPTEMBER, picking grapes, design 957, painted by Julie Wills, issued 1975.

OCTOBER, sowing winter corn, design 938, painted by Julie Wills, issued 1975; NOVEMBER, gathering acorns to feed the pigs, design 937, painted by Susan Pottinger, issued 1975; DECEMBER, pig killing, design 897, painted by Susan Pottinger, issued 1975.

Stoneware Sculptures by Barbara Linley Adams

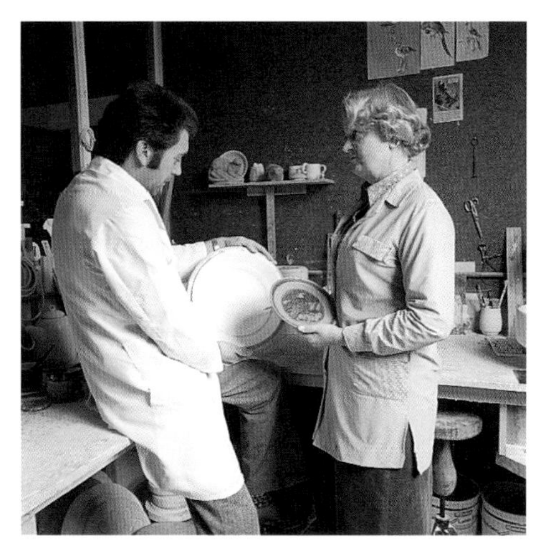

Barbara Linley Adams and Joe Leadbeater discussing a master mould.

Linda Garwood restoring a cast to the condition of the original model.

Eunice Menke applying an oxide wash which provides the black detail after firing.

Mallard 707, first made 1973, mark No.29 and No.60, modified, 'mallard anas platyrhynchos stoneware sculptures by BARBARA LINLEY ADAMS, Limited edition of 1,000', B. Linley Adams incised in script; fawn 717, first made 1977, mark No.29, and B. Linley Adams incised in script; barred owl 705, first made 1973, finished by Janet Stone, mark No.29; cat 720, first made 1978, finished by Susan Dipple, mark No.29; pair of grouse 711, first made 1974, finished by Janet Stone, mark No.29 and No.60, modified, 'Grouse lagopus stoneware sculptures by BARBARA LINLEY ADAMS, Limited edition of 1,000', B. Linley Adams incised in script. Height of barred owl 13ins (33cm).

Merlin 716, first made 1977, finished by Susan Dipple, mark No.29; kookaburra, first made 1984, finished by Lindsay Loader, mark No.29; otter 729, first made 1980, finished by Joanna Durant, mark No.29; squirrel 719, first made 1977, mark No.29; pony 736, first made 1981, mark No.29; hound 701, first made 1985, finished by Susan Dipple, mark No.29. Height of hound 7½ins (19cm).

Guinea pig 792, first made 1984, mark No.29; toad 714, first made 1975, mark No.29; standing rabbit 715/4, first made 1977, mark No.29; puppy on slipper 636, first made 1988, finished by Nicola Masserella, mark No.29; shetland pony head 730, first made 1980, mark No.29; tortoise 727, first made 1979, mark No.29; puffin, first made 1974, marked POOLE, painted; quail 709, first made 1974, finished by Jane Freeborn, mark No.29; bluetit 726, first made 1980, first coloured 1991, finished by June Cole, painted by Nicola Masserella, mark No.29; alligator 779, designed and modelled by Tony Morris, first made 1982, mark No.29; small fawn on stand 772, first made 1979; mouse on apple 703, first made 1972, finished by Janet Stone, mark No.29; seal 768, first made 1979, transfer printed mark WORLD WILDLIFE FUND with panda motif; robin on flower pot 725, first made 1979, finished by Nicola Masserella, mark No.29, made for the Royal Society for Protection of Birds. Height of quail 5ins (12.5cm).

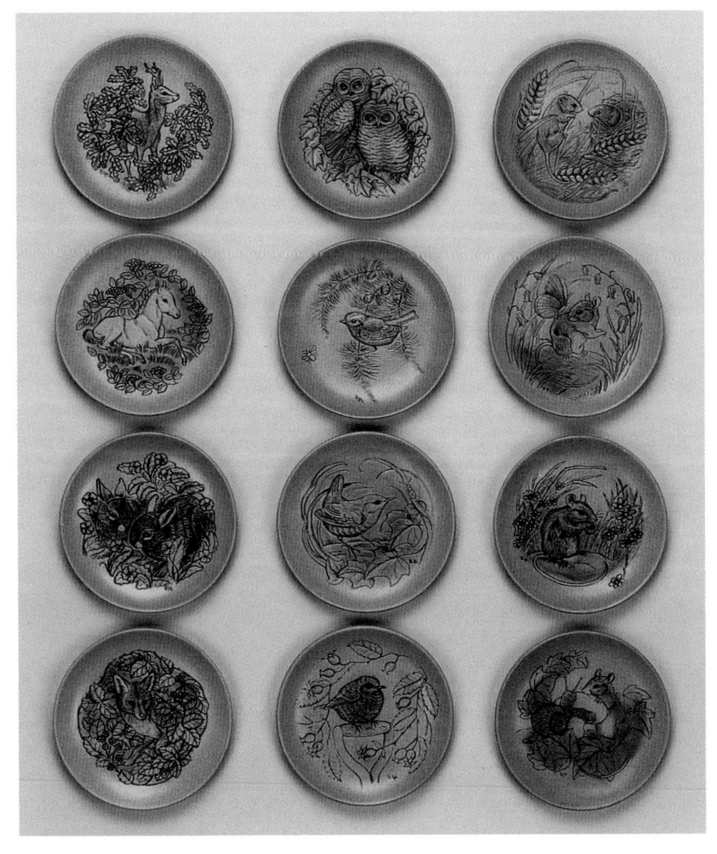

Above: the Wildlife Collection of stoneware dishes, issued 1982-1984. The series entitled New Forest animals, birds, mice, cats, wild animals and dogs. Diameter of dish 5ins (13cm). Examples showing alternative images have also been identified.

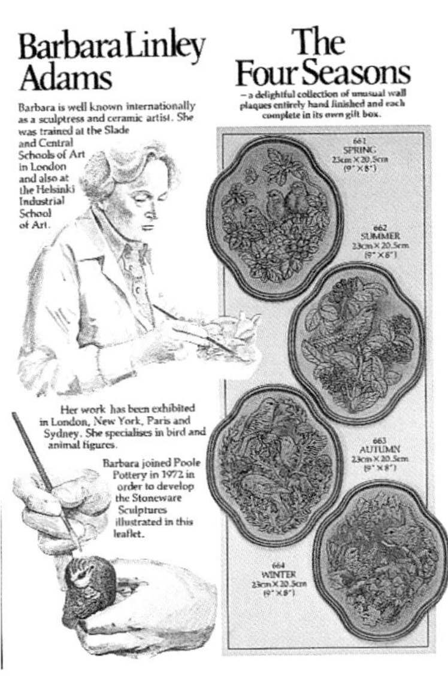

Left: illustration sheets showing British Birds limited edition plates, issued 1978; Game Bird plates and The Four Seasons wall plaques, issued 1982-1983.

Left: Birds of North America series, issued in 1978 in limited editions: mallard, heron, horned owl and bald eagle. Diameter 8¼ins (21cm).

Below: Bert Baggaley, modelling the medium size Dolphin, 1979.

Seal plate, 1979, moulded in low relief with inscription: 'This Seal plate No.10 of a limited edition of 7,500. Designed by Barbara Linley Adams and produced in co-operation with the World Wildlife Fund.' Poole Pottery mark No.74 and the logo for The World Wildlife Fund incorporated. Diameter 8¼ins (21cm). Christmas plate, 1986, 'Away in a Manger', limited edition of 10,000, designed and modelled by Barbara Linley Adams, mark No.68, modified. Other plates depicting birds and animals in this series, 'Santa's Helpers', 1978; 'Three Wise Men', 1979; 'Temptation', 1980; all limited editions of 10,000; 'Christmas Carol', 1981; 'Waiting for Santa', 1982; 'Playmate', 1983; Expectation', 1984; 'Carol Singers', 1985; all limited editions of 5,000. Diameter 8¼ins (21cm).
In the same series Mother's Day plates were also designed by Barbara Linley Adams, mark No.75. 'Tenderness', 1979; 'Devotion' 1980; limited editions of 10,000; 'For You', 1981; 'Family Frolics', 1982; 'Patience', 1983; 'Puppy Love', 1984; all limited editions of 5,000. Diameter 8¼ins.(21cm).

Dolphin embossed tray, shape 402, designed by Tony Morris, 1967. Silk screen transfer printed, back mark incorporating E.N.A.E.M. INSTITUTE, ROTARY INTERNATIONAL, BOURNEMOUTH 1979 and Poole Pottery, mark No.74.

Earthenware figures in dolphin blue glaze, 1989-1990. Introduced in 1967, this range included other figures and glazes, some of which were hand painted.

Above: A group of embossed trays, shape 402, owl, seagull, squirrel, deer and penguin, designed by Tony Morris, 1974 and covered in olive green transparent glaze, mark No.62. Other figures including a fish and zebra were also produced in this series and alternative transparent glazes were used - dolphin blue, midnight blue and chestnut. Illustrated as a mirror image.

Left: Elegance figurines in white earthenware, designed and modelled by John Bromley, 1980-1981. The gold and other transfer decoration, with hand painted details on a tin based vellum glaze, designed by Ros Sommerfelt. Left to right: Katherine, Elizabeth, Abigail, Eleanor, Victoria and Lillie, mark No.73, modified with name added. In 1982 these figures were made in bone china. Tallest figure height 10ins (25.5cm).

Dorset Collection and Cache Pots

A factory promotional photograph showing a selection of wares from the Dorset Collection, 1977. Thrown or moulded in white earthenware covered with a red clay slip, the patterns, designed by Ros Sommerfelt, were painted onto the biscuit with a copper/iron oxide wash and oversprayed with Delphis red glaze.

Wicker effect cache pots in snow white glazed white earthenware. Designed by Tony Morris, 1980.

Embossed white earthenware cache pots glazed in chestnut, olive green and gold transparent glazes. Designed by Tony Morris, 1980.

The Dorset Collection, 1979, comprising a range of cache pots decorated with sgraffito, copper/iron wash and latex painting techniques. The patterns designed by Elaine Williamson, Ros Sommerfelt, Carolyn Walters and other paintresses.

Ros Sommerfelt designed the Bamboo pattern in 1979 and this was painted in three sizes exclusively for Marks & Spencer.

Hexagonal white earthenware cache pots designed with the Blue Floral on-glaze transfer pattern (centre) by Elaine Williamson, 1985.

White earthenware cache pots designed by the Queensberry Hunt Partnership, with patterns in soluble and re-active colours designed by Elaine Williamson and Ros Sommerfelt, 1983, painted under the glacier glaze.

Olympus, Calypso and Domino

A selection of white earthenwares, the two left hand vases of the Contrast design decorated with chestnut and snow white glazes in a re-active technique developed by Leslie Elsden, 1977, shape 34, mark No.47, shape 83, mark No.47. Other shapes in the Contrast range include: plates 3A and 4A, vases 15, 31 and 84, dishes 41, 42, 49, 81, 91 and 361, bowls 57, 94, 95 and 96, ashtrays 801 and 802. Dish and two vases of the Sienna pattern, handcrafted in the art nouveau style with scolloped edging, sprayed with a base glaze and muted colours over a free-style hand painted pattern in latex resist to complement the shape. Designed and developed by Tony Morris and Jacqueline Leonard, 1978. Shallow dish shape 588, mark No.47; vase shape 583, mark No.34; vase shape 580, mark No.47. Tallest vase height 11¼ins (28.5cm). Other shapes in the Sienna range include: bowls 485, 486, 584, 585, 587 and 592, ginger jars 490, 491 and 492, cache pots 497, 498, 499 and 500, vases 579, 581 and 582, dish 589.

A selection of Olympus, once fired, grey stoneware. The hand thrown shapes and seashore pattern designed by Rosalind Sommerfelt, 1977. The decorative border painted directly onto the clay in black outline and filled in with re-active glazes. From left to right: powder bowl shape 62, sprayed with black panther glaze, thrown by Alan White, mark No.58; vase shape 60C, sprayed with dusk glaze, painted by Susan Barfoot, mark No.70; vase shape 60A, sprayed with magnolia glaze, painted by Jacqueline Mackenzie, mark No.70; bud vase shape 63, sprayed with ice green glaze, mark No.70. Tallest vase height 6¼ins (16cm).

A selection of wares from the Calypso range - a 1977-1978 revival, by Leslie Elsden, of the Picotee spray banding technique as developed by him in 1932. The coloured bands are applied to the unfired snow white glaze on the following range of white earthenware shapes: vases 15, 31, 34, 83, 84, 85 and 93, dishes 42 and 49, bowl, 56 and 57, plant pots 72 and 73, fruit bowls, 94, 95 and 96, ashtrays 801 and 802. Vase 85 height 16ins (40cm).

A selection of white earthenwares from the Domino range, decorated in black panther and snow white glazes, introduced in 1976-1977, which included the following shapes: vases 15, 31, 34, 84 and 93, plant pots 72 and 73, fruit bowls 94, 95 and 96; heart tray 392 (white only), club tray 393 (black only), diamond tray 394 (white only) and spade tray 395 (black only).

The Olympus range of shapes decorated in the Rosalinde pattern, designed by Ros Sommerfelt, 1977.

Parkstone, Broadstone and other Tablewares

A group of slip outline glazed white earthenwares, designed and decorated by Cynthia Bennett, 1980-1981. Bowl shape 57, dish shape 6, powder box shape 462 and dish shape 3. Largest dish diameter 12½ins (32cm).

A selection of white earthenware mugs introduced 1980, with in-glaze transfer decorations, from top to bottom: Facade and Window Box, designed by Ros Sommerfelt, Fashion and Floral, designed by Elaine Williamson.

Promotional leaflets for Compact tableware decorated with glaze re-active lithos on Parkstone glaze, left, and Broadstone glaze, right, 1975-1976.

Poole Pottery stand at the Birmingham International Gift Fair, 1978.

Beardsley and Camelot

The Beardsley collection of on-glaze transfer decorated white earthenwares, developed by Ros Sommerfelt and introduced in 1979. Top: mug 482, ginger jars 490 and 491, candy tray 481, bud vase 480. Centre: candlestick 483, Regency candy jar 487, bowls 485 and 486, jug 489, vase 488. Bottom: ashtray 476, bonbon tray 478, twin server 484, heart-shaped lidded box 479 and coaster 477. Added to the range in 1980: small heart-shaped box 456, round pill box 459, powder box 462, shell dish 465. Added to the range in 1981: bell 450, small egg 451, large egg 452, plant pots 497, 498 and 499. Ginger jar 491 height 9ins (23cm).

Vase in white earthenware, thrown by Alan White, 1977. The pattern in best burnished gold on black panther glaze designed and painted by Karen Hickisson, mark No.28. Height $19\frac{1}{2}$ins (50cm).

Camelot plates designed in 1977, hand painted with best burnished gold on a black enamel transfer print. Design 513 Lady of Shalott and design 512 Arthur and Guinevere by Ros Sommerfelt. Design 511 Voyage to Avalon and design 510 Excalibur by Tony Morris, mark No.69. Diameter $8\frac{1}{2}$ins (21.5cm).

An original hand thrown vase, painted by Susan Pottinger when recreating the designs of Aubrey Beardsley in 1978, leading to the development of the Beardsley range, mark No.28. Height $13\frac{1}{2}$ins (34cm).

Gift Wares

Fleurie, a group of wares featuring women with flamboyant hair styles and flowing costumes typical of the art nouveau period. Designed by Ros Sommerfelt and in production 1979-1980 as an on-glaze transfer decoration over alpine white glaze. Applied to the same range of moulded white earthenware shapes which, in 1980, comprised the Beardsley collection: bud vase shape 480, bowl shape 486 and coaster shape 477, all mark No.74 modified. Bowl diameter 8ins (20.5cm).

Above: a selection of the Kandy giftware range designed by Ros Sommerfelt and in production 1982-1983.

A selection of the Wren & Robin giftware range with patterns designed by Barbara Linley Adams and in production 1982-1984.

Above: a selection of the Wild Garden giftware range designed by Elaine Williamson and in production 1981.

Right: a selection of the Bow Bells giftware range designed by Ros Sommerfelt and in production 1981.

Far right: a selection of The Country Lane giftware range designed with an open stock pattern, and in production 1979-1983.

A selection of the bone china giftware range designed by Elaine Williamson and Ros Sommerfelt. The slightly art deco Polygon shape and all on-glaze transfer patterns designed by Elaine Williamson. Left: Rosalind pattern in production 1983-1987. Centre: Iona pattern, in production 1986-1987. Right: Athena pattern, in production 1986-1987. All mark No.78 with pattern name added. The Ophelia pattern 1983-1987, Cymbeline 1984-1987 and Trelissick on the Polygon shape, 1986-1987, were also designed by Elaine Williamson.

A selection of bird and animal figures by Barbara Linley Adams and others, reissued in the fine bone china body with gold painted eyes and in production 1985 and 1986.

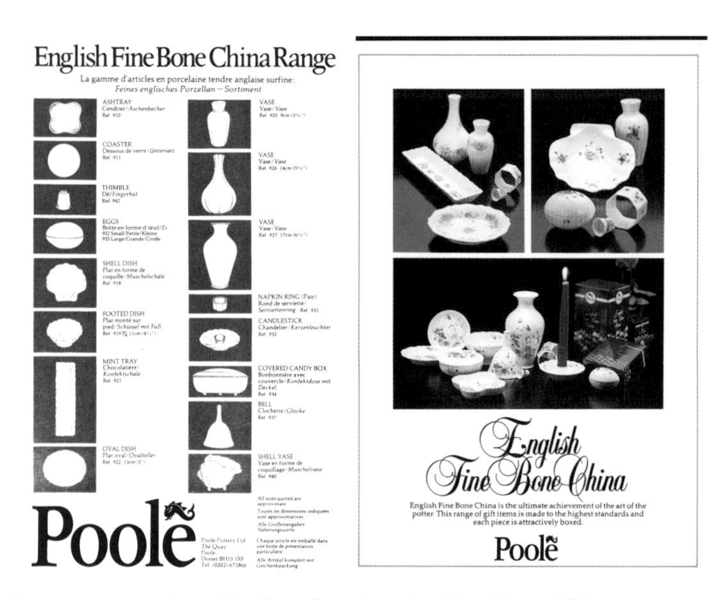

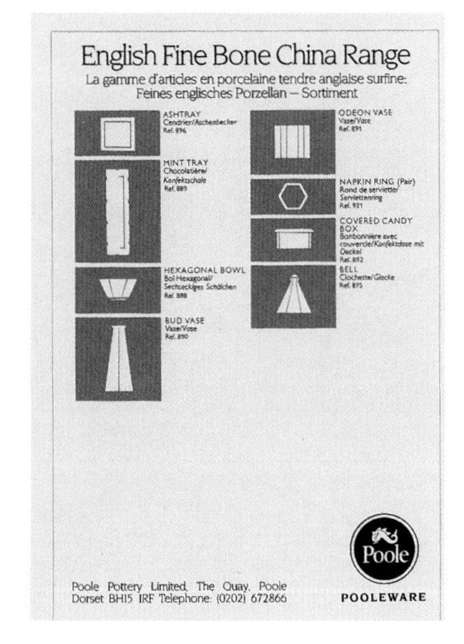

Factory promotional leaflets showing the Fine Bone China range.

Scenic plates with on-glaze open stock transfer patterns. Top row: a set of four plates issued in 1990 with patterns of English cottages, Rose Cottage pattern 793, River Bridge pattern 792, Tall Chimneys pattern 794 and The Manor House pattern 795. Bottom row: Bavarian town scenes by Barbara Furstenhofer, from a set of eight designs issued in 1983, Munchen pattern 431, Marktbreit pattern 432, Mespelbrunn pattern 433 and Chriskindlesmarkt pattern 434, mark No.77. Diameter 6ins (15cm). Between 1983 and 1994, forty-seven known titles in sets of four, six and eight plates, covering almost two hundred and fifty different subjects were portrayed on Poole scenic plates.

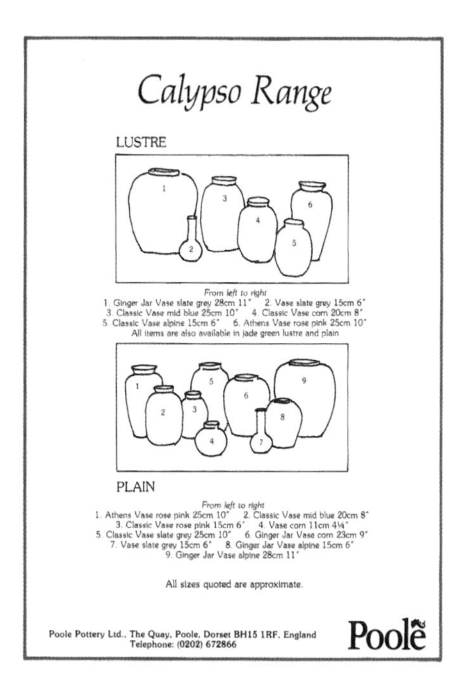

Factory promotional photograph showing the Calypso pastel range developed for Poole by the Queensberry Hunt Partnership and introduced 1984, with leaflets showing a development of the range in 1987.

A selection of the Corinthian range in white earthenware designed by the Queensberry Hunt Partnership and in production 1987.

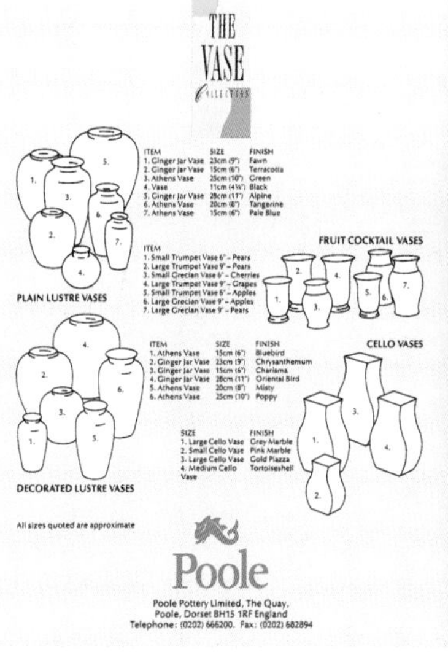

Right: factory promotional leaflets for the lustre, lustre decorated and Cello vase collections introduced in 1990. The Cello range designed by the Queensberry Hunt Partnership.

The Aztec range in white earthenware decorated with a Mary Jones Design pattern by Liane Hutchings and in production 1988-1989.

Studio vases in white earthenware. Left: the Athens vase, freely painted and signed by Ros Sommerfelt using a rubber resist technique, 1986; right: the Classic vase freely painted and signed by Anita Harris using a paper resist technique, 1993. Taller vase height 10ins (25.5cm). Centre: Ros Sommerfelt painting in the design studio, 1987. Right: Carnation, a broad brushwork design by Sara Pearch, 1991, freely painted on alpine glazed white earthenware dish shape 5 and Athens vase, mark No.86 and '© Sara Pearch' transfer printed in script. Vase height 10ins (25.5cm). Other shapes in this range include Athens vases 6ins and 8ins, ginger jar vases 6ins, 9ins and 11ins, ginger jar lamp base 11ins, shape 3 dish 8ins, shape 4 dish 10ins, shape 54 dish 16ins and shape 57 dish 10ins.

A series of six white earthenware plates made for the National Trust, 1990 and decorated with in-glaze Cobalt blue transfers on a crystal glazed ground. Each plate is a replica of a cat plate in the servants' hall at Kingston Lacy, Dorset. Cat on table, cat on armchair, cat with goldfish, cat on dresser, cat with umbrella and cat with butterfly. A specially designed printed back mark states that the original plates were hand painted, c.1888. Diameter 10ins (25.5cm).

A design painted by Phillip Sutton on an alpine glazed white earthenware dish, 1986, mark No.62 and signed by the artist. Diameter 16ins (40.5cm).

Modern Tablewares

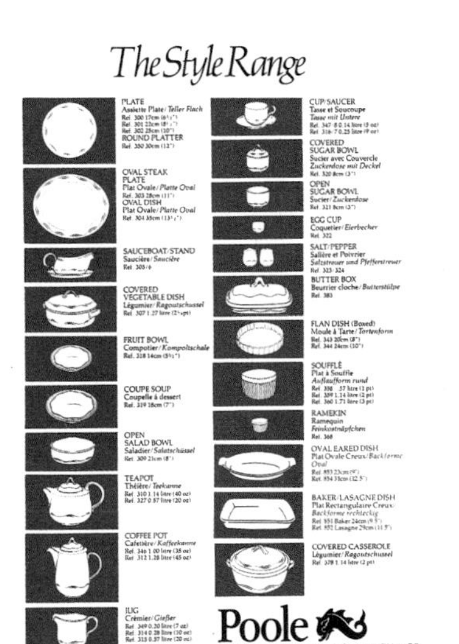

Factory promotional leaflet for the Style range designed by Robert Jefferson and in production in various patterns, 1979-1988.

Factory promotional leaflet for the Compact range designed by Robert Jefferson and in production in various patterns, 1965-1992.

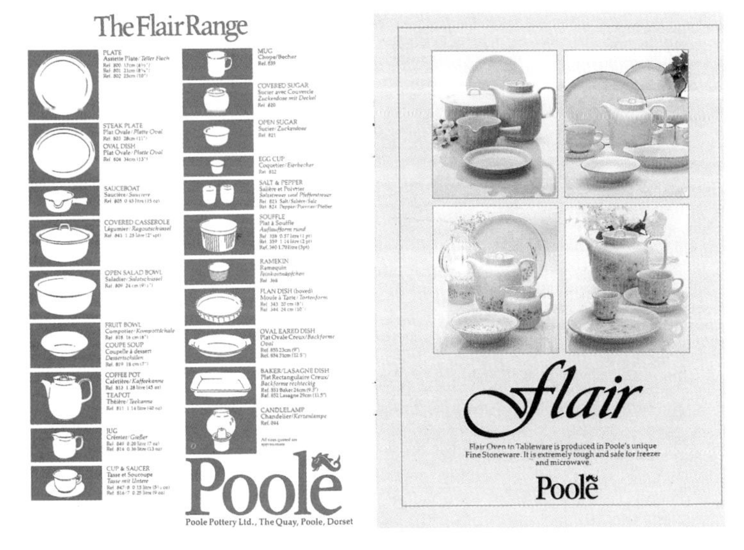

Factory promotional leaflet for the Flair range designed by the Queensberry Hunt Partnership and in production in various patterns, 1983-1986.

Factory promotional leaflet for the Concert range designed by Elaine Williamson and the Poole design team and in production in various patterns, 1985-1992.

A selection of tablewares from the Flair, Concert and Compact ranges.

A selection of tablewares from the Astral, Campden and Next ranges.

Factory promotional leaflet for the Astral range designed by John Horler of the Queensberry Hunt Partnership and in production in various glaze finishes, 1989-1990.

Factory promotional leaflets for the Campden range designed by Robert Welch and in production in various patterns, 1989-1991.

Factory promotional photograph for the Homespun ovenware range designed by Alan White and in production 1989.

Factory promotional leaflet for the Microlyte ware, designed by Trevor Wright, in production 1988-1990.

Factory promotional leaflet for the Oven Ware range designed and extended to various glaze finishes and tableware patterns, 1975-1994.

Chapter Ten

Nursery Ware

Since the earliest days of Carter, Stabler & Adams, nursery wares have been an important part of Poole production. The initial impetus probably came from Truda Adams, and the first designs aimed specifically at the children's market may have been her series of birds, animals and fish used on John Adams toilet and teaware shapes, and illustrated in the 1922-1923 catalogues. The first identifiable nursery ware ranges also date from this time, notably Dora Batty's Nursery Toys and Nursery Rhymes series. These designs were also used to decorate tiles from the early 1920s, along with other early series such as Harold Stabler's Water Birds, and examples were illustrated in the 1924 *Studio Year Book of Decorative Art*. Contemporary advertisements suggest that these tiles may have initially been produced for nursery use. However, it was not until the 1930s that there was any significant expansion of the nursery ware ranges. A number of new designs were introduced between 1934 and 1936, including Stories and Rhymes by Dora Batty, and Toys, Kensington Gardens and London Characters by Truda Carter. Contributions were also made by artists outside the factory, such as Alfred Read, whose 1935 Play Box series was used on both nursery ware and tiles. Even more important was Eileen McGrath, sister of the famous interior designer Raymond McGrath, who supplied Poole with a stylish series of nursery ware designs in about 1934, The Circus, The Picnic and The Zoo. From the early 1930s, pieces from the nursery ware ranges could be personalised by the addition of children's names, a service featured in catalogues, advertisements and contemporary magazine articles. In its report of the visit by the Duke and Duchess of York to the Carter, Stabler & Adams stand at the 1935 British Industries Fair, *The Pottery Gazette* noted the Royal order for two sets of nursery ware with the addition of painted names, presumably 'for the use of the Princess Elizabeth and the Princess Margaret Rose.' Some of these ranges remained in production over many years, with slight alterations and adaptions and no new nursery ware series was introduced until 1963, when Robert Jefferson designed a three piece children's set decorated with drawings by him of animals screen printed, colour washed and contrasted with Sunshine Yellow and Blue Moon glazes. There was then another gap until 1979 when Elaine Williamson's Nursery Rhymes design was introduced, transfer-printed onto a four piece children's set. This was followed in 1985 by her adaptation of the Hambro Industries My Little Pony designs, a rare example of Poole merchandising. In 1994 a far more comprehensive children's ware range of nine shapes was introduced. Entitled The Mad Hatter's Tea Party and sold individually and in boxed sets, these are decorated with a coloured version of Sir John Tenniel's illustrations for *Alice in Wonderland* and *Alice Through the Looking Glass*, a design developed by Sarah Chalmers from an idea by Christopher Woodhead.

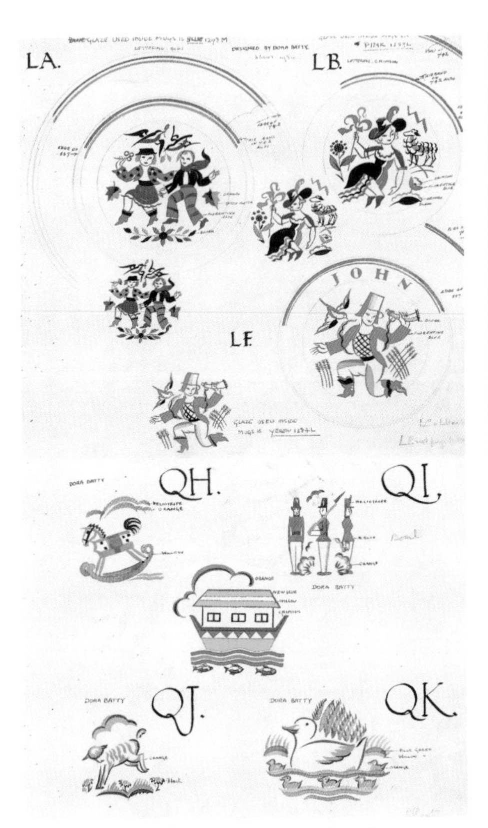

Pages from a factory pattern book showing the Nursery Toys designs by Dora Batty, 1921-1922, and designs from Stories and Rhymes, 1934.

Left to right, back: white earthenware bowl 296/LO Bo-peep from Nursery Rhymes designed by Dora Batty, 1934 and painted on white glaze by Marian Heath, 1937-1938, mark No.29; white earthenware bowl 366A/DH elephant ride from The Zoo designed by Eileen McGrath, 1934-1935 and painted on white glaze by Gwen Haskins, 1940-1946, mark No.29; white earthenware egg cup stand 712/LI rocking horses from Toys designed by Truda Carter, 1934 and painted on white glaze by Doris Marshall, 1934-1936, mark No.19. Front: white earthenware mug 648/HM drummer boy from Play Box designed by Alfred Read about 1935 and painted on white glaze by Gwendoline Selby, 1951, mark No.29; red earthenware tea plate 557/QK duck with ducklings from Nursery Toys designed by Dora Batty, 1921-1922 and painted on clear glaze over white slip by Ruth Pavely, 1925-1927, mark No.20; red earthenware tea plate 557/QH rocking horse from Nursery Toys designed by Dora Batty, 1921-1922 and painted on clear glaze over white slip by Gertie Warren, 1925-1927, mark No.20. Largest bowl diameter 7¼ins (18.5cm).

Pages from a factory pattern book showing nursery ware and children's toilet set designs.

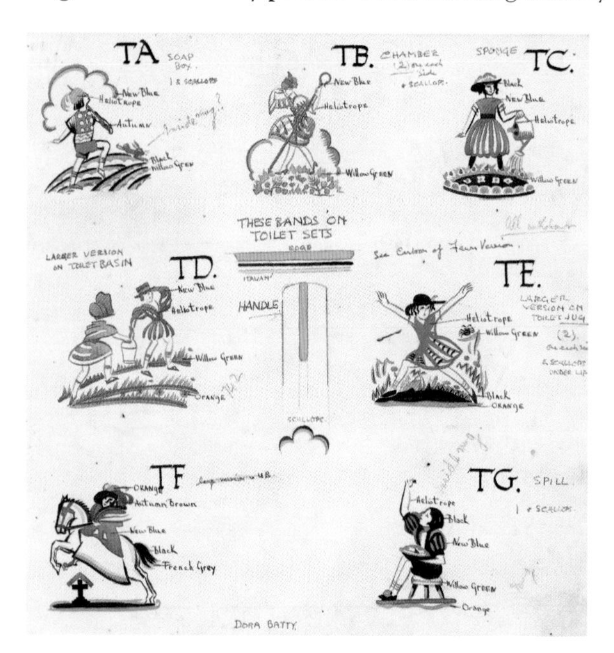

Designs from the Nursery Rhymes series by Dora Batty, 1921-1922.

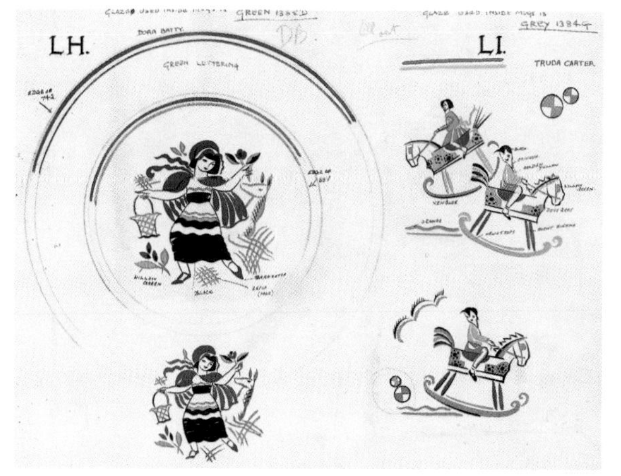

Red Riding Hood from the Stories and Rhymes series by Dora Batty, 1934, and a rocking horse from Toys by Truda Carter, 1934.

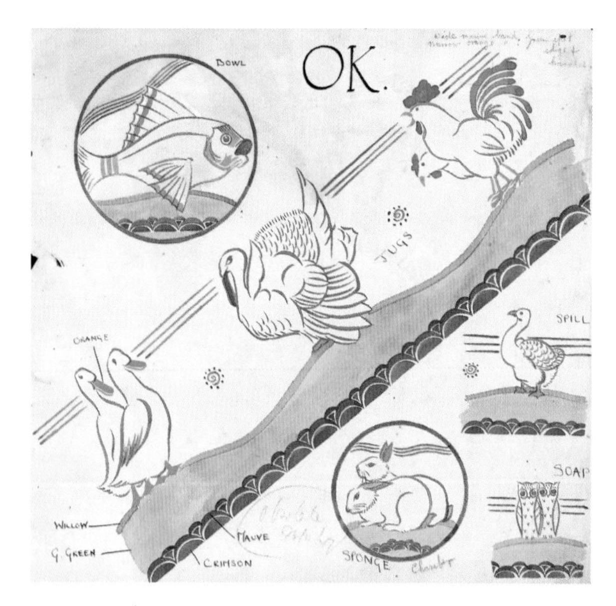

Patterns designed by Truda Adams for nursery toilet sets and children's tea ware.

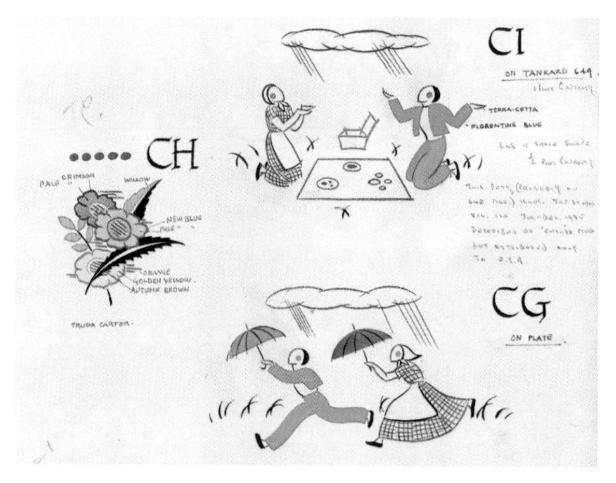

The Picnic designed by Eileen McGrath, 1934-1935.

London Characters designed by Truda Carter, 1934-1935.

Nursery Toys designs by Truda Carter, 1935-1936. Seven patterns from a series of eight which included XZ penguins and fishes, not shown.

The Zoo designed by Eileen McGrath, 1934-1935.

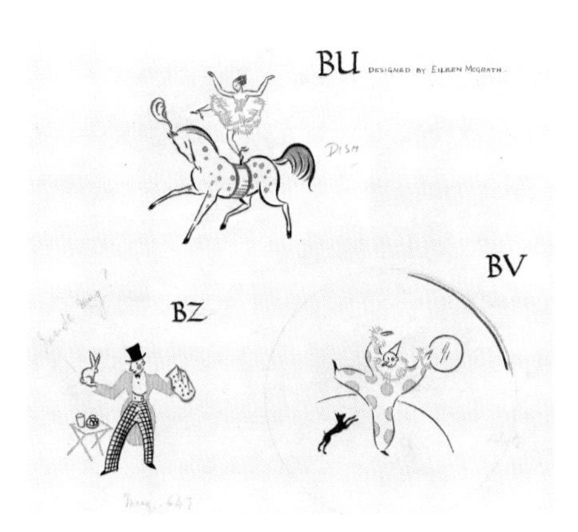

Factory pattern sheet showing The Circus designs by Eileen McGrath, 1934-1935.

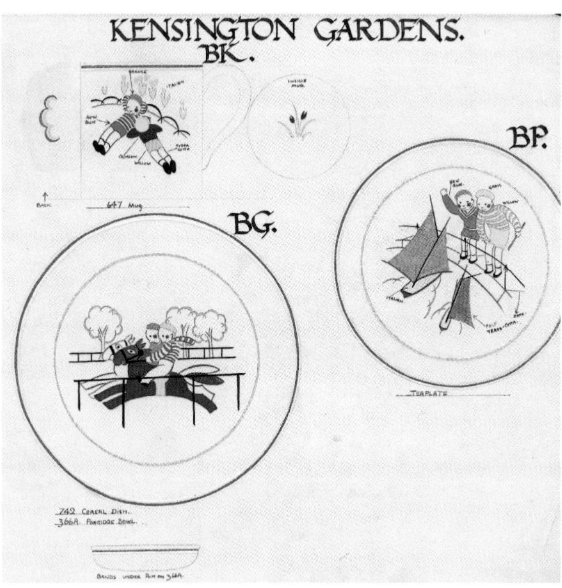

Factory pattern sheet showing Kensington Gardens designs by Truda Carter, 1934-1935.

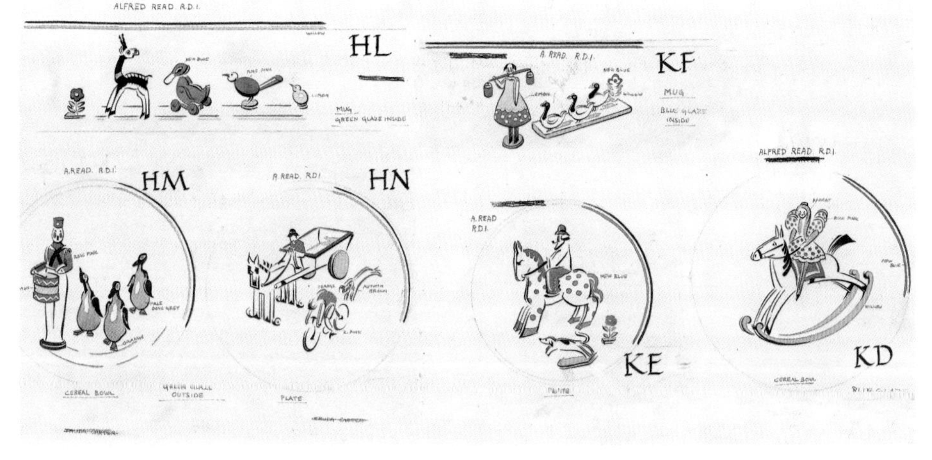

Factory pattern sheets showing Play Box designs by Alfred Read, about 1935.

Children's sets in white earthenware. Left to right: in-glaze transfer printed 'Nursery Rhymes' designed by Elaine Williamson, 1979, mark No.74 modified; silk screen transfer printed and colour washed zoo animals designed by Robert Jefferson, 1962, mark No.48: in-glaze transfer printed 'My Little Pony', a Hambro Industries design adapted by Elaine Williamson, 1985, mark No.73 modified.

Left: page from a Robert Jefferson sketch book showing preliminary drawings for his children's ware range.
Right: the Mad Hatter range, introduced in 1994. The designs, a coloured version of the original Alice illustrations by Sir John Tenniel, were developed by Sarah Chalmers from an idea by Christopher Woodhead.

Chapter Eleven

Commemoratives

Although well used from its earliest days to the design and manufacture of limited production runs, Poole has never been known for commemorative wares. An early example is the range of portrait tiles shown on page 23. Throughout the 1920s, vases and other wares with special inscriptions, often lettered by Margaret Holder, were frequently made on a one-off basis, but for private rather than general commemorative use. Such wares have been made at Poole throughout its history, and often have interesting local associations. It is actually quite hard to identify the first example of a general commemorative piece to have been made at Poole, but one of the earliest may have been the Jubilee bell, issued in 1935. There were a number of other 1930s examples, celebrating the coronations of Edward VIII and George VI, but the first definable range was probably that planned for the Festival of Britain in 1951 by Claude Smale, but never issued in quantity. More successful was the group of wares designed by Alfred Read for the coronation of 1953. Linked to these two events were the series of large presentation vases painted in traditional styles with coats of arms and inscriptions by Ruth Pavely. Since the 1960s Poole commemoratives have often taken the form of limited editions, linked to particular events, such as the 600th anniversary of the Montacute Charter in 1971, the Thomas Hardy Festival in 1968, the Silver Jubilee of 1977 and the marriage of Prince Charles and Lady Diana Spencer in 1981, this occasion inspiring a surprisingly wide range of wares. Other events celebrated by Poole include European Architectural Heritage Year and the 50th anniversary of the D-Day landings, along with more local occasions such as the factory's centenary in 1973, when each employee was given a commemorative mug and the Royal visit of 1979. Since the 1970s mugs and coasters have frequently been made to special order, with painted or printed decorations to mark events of both local and national significance.

Above, left to right: Jubilee Bell, inscription, floral sprig and GM (George and Mary) painted on white glaze by Doris Marshall, 1935, mark No.19; King Edward VIII wall plaque, modelled in low relief by Harold Brownsword prior to the abdication in 1936, spray glazed in vellum ice green, mark No.28; Poole Swimming Club vase 857, three floral sprigs and inscription painted on white glaze by Ruth Pavely, 1937, mark No.28 and Made in England stamped; Sunday Points plate, part of a tea set probably a yacht race trophy, painted on white glaze by Margaret Holder, 1939, mark No.19; bowl 502 with Festival of Britain painted on alpine white glaze by Susan Nunns, 1951, mark No.36; plate with C.R. Andrews for long service, painted on alpine white glaze by Susan Russell, 1977, mark No.62; beaker 128 with Coronation E II R 1953, designed by Alfred Read, stencilled and painted on alpine white glaze by Jean Cockram, mark No.37. Height of wall plaque 11$^{1}/_{4}$ins (28.5cm).
Far right: dish 15 from a limited edition of 25 pieces made in 1953. The Coronation decoration was designed by Alfred Read and painted by Ruth Pavely. The shape 528 was designed by John Adams, thrown in white earthenware and covered with alpine white glaze. Alfred Read produced a number of designs for Coronation ware, mostly based on the royal coat of arms, the E II R monogram and various celebratory phrases, surrounded by either calligraphic patterning or coloured bands. Diameter 15$^{1}/_{2}$ins (39.5cm).

Festival of Britain hors d'oeuvres dish 362, designed by John Adams, 1936-1938. The pattern designed by Claude Smale and painted on alpine white glaze by Gwen Haskins, 1951, mark No.29 and /FOB 10 painted.

Factory design sheet for a plate to commemorate the Festival of Britain, 1951, by Claude Smale. This, and its accompanying range, were probably only produced in small quantities because of delays in the issue of the necessary production permits by the Board of Trade.

White earthenware plaques, shape 6, decorated with stained glass window designs by Tony Morris and incorporating the following inscriptions, left to right: 'The Marriage of The Prince of Wales and Lady Diana Spencer, July 29th, 1981.' Trial plaque of an edition limited to 250 painted by Carolyn Walters, 1981, mark No.29; 'The Saint George', plaque 302 of an edition limited to 1,000, painted by Laura Wills, 1977-1978, mark No.29; 'The Queen's Silver Jubilee, 1952-1977', plaque 34 of an edition limited to 250 painted by Julie Williams, 1977, mark No.29. Diameter $12^{1}/_{2}$ins (32cm).

Montacute Charter plaques, number 2 from a limited edition of twenty-five pairs made to mark the 600th anniversary of the Montacute Charter, granted to the Town of Poole by William Montacute, Earl of Salisbury, in 1371. The plaque on the left represents the Seal of William Montacute, and on the right, the Common Seal of Poole, both seals were affixed to the Charter. Made in white slipped red earthenware body with sgraffito decoration and crystal glaze by Tony Morris in 1971, mark No.29 and No.28. Diameter $10^{1}/_{2}$ins (26.5cm).

White earthenware dish shape 54, decorated with a line drawing and hand coloured map of Hardy's Wessex, designed by Tony Morris. An inscription on the reverse states 'A limited edition of 250 hand made in England by Poole Pottery for the Thomas Hardy Festival, Dorchester, July 1968, No.101.' Diameter 16ins (40.5cm).

Replicas of presentation vases, shape 661, hand thrown in white earthenware by Guy Sydenham and painted on alpine white glaze by Ruth Pavely, depicting, left to right: the Rhodesian Coat of Arms with the inscription 'Presented to the town of Bishop's Stortford by the makers of Poole Pottery in 1953, in commemoration of the centenary of the birth of Cecil Rhodes', mark No.29; the Poole Coat of Arms with the inscription 'Presented to the Borough & County of the Town of Poole by the makers of Poole Pottery, in commemoration of the Festival of Britain, 1951', mark No.29; the Bulawayo Coat of Arms with the inscription 'Presented to the City of Bulawayo by the makers of Poole Pottery in the year 1953, on the occasion of the Central African Rhodes Centenary Exhibition', mark No.29. Height of centre pot $14^{1}/_{2}$ins (37cm).

Above left: white earthenware plate, number 7 in a limited edition of 100, the symbolic decoration designed and painted on alpine white glaze by Donna Ridout, mark No.62. Diameter 10½ins (26.5cm). Right: European Architectural Heritage Year plate 1975, produced in a limited edition of 1,000. A silk screened line drawing coloured by hand on white earthenware, designed by Graham Smith of Poole Museum Services, mark No.63; white earthenware replica of a commemorative plaque, hand painted by Pat Summers and presented to HM The Queen and The Duke of Edinburgh by Dorset Police on 23rd March, 1979. Decorated with an on-glaze transfer and made in limited numbers for members of the constabulary, mark No.74; loving mug commemorating the marriage of HRH The Prince of Wales and Lady Diana Spencer on July 29th, 1981. Hand made in white earthenware and depicting the Prince of Wales feathers with dragon on reverse, painted on alpine white glaze by Susan Russell, mark No.28, number 33 of an edition limited to 100 pieces; plaque commemorating the marriage of HRH The Prince of Wales and Lady Diana Spencer, July 29th, 1981. Made in grey stoneware from an original design modelled in low relief by Barbara Linley Adams, the lettering by Alan Pepper, finished in clay by Hazel Jones, mark No.29 and No.73 modified, number 1 of edition limited to 2,000; a set of two bone china busts representing HRH The Prince of Wales and Lady Diana, from an original pair designed and modelled by Bert Baggaley and finished unglazed, mark No.29, edition limited to 2,000 pairs. Plaque diameter 9ins (23cm).

Hand thrown and carved by Guy Sydenham, this model bottle kiln in red stoneware was made to commemorate the centenary of Poole Pottery in 1973, mark No.29. Height 13½ins (34.5cm).

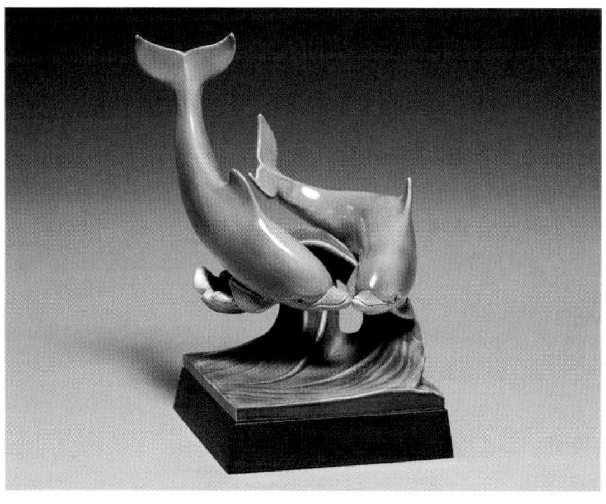

Replica of a dolphin sculpture, designed and modelled in white earthenware by Tony Morris and presented to HM The Queen and HRH The Duke of Edinburgh on their visit to Poole Pottery, 23rd March, 1979. Height 12½ins (32cm).

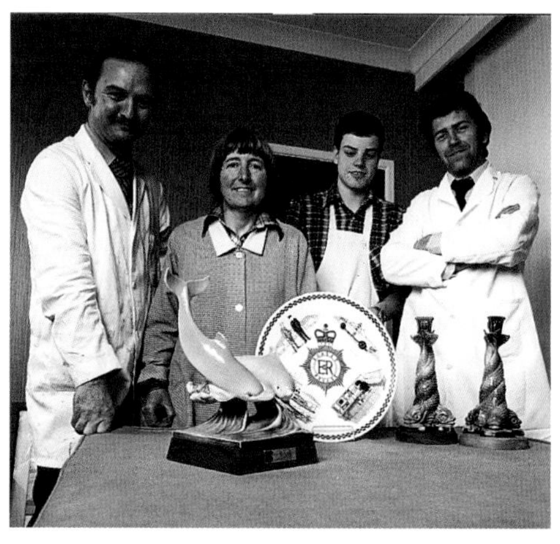

Tony Morris, Pat Summers, Alan Pepper and Joe Leadbeater, designers and modellers, with Royal Visit presentation pieces commissioned by the Borough of Poole, Dorset Constabulary and Poole Pottery.

A group of coasters in white earthenware decorated with on-glaze transfers. The non-pictorial coaster commemorating the royal wedding and 'Operation Friendly Invasion, 1944-1979' are both limited editions of 2,500 and 1,000 respectively. All mark No.74 except the Ryvita Company's 50th anniversary, mark No.29 plus a Queen's award inscription, the Beardsley, mark No.72, and the Portsmouth D-Day Celebrations 1944-1984, for which a special mark was designed.

White earthenware commemorative mugs, 1974-1990. Broadstone Golf Club, mark No.62, Fisherman's Mission Centenary, mark No.74, Parkstone Yacht Club, mark No.64, Society of Poole Men, mark No.62, Poole Rotaract Pram Prix, 1980. Dorset Seasons Winter – Corfe Castle, and Spring – Durdle Door, mark No.74, Poole Quay, mark No.62, The Rows, Chester, mark No.74.

Chapter Twelve

Tiles & Tile Panels

The production of tiles and architectural ceramics was the backbone of the ceramic industry in Dorset throughout the second half of the 19th century and well into the 20th, and all subsequent developments at Poole should be seen in this context. Early decorative wares were inevitably overshadowed by this core business and, although some independence was established before the First World War, it was not until the establishment of Carter, Stabler & Adams in 1921 that the decorative wares were really able to stand on their own. With tile manufacture centred on Hamworthy, Carter & Company were able to make the most of the commanding market position they had established in the late 19th century. From the 1920s the two arms of the business operated independently, a pattern maintained over subsequent decades, but there were inevitably many areas of co-operation and common interest, underlined by the lasting influence of the Carter family. Painters and other skilled employees moved between the manufacturing units, but more important was the role played by the tile factory as a breeding ground for design. A number of artists were drawn to Poole initially by Carter & Company, including Edward Bawden, Cecil Aldin and Reginald Till, while others, for example Dora Batty, Harold Stabler and Alfred Read, designed successfully for both companies. The range of tiles made at Poole since the 1920s is enormous and warrants detailed study in its own right, based on the extensive Carter & Company archives. This chapter features examples of painted and printed tiles largely from series designed by major artists, in production between the 1920s and the 1960s, along with the key tile catalogues issued by Carter & Company, and subsequently by Pilkington since the Second World War. These reveal the longevity of some series, with designs from the 1920s still available in the 1950s. Series by known designers are, of course, only a small part of Carter's tile output, and included also are examples of architectural and pictorial tile panels, an important area of Carter production from the 1920s to the 1950s, along with commemorative tile plaques and the silk screen decorated tiles made from the late 1950s.

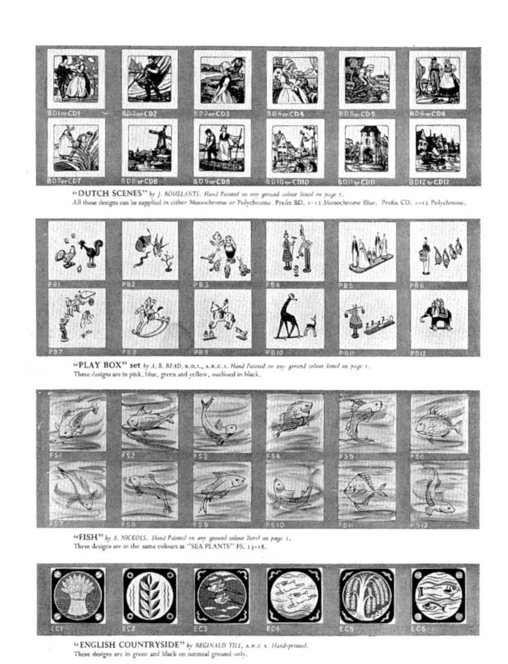

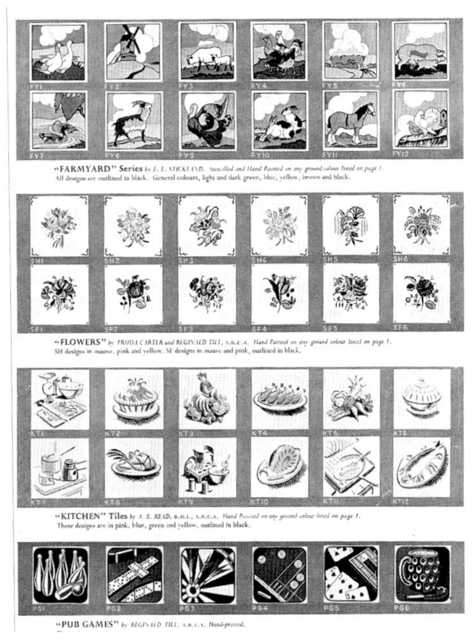

Carter & Company promotional leaflet of the early 1950s showing sets of decorated tiles; Sea Plants by Phyllis Butler, Sea by Susan Williams-Ellis, Nursery Toys by Dora Batty, Sporting by Edward Bawden, Dutch scenes by J. Rouelants (sic), Play Box by Alfred Read, Fish by A. Nickols, English Countryside by Reginald Till, Farmyard by E.E. Stickland, Flowers by Truda Carter and Reginald Till, Kitchen by Alfred Read, Pub Games by Reginald Till, Chase by Edward Bawden, Water Birds by Harold Stabler, Dog by Cecil Aldin, Ships by Reginald Till and Nursery Rhymes by Dora Batty.

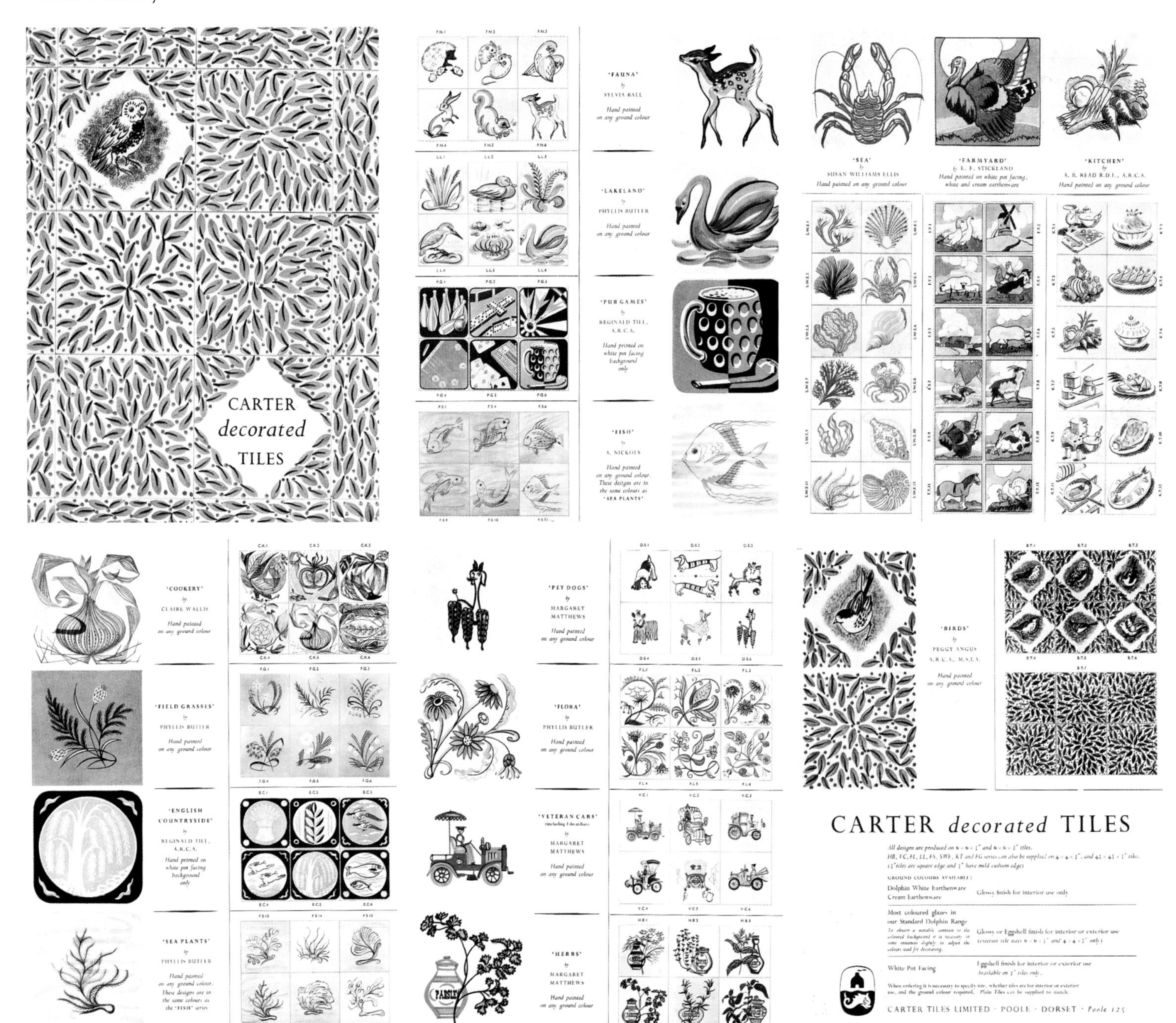

Carter & Company promotional leaflet of about 1960 showing sets of decorated tiles: Fauna by Sylvia Ball, Lakeland by Phyllis Butler, Pub Games by Reginald Till, Fish by A. Nickols, Cookery by Claire Wallis, Field Grasses by Phyllis Butler, English Countryside by Reginald Till, Sea Plants by Phyllis Butler, Pet Dogs by Margaret Matthews, Flora by Phyllis Butler, Veteran Cars by Margaret Matthews, Herbs by Margaret Matthews, Sea by Susan Williams-Ellis, Farmyard by E.E. Stickland, Kitchen by Alfred Read and Birds by Peggy Angus.

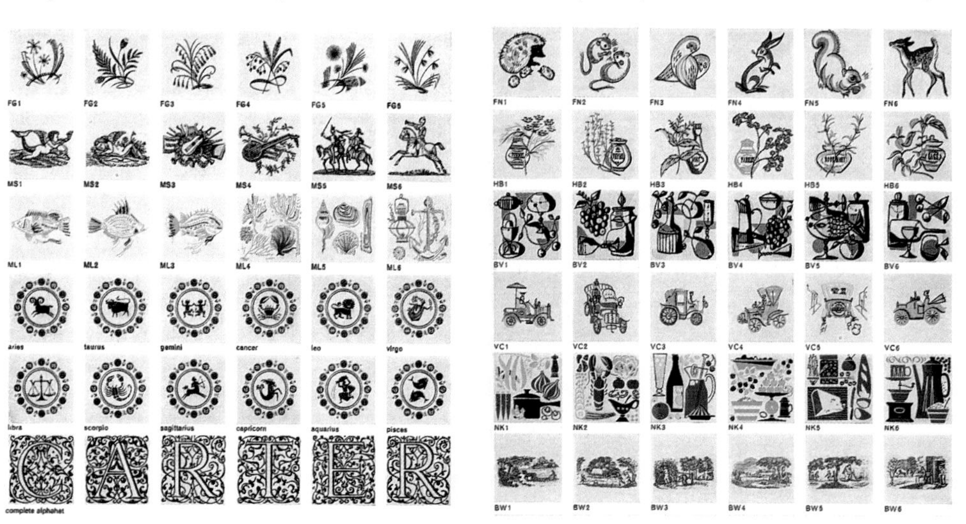

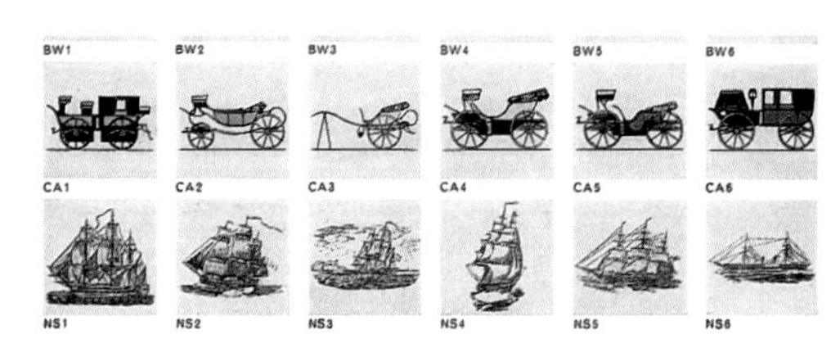

Decorative tile sets by Sylvia Ball, Phyllis Butler, Una Hart, Brian Moore, Daphne Padden, Margaret Matthews and others, illustrated in a Carter catalogue of ceramic products issued March 1964.

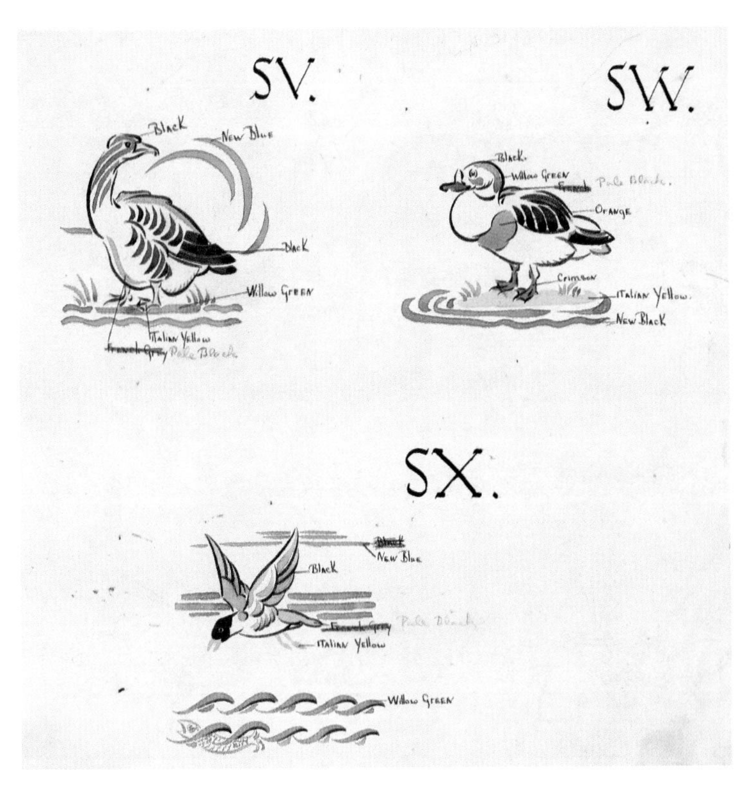

Designs for Harold Stabler's Water Birds series, c1922, used on both tiles and nursery ware.

Tiles hand-painted with water birds by Harold Stabler, 1920s-1950s.

Examples of hand-painted tiles from decorative sets: top left, Nursery Rhymes by Dora Batty, 1920s-1950s; top right: Sporting by Edward Bawden, 1920s-1950s; bottom left: Dog by Cecil Aldin, 1930s-1950s; bottom centre: Play Box by Alfred Read, 1930s-1950s; bottom right; similar to Flowers by Truda Carter, 1920s-1950s.

Examples from stencilled and painted Farmyard series designed by E.E. Stickland about 1922.

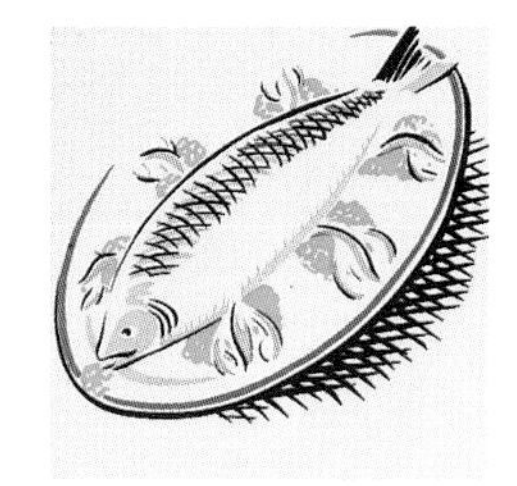
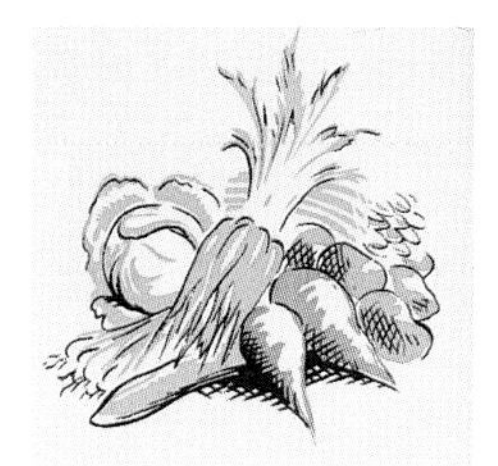

Examples from painted Kitchen set by Alfred Read about 1923.

Right: examples from painted Chase set, designed by Edward Bawden about 1922.

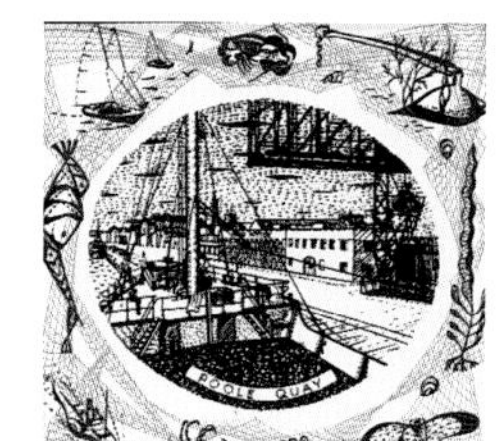

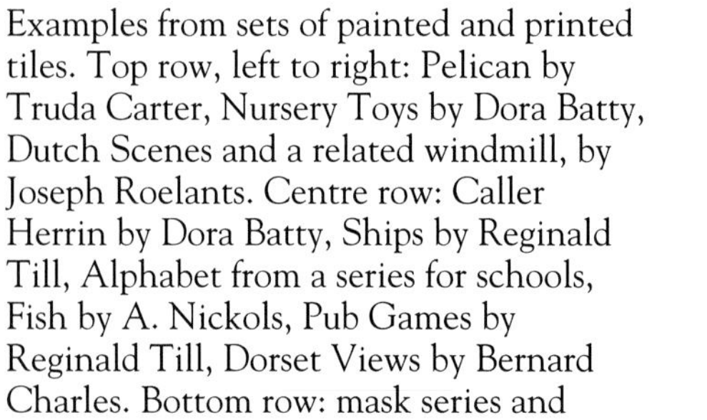
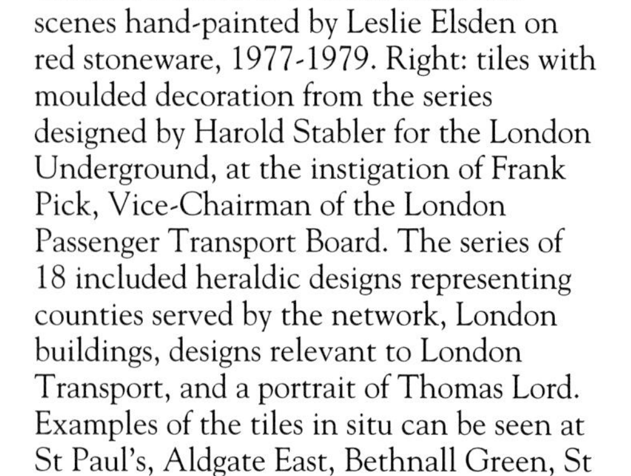

Examples from sets of painted and printed tiles. Top row, left to right: Pelican by Truda Carter, Nursery Toys by Dora Batty, Dutch Scenes and a related windmill, by Joseph Roelants. Centre row: Caller Herrin by Dora Batty, Ships by Reginald Till, Alphabet from a series for schools, Fish by A. Nickols, Pub Games by Reginald Till, Dorset Views by Bernard Charles. Bottom row: mask series and scenes hand-painted by Leslie Elsden on red stoneware, 1977-1979. Right: tiles with moulded decoration from the series designed by Harold Stabler for the London Underground, at the instigation of Frank Pick, Vice-Chairman of the London Passenger Transport Board. The series of 18 included heraldic designs representing counties served by the network, London buildings, designs relevant to London Transport, and a portrait of Thomas Lord. Examples of the tiles in situ can be seen at St Paul's, Aldgate East, Bethnall Green, St John's Wood and Swiss Cottage.

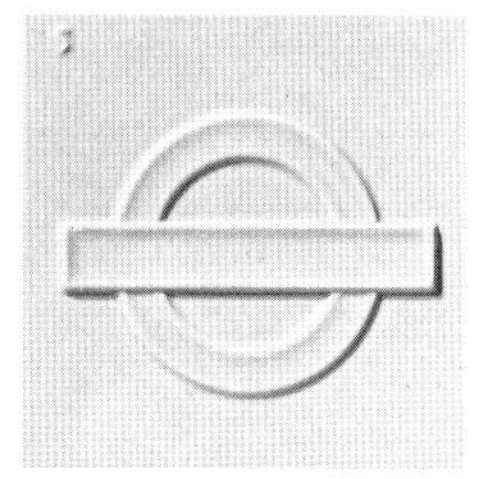

Tubelined tile panel designed by Arthur Nickols, from a series of town maps and markers made by Carter & Company in the 1950s. This example is now in the Poole Pottery Museum collection. Other towns featured included Swanage and Wareham.

Tiled staircase in the former showroom area of the East Quay factory showing, left: pressline tiles designed by Reginald Till for Carter's stand at the Ideal Home Exhibition, 1927, and right: a decorative tubelined panel designed by him for the Building Trades Exhibition, 1930.

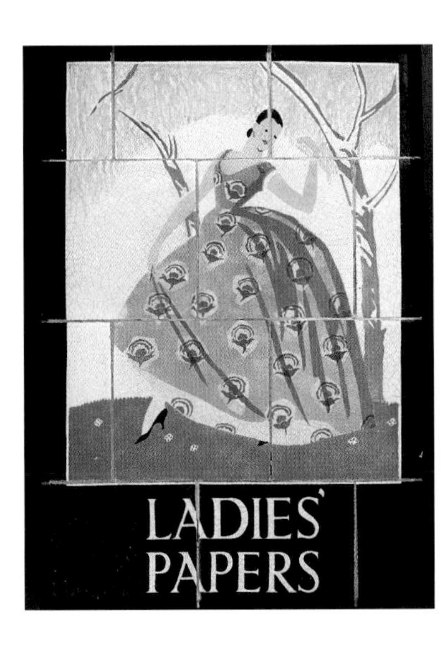

Examples from a series of tile panels produced by Carter & Company in the 1920s for the decoration of W.H. Smith shops, with the style of lettering designed for them by Eric Gill. It is not known who designed the images. Panels still in situ can be seen in shops in Torquay, Devon and Newtown, Powys.

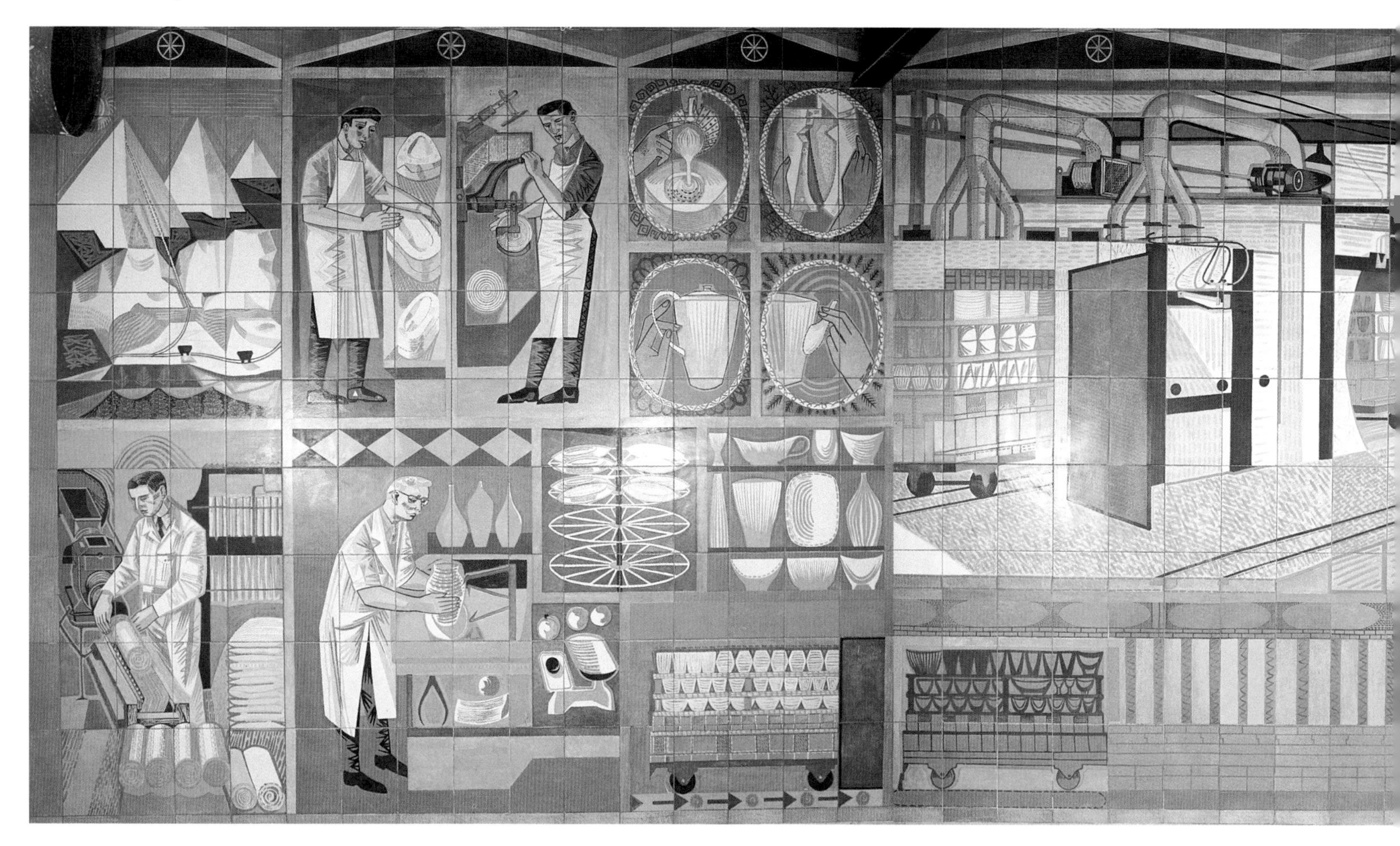

Tile mural designed by Joseph Ledger in 1955, featuring the processes of pottery making at Poole, from the claypit to the packing shed or department. Included in the scenes painted by Catherine Stern are cameo portraits of Arthur Hurd pugging, Guy Sydenham throwing,

Carter & Company tubelined tile panel (part) c1930. Designer and original location unknown.

Rock-a-Bye Baby hand-painted tile panel, designer unknown. Made by Carter & Company for the Prince Edward of Kent children's ward at the Ealing Hospital, 1934-1935, and now in the Pottery Museum.

Carter & Company hand painted tile panel c1935. Designer and original location unknown.

Harold Barnett platemaking, Ruth Pavely checking a painted vase and Bill Dopson packing.

Left: Faience slabs depicting crustacean and other marine life, designed and modelled in low relief by Tony Morris, 1967, and used as a feature on a staircase in the former craft section.

Right: Faience panel, Europa and the Bull, designed by Joseph Ledger for the Carter & Company stand at the Building Trades Exhibition, 1953, and now in the East Quay factory.

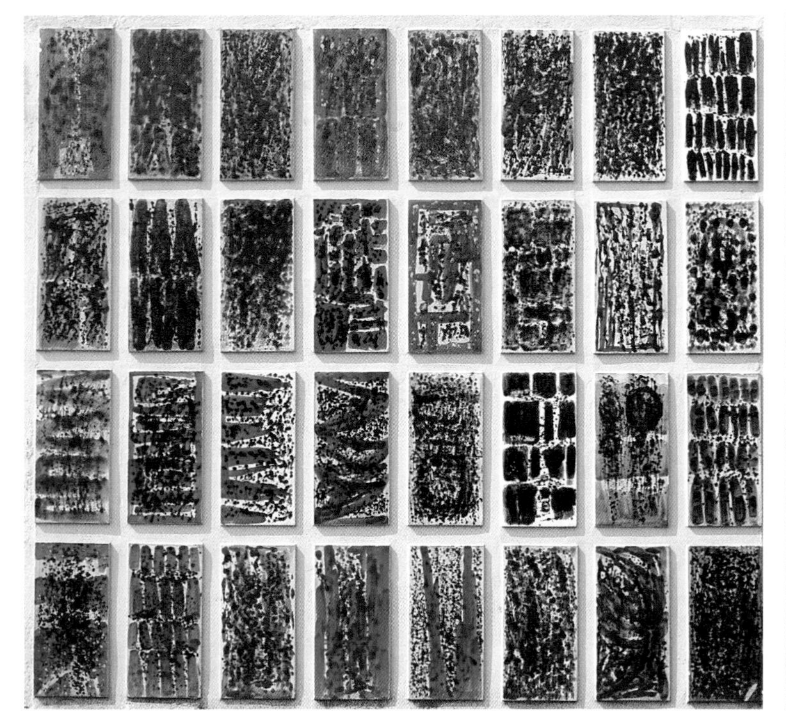

Decorative faience slabs, glazed byTony Morris and fixed to the Fishermans Road elevation of the Pottery in 1963.

'D' Day memorial plaque designed by Irene Reeve, made by Alan White, and fixed to the harbour facing wall of the Pottery in 1994.

Pauline May silk screen printing Carter tiles, c1960.

Carter & Company stand at the Building Trades Exhibition, 1953.

A slip outline, hand-painted and screen printed tile panel, designed by Peggy Angus for the Crown public house, Charing Cross Road, London in the 1950s.

Tile Plaques

Commemorative plaques to mark buildings in London with historical associations were first made in pottery in the late Victorian period. Royal Doulton were the primary manufacturer and it was they who introduced the familiar blue plaque with its raised slip lettering in 1937. In 1955 Carter & Company took over the making of the blue plaques, having been involved since the early years of the century with the production of similar architectural commemorative wares. Initially the blue plaques were made by the Faience Department at Hamworthy, but in 1977 production was transferred to the East Quay. From then until 1981 when, for various reasons, Poole stopped making them, over seventy blue plaques were made by Cynthia Bennett, Julie Williams and Hilda Smith, decorators who specialised in this highly skilled area of production. Among those commemorated by Poole blue plaques are the painter Augustus John, the actress Lillie Langtrey, the politician Herbert Morrison, the writer George Orwell and the scientist Sir Alexander Fleming.

Stages in the design and manufacture of a commemorative faience blue plaque, showing the original slip trailed lettering.

Poole Swimming Club stoneware plaque made by Carter & Company about 1932.

Della Robbia style plaque made by Carter & Company and erected at a model farm in Kent for tuberculous ex-soldiers after the First World War.

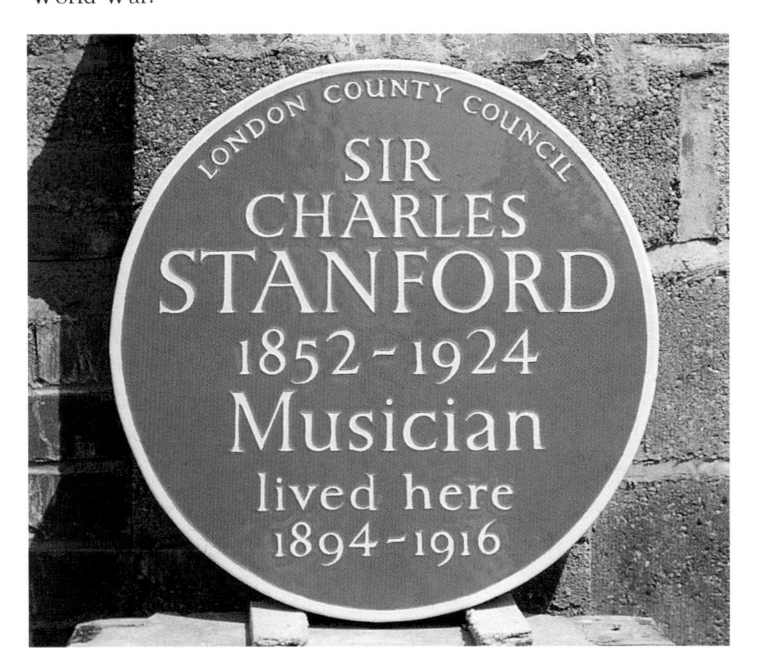

L.C.C. blue plaque made by Carter & Company.

Chapter Thirteen

Poole Pottery in the 1990s

Over the years, Poole's reputation as a trend setter and style leader has helped to maintain its position in the market place. In the face of an increasingly competitive international market, this has given the Pottery a vital foundation for success. In the 1980s a distinctive new image began to emerge, with the emphasis on more informal and casual styles that used traditional techniques in an up-to-date and immediate way. The start came in 1986, when Hinchcliffe and Barber, an external design partnership, created a new range featuring sponged decoration in blue. This became the foundation for a whole new tableware style based on broad, naturalistic patterns applied to the pottery by sponging, hand-painting and transfer printing techniques. The pattern that really established this new style was Alan Clarke's Dorset Fruit, introduced in 1990 as a bold exploitation of the fashionable sponging process. The appointment of David Queensberry as design director two years later launched a creative explosion that brought many new talents to the fore, including Sarah Chalmers, Nicola Wiehahn, Kate Byrne and, notably, Anita Harris, whose designs such as Vineyard, Blue Vine and Vincent quickly established Poole's new image. At the same time, the Pottery experienced a major revolution in the form of a management buy out, led by Peter Mills, formerly sales and marketing director of Dartington Crystal. In October 1992 Mills and his team took the Poole Pottery out of BTR, parent of Pilkington's Tiles, owners of Poole since the early 1960s, with the aim of building a company that looked to the future while drawing on the strengths of the past. The achievements of the 1990s were considerable, with Poole once again seen in Britain and around the world as a style leader. The Pottery also became a major exporter, with up to fifty percent of production going overseas, notably to North America and the Far East. The secret of Poole's success was the ability to respond quickly to market forces, such as the move towards casual dining that reflects the new spirit of informality that dominates interior design and family living today.

During the decade tableware was established as the dominant element in the carefully maintained market balance with giftware production, and the late 1990s witnessed some striking tableware success stories, such as Vineyard, introduced in 1995, Vincent of 1996, aimed particularly at the North American market, and Omega, Fresco and Terracotta, launched in 1997. These three, designed externally, by Fenella Mallalieu, and Rachel Barker and Andrew Brickett, revived traditional techniques in an entirely new and modern way. Bluebell and Fraiche, designed by Anita Harris and introduced in 1998, developed further the new Poole image and set the Pottery on track for the millennium. At the same time, Poole has created related ranges for particular markets and clients, for example MFI, John Lewis, Laura Ashley, Heal's, Harrods, the National Trust and, in the United States, for Tiffany's. While his eyes were set firmly on the future, Mills understood clearly the importance of the past.

Poole's position as one of the great names of 20th century ceramics is constantly underlined by its expanding appeal to collectors all over the world. Many auction houses hold regular specialist Poole sales and high prices are realised for Poole productions of all periods. The current world auction record for a single piece is £19,000, realised by Cottees of Wareham in October 2001 for a large 1920s vase painted by Anne Hatchard with a floral pattern on a black ground. This book, first published in 1995 and now in its third revised edition, has also broadened the pottery's appeal. However, the interests of collectors are not limited to the wares of the past but are always an important part of the modern Poole story. The new Poole Studio collection was launched in 1996, with ranges by leading artists and designers such as Sir Terry Frost, Janice Tchalenko and Charlotte Mellis. However, the most significant contribution has been made by Sally Tuffin, and one of her designs for a time took the Poole style around the world in the exclusive group of fifteen designs created by international artists for display on the tailfins of British Airways' aircraft. Interests of collectors were also catered for by the Collectors Club, which now has over 1000 members worldwide, who enjoy a regular magazine and a wide range of events and activities, including the annual Pottery gala day. On a broader front, the appeal of Poole is universal and much was done to increase the range of visitor attractions. A large complex of factory shops and retail units, Pottery tours, interactive areas where children and their parents can try their skills at throwing, painting, decorating and other ceramic techniques and a restaurant helped to bring over a million visitors a year to the Poole Pottery, keen to enjoy the magnificent harbourside site in a major resort area. In 1998 the Poole Pottery celebrated its 125th anniversary, which provided an opportunity to look back over a distinctive and memorable history, and to look forward towards another century of trend setting in the ceramic industry.

In the event, the close of the twentieth century was marked in a spectacular manner with the launch in 1999 of the new Living Glaze ranges, whose success shifted the balance once again from tableware towards giftware. Bright colours, abstract patterns and explosive glaze effects represented a new direction for Poole, even though the inspiration came in part from the Delphis wares of the 1960s. With a combination of defined series patterns, limited editions and a wide range of adventurous individual studio wares by artists such as Tony Morris, Janice Tchalenko, Alan Clarke and Anita Harris, Living Glaze took the market by storm and underlined once again Poole's ability to be determinedly modern.

David Queensberry, Art Director 1992-1997.

The new Delphis restaurant opened by Poole Pottery in 1993.

The Poole Pottery Museum enlarged and redesigned in 1993.

Peter Mills, Managing Director 1992-2001.

A harbour view of the Delphis restaurant.

Poole Blue sponge decorated wares by Hinchcliffe and Barber, an external design partnership, first shown in 1986, mark No.81. Although production was limited, these wares brought new ideas to Poole and laid the foundations for the design developments of the 1990s.

A range of wares decorated with the Dorset Fruit pattern designed by Alan Clarke. First introduced in 1990, this pattern established the traditional sponged decorative technique at Poole.

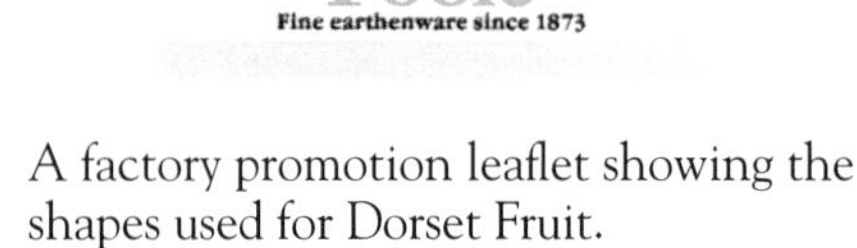

A factory promotion leaflet showing the shapes used for Dorset Fruit.

Paintresses Lindsey Stevens, left and Wendy Low demonstrating the sponging technique with the Blue Vine pattern.

Legumes, a hand painted underglaze pattern, introduced 1992, designed by Sarah Chalmers, a freelance painter and ceramicist. Shown on a vitrified 614 casserole and white earthenware plate, mark No.90; Black Horse mug, commissioned by Lloyds Bank plc, 1993, mark No.90 and L.B.I.S. stamped (Lloyds Bank Investment Services); Brush Strokes Floral, introduced 1992, a hand painted in-glaze pattern, by Anita Harris, freelance designer. Shown on a white earthenware ginger jar vase, mark No.88 and small footed bowl, mark No.90. Plate diameter 10½ins (26.5cm).

Three underglaze patterns designed by Anita Harris: Gypsy, a stencilled and hand painted pattern, introduced 1992, shown on a white earthenware plate, tea cup and saucer, mark No.90; Reflections, a hand painted and sponge decorated pattern, introduced 1992, shown on a white earthenware plate, mark No.90 with 'REFLECTIONS BY ANITA HARRIS' added, and jug, mark No.90; Vineyard, a sponge decorated pattern, introduced 1993, shown on a white earthenware plate and jug, mark No.90. Largest plate diameter 10¼ins (26cm).

Four underglaze, hand painted and sponge decorated patterns designed by Anita Harris: Blue Vine, introduced 1993, shown on a vitrified 854 oval-eared dish and white earthenware tea cup and saucer, mark No.90; Blue Leaf, introduced 1994, shown on a white earthenware 042 candlestick, mark No.34 and 067 classic vase, mark No.90; Green Leaf, introduced 1994, shown on a white earthenware plate, mark No.90; Barley, introduced 1994 exclusively for Whittards of Chelsea, shown on a white earthenware jug with a specially designed back mark. Diameter of plate 9ins (23cm).

Three underglaze hand painted and sponge decorated patterns designed by Anita Harris: Winter Vine, introduced 1994, shown on a white earthenware plate and 043 candlestick; Vincent, introduced 1994, shown on a white earthenware plate and breakfast cup and saucer, mark No.90; Acorn and Oak Leaves, introduced 1994 exclusively for the National Trust, shown on a white earthenware 611 jug and 043 candlestick with a specially designed back mark. Diameter of plate 10½ins (26.5cm).

Four in-glaze transfer decorations on white earthenware: Polka, designed by Queensberry Hunt, introduced 1994, shown on a breakfast cup and saucer and plate, mark No.91; Morning Glory, designed by Nicola Wiehahn, introduced 1994, shown on a tea pot and plate, mark No.90 modified; Stourhead, designed exclusively for the National Trust by Julie Depledge, introduced 1991, shown on a cup and saucer from the Concert range of tableware with a specially designed back mark. The design is based on a late 18th century Indo Portuguese ebony and inlaid ivory work box in the house at Stourhead, Wiltshire; Nasturtium, designed by Bryony Langworth, introduced 1991, shown on the 839 mug, mark No.87. Larger plate diameter 9ins (23cm).

A selection of white earthenwares made exclusively for Tiffany & Co. Alfama, an underglaze painted and sponge decorated dish, the pattern adapted by Anita Harris from a 200 year old Portuguese tin glazed and low fired Majolica dish, first made 1994; Tiffany Tulips, an on-glaze transfer decorated trumpet vase shape 019, first made 1992; Tiffany Spice 'Chocolate theobroma cacao', an in-glaze transfer decorated plate, first made 1994; Peony, an in-glaze transfer decorated round lidded box shape 659, first made 1994; New York Toile, an in-glaze transfer decorated plate first made 1994. These further commissions are based upon patterns supplied by Tiffany & Co. and carry a specially designed back mark. Vase height $8^{1}/_{2}$ins (22cm).

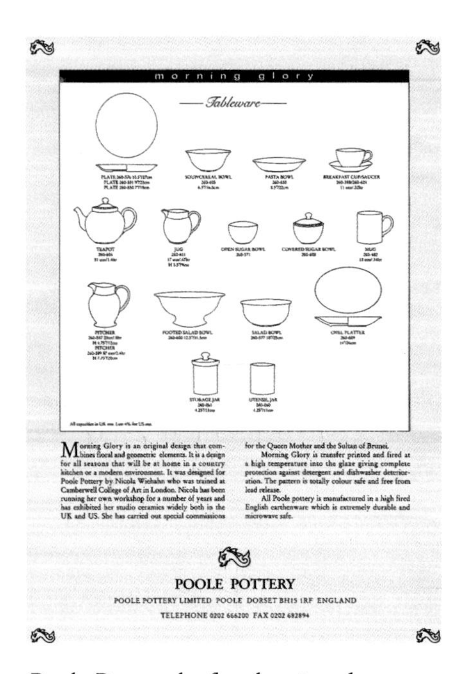

morning glory

Tableware

PLATE / SOUP/CEREAL BOWL / PASTA BOWL / BREAKFAST CUP/SAUCER

TEAPOT / JUG / OPEN SUGAR BOWL / COVERED SUGAR BOWL / MUG

PITCHER / FOOTED SALAD BOWL / SALAD BOWL / OVAL PLATTER

STORAGE JAR / UTENSIL JAR

Morning Glory is an original design that combines floral and geometric elements. It is a design for all seasons that will be at home in a country kitchen or a modern environment. It was designed for Poole Pottery by Nicola Wiehahn who was trained at Camberwell College of Art in London. Nicola has been running her own workshop for a number of years and has exhibited her studio ceramics widely both in the UK and US. She has carried out special commissions for the Queen Mother and the Sultan of Brunei.

Morning Glory is transfer printed and fired at a high temperature into the glaze giving complete protection against detergent and dishwasher deterioration. The pattern is totally colour safe and free from lead release.

All Poole pottery is manufactured in a high fired English earthenware which is extremely durable and microwave safe.

POOLE POTTERY

POOLE POTTERY LIMITED POOLE DORSET BH15 1RF ENGLAND

TELEPHONE 0202 666200 FAX 0202 682894

Poole Pottery leaflet showing shapes available in the Morning Glory range.

An illustration from a Poole Pottery leaflet showing a range of wares decorated with the Orchard in-glaze transfer pattern, designed by Kate Byrne, 1994.

White earthenware trumpet vase shape 031 and footed cache pot shape 538, introduced 1994, with Gold Leaf design, decorated on-glaze with gold ceramic pigment on snow white and black panther glazes and a combination of sponging, painting and stencilling, mark No.80. Vase height 13ins (33cm).

New England, a range of tablewares with pattern designed by Anita Harris, 1995, all mark No.90 and introducing a new sponged technique of layered colours.

Two hand painted and sponge decorated underglaze designs by Anita Harris: Charlotte, introduced 1995 exclusively for M.F.I., shown on a white earthenware classic vase and candlestick, mark No.96; Sweet Pea, introduced 1996 exclusively for the National Trust, shown on a white earthenware coffee pot and open sugar bowl, mark No.99. Height of coffee pot $7^{3}/_{4}$ins (19.5cm).

Calabash, a stencilled and hand painted underglaze design by Anita Harris, introduced 1995, shown on a range of white earthenware including a vitrified casserole, mark No.90. Height of pasta storage jar 14ins (35.5cm).

Seed Packets, an in-glaze transfer decoration after designs used on American seed packets in the late 1800s, introduced in 1996, shown on a range of white earthenware, mark No.90 modified. Length of oval platter 14ins (35.5cm).

Omega, a slip trailed and painted underglaze design by Fenella Mallalieu, introduced 1997, shown on a range of white earthenware, mark No.90 modified. Diameter of plates 10½ins (26.5cm).

Country Rose, a stencilled and hand painted underglaze design by Lindsey Stevens, introduced 1996 exclusively for M.F.I., shown on a white earthenware plate, cup and saucer, mark No.96. Highland Cattle and Sheep, two stencilled and hand painted designs by Anita Harris, introduced 1996 exclusively for Edinburgh Woollen Mills, shown on a white earthenware mug, pickle dish and storage jar, mark No.90. Diameter of plate 8½ins (21.5cm).

Terracotta, a brushed slip, sgraffito and hand painted underglaze design by Rachel Barker and Andrew Brickett working with Alan White introduced 1997, shown on a range of dishes and bowls hand thrown in a red terracotta body, mark No.90 modified. Diameter of large bowl 12½ins (32cm).

Andrew Brickett.

Rachel Barker.

Fresco, a brushed slip, sponged and hand painted underglaze design by Rachel Barker and Andrew Brickett, introduced 1997, shown on a range of white earthenware, mark No.90 modified. Diameter of dish 13½ins (34.5.cm). A version of this design, with the olive replaced by a chilli, was specially made for Heal's.

Cranborne, a textured, brushed slip stamped and hand painted underglaze design by Rachel Barker and Andrew Brickett, introduced 1997 exclusively for Laura Ashley, shown on a white earthenware plate and mug, mark No.103. Diameter of plate 7ins (18cm).

Rustic Wash, a textured, brushed slip underglaze pattern adapted by Anita Harris from a design by Rachel Barker and Andrew Brickett, introduced 1998 exclusively for Alders, shown on a white earthenware classic vase and two oval vases, mark No.90; Sahara, a ceramic pencil and hand painted underglaze design by Anita Harris, introduced 1998 exclusively for Alders, shown on a white earthenware classic vase, mark No.90. Height of large oval vase 8¾ins (22cm).

Bluebell, a brushed slip, stamped and hand painted underglaze design by Anita Harris, introduced 1998, shown on a range of white earthenware, mark No.90. Diameter of plate 9¾ins (24.5cm).

Anita Harris, demonstrating the brushed slip technique.

Fleur Jaune a stamped and hand painted underglaze design by Anita Harris, introduced 1997 exclusively for Harrods, shown on a white earthenware plate and mug, mark No.102. Diameter of plate 9ins (23cm).

Chickens, a stencilled and hand painted underglaze pattern adapted by Anita Harris from a B.H.S. design, introduced 1998 exclusively for British Home Stores, shown on a white earthenware plate and conical jug, mark No.90 modified; Fresco Wash, a brushed slip underglaze design by Rachel Barker and Andrew Brickett, introduced 1997, shown on a range of white earthenware, mark No.90 modified; Citrus Grove a stencilled, hand painted and airbrushed underglaze design by Anita Harris, adapted for airbrush by Alan Clarke, introduced 1998 exclusively for British Home Stores, shown on a white earthenware cake plate and conical jug, mark No.90 modified. Diameter of cake plate 12¾ins (32.5cm).

Faberge, a stencilled and hand painted underglaze pattern adapted from M.F.I. fabric and wallpaper by Anita Harris, shown on a white earthenware cache pot and vase; Ferruccio, a stencilled hand painted and sponge decorated underglaze design by Anita Harris, shown on a white earthenware classic vase and round lidded box; Vermont, a stencilled underglaze pattern adapted from M.F.I. fabric by Anita Harris, shown on a white earthenware pitcher. The three patterns introduced 1996 exclusively for M.F.I., mark No.96. Height of pitcher 10¼ins (26cm).

Da-Vinci, a hand painted underglaze pattern adapted from M.F.I. fabric by Anita Harris, shown on a white earthenware classic vase; Matisse, a hand painted underglaze design by Sue Green of Queensberry Hunt Partnership, adapted to complement M.F.I. fabric by Anita Harris, shown on a white earthenware classic vase and candlestick; Bellinni, a ceramic pencil underglaze pattern adapted from M.F.I. fabric by Anita Harris, shown on a white earthenware pitcher; Indigo, a sgraffito and hand painted in-glaze pattern adapted from M.F.I. fabric and wallpaper by Anita Harris, shown on a white earthenware pitcher and classic vase. The four patterns introduced 1995 exclusively for M.F.I., mark No.96. Height of large classic vase 9¾ins (24.5cm).

Continuing the tradition of stoneware wildlife sculptures started by Barbara Linley Adams in the 1970s, these stoneware cats, designed by the Ceramic Undertones Craft Centre, Poole, have been made at Poole Pottery since 1996.

Fraiche, a stencilled and hand painted design by Anita Harris, adapted for airbrush by Alan Clarke, introduced 1998, shown on a range of white earthenware, mark No.90. Diameter of large plate 10½ins (26.5cm).

Alan Clarke, master of the airbrush technique, was trained by Leslie Elsden and worked as his assistant in the development of the Aegean range 1972-1974. He later became responsible for the production of the blue glazed Dolphin range and in the late 1980s carried out trials which led to the establishment of sponge decorating and the introduction of his popular Dorset Fruit pattern.

Three stencilled and airbrushed underglaze designs by Alan Clarke: Moonlight, introduced 1998 exclusively for Alders, shown on a white earthenware classic vase, mark No.90; Clouds, introduced 1996 exclusively for the John Lewis Partnership, shown on a white earthenware Athens vase, mark No.90; Shadow Stripe, introduced 1997 exclusively for the John Lewis Partnership, shown on a white earthenware classic vase, mark No.90. Height of large classic vase 9¾ins (24.5cm).

Yvonne Morris, technical manager, research and development and David Walton, consultant who both joined the company in the 1960s.

Poole stand at the International Spring Fair, NEC, Birmingham, 1998.

Visual jokes created by the humorous illustrator Glen Baxter reproduced in a series of on-glaze transfer decorated white earthenware mugs and plates, below right, in 1995, mark No.95. Diameter of plates 9ins (23cm). A small Glen Baxter motif is featured on the back of each mug, illustrated above.

One from a series of mugs in white earthenware decorated with on-glaze transfer patterns based upon 18th-century prints, commissioned in 1995 by the Museum of Garden History at the Church of St. Mary-at-Lambeth, London, mark No.94. Height 3½ins (9cm).

Liberty year mug 1998 in white earthenware decorated with an on-glaze transfer pattern based upon a print from the Liberty & Co. archive, mark No.104. Height 3½ins (9cm).

Poole Studio Collection

The creation of individual designs and the production of studio-type wares has been a feature of the Poole Pottery since its early days, with plenty of memorable examples dating from the 1920s and the 1930s. Individuality of design and handcraftsmanship were also features of the 1950s, a tradition carried on into the 1960s by the setting up by Robert Jefferson and Guy Sydenham of the Poole Studio. Their distinctive creations led directly to ranges like Delphis, Aegean and Atlantis, and the development of studio production on a commercial scale. With this tradition in mind, the Poole Studio was re-established from 1995 and a number of artists and designers were asked to create new handcrafted styles to be produced in limited editions and for sale to members of the Collectors Club. Sally Tuffin, a former Royal College of Art student famous for her fashion and textile designs, and for her work as a ceramic designer for Moorcroft and the Dennis China Works, created the modern Poole studio look with a series of distinctive designs often inspired by the pottery's maritime associations. Others have also played a part, including Sir Terry Frost, Britain's leading abstract artist and a key figure in postwar West Country painting. He created two designs in 1996 to mark his 80th birthday, produced in association with the Royal Academy of Arts. The following year saw the production of decorative ranges by Janice Tchalenko, also from the Royal College of Art and a leading experimental potter and colourist, and Charlotte Mellis, an independent artist based in the north of England who has pioneered a distinctive decorative style. The most recent contribution has been by Karen Brown, whose powerful Dorset landscapes link Poole closely to its environment. At the same time, Alan White, Poole's master thrower who has been associated with the pottery since 1966, has produced a range of individual studio wares that reflect not only his skill as a thrower but also his inventive use of traditional techniques and materials such as terracotta, opaque white tin glaze and majolica colours.

Sally Tuffin, working on the Blue Poole designs for British Airways.

Gala Day dishes 1995 and 1996 in white earthenware designed by Sally Tuffin and hand painted on alpine white glaze, mark No.97. Diameter $6^{1}/_{2}$ins (16.5cm).

Parasols design by Sally Tuffin for the Poole Collectors Club, from 1996. Diameter of dish $10^{1}/_{4}$ins (26cm).

The Yaffle (green woodpecker), a shallow-footed bowl in white earthenware designed by Sally Tuffin after the plaque above the door at Yaffle Hill, Cyril Carter's former home at Broadstone. Hand painted on alpine white glaze by Lindsey Stevens mark No.62. Diameter $10^{1}/_{2}$ins (26.5cm).

Sally Tuffin's original artwork for the Strolling Leopard vase.

Year vases and plate in white earthenware with designs by Sally Tuffin. Strolling Leopard, 1995 and Forest Deer, 1996 hand painted with soluble ground colours and brush stroke details. The plate 1997 hand painted in the traditional manner, commemorates the Brede class Poole lifeboat, mark No.97. Diameter of plate 10½ins (26.5cm).

Members of the Poole Collectors Club outside Yaffle Hill with Mr. and Mrs. Holguette, the present owners.

Peter Mills presenting Mrs. John Major with the *Flags* charger.

A white earthenware urn and dish hand painted with flags signalling the five letters P O O L E, provides a nautical flavour to this studio design created by Sally Tuffin in 1996, mark No.97. Diameter of dish $10^3/_4$ins (27.5cm).

Promotional leaflet showing Sally Tuffin's designs for the Poole Studio from 1996.

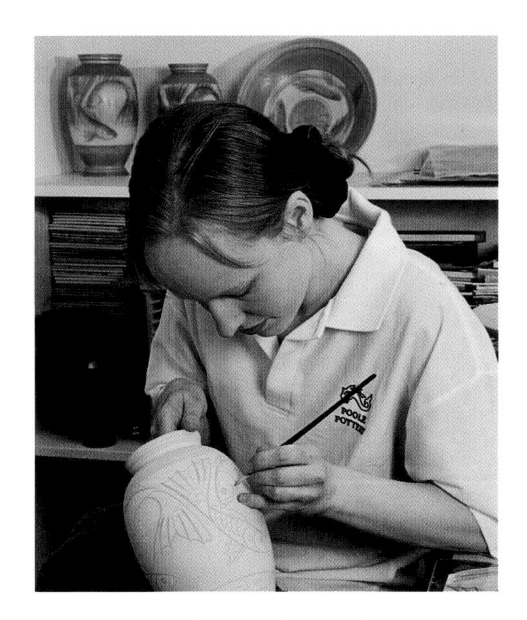

Sarah Westlake painting a fish design vase.

Seagull and fish designs by Sally Tuffin, hand painted on a white earthenware urn, vase and dishes represented in the studio collection 1996, mark No.97. Diameter of large dish $12^1/_2$ins (32cm).

Blue Poole, designed by Sally Tuffin for British Airways and painted by Karen Brown. These unique pieces, inspired by the Seagull range, were created for the British Airways Collection, 1997.

British Airways aircraft, Blue Poole, with the Sally Tuffin's tailplane design as part of the new livery.

Sally Tuffin, The Lady Mayor of Poole, Mrs Annette Brooke and Peter Mills at the launch of the Blue Poole livery design, 1997.

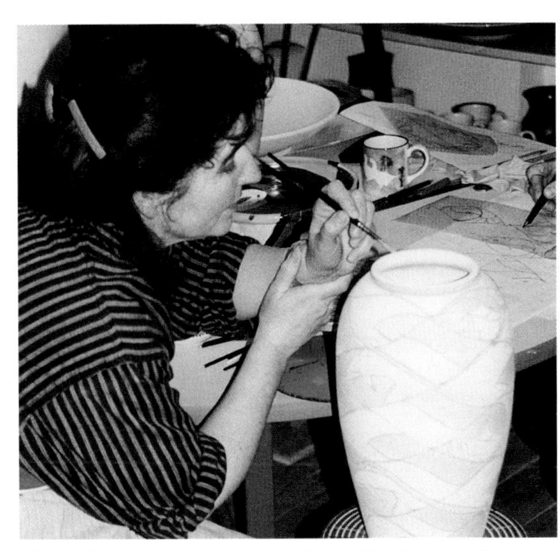

Karen Brown painting the Blue Poole vase for British Airways.

Sir Terry Frost R.A., foremost abstract painter of the post-war generation, in the Poole Studio 1996. His two designs Arizona Blue and Trewellard Red on white earthenware dishes were hand painted by Lindsey Stevens in limited editions of 100 each, mark No.98. Diameter 16¼ins (41.5cm).

Trewellard Red.

Arizona Blue.

Isle of Purbeck studio collection available only to members of the Poole Collectors Club, in white earthenware with designs by Karen Brown hand painted on alpine white glaze, 1997-8. The abstract design on the dish and small vase is that of Old Harry Rocks while the large vase is based upon Corfe Castle, mark No.97. Tallest vase height 8ins (20.5cm).

Promotional leaflet showing ranges by Janice Tchalenko for the Poole Studio, from 1996.

Janice Tchalenko in her studio.

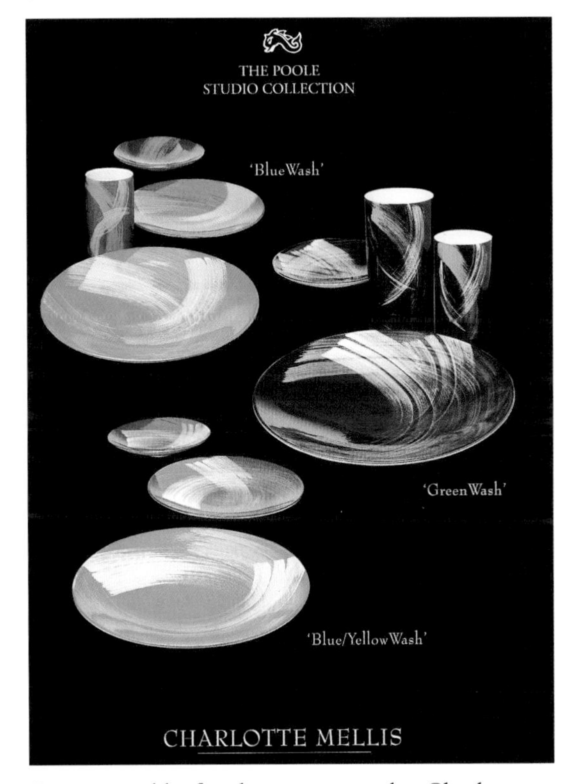

Promotional leaflet showing ranges by Charlotte Mellis for the Poole Studio, from 1997.

A new range of studio figures, modelled in the Poole tradition of the 1930s, introduced in 1998, The four figures, Leaping Deer, Galleon, Elephant and Bear, are made in a variety of richly coloured glazes.

Special Productions

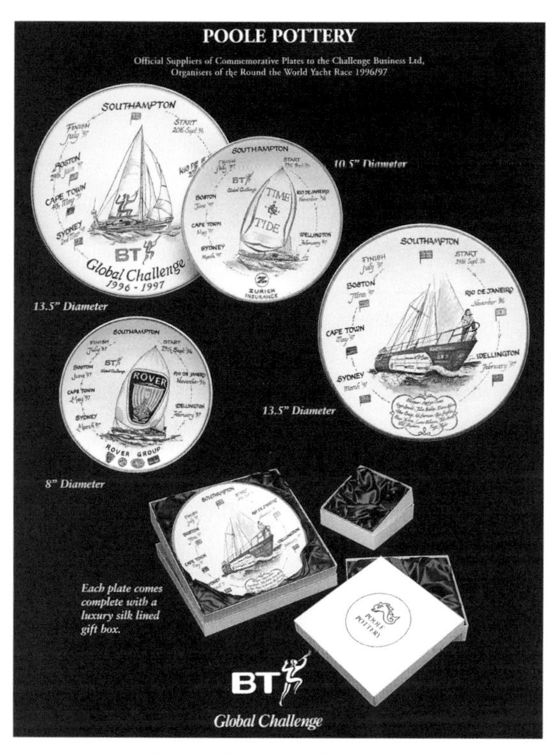

Promotional leafletshowing the commemorative range made for the BT Challenge in the Round the World Yacht Race, 1966/7.

Commemorative white earthenware plate marking the 50th anniversary of 'Victory in Europe 8 May 1945', No.1 from an edition of one hundred, designed and painted on alpine white glaze by Lindsey Stevens, mark No.62. Diameter 10ins (25.5cm).

This commemorative plaque was created for the Friends of Upton House.

A charming family plate with footprints in the foxgloves.

First prize for the *Song of Poole* Competition for local schools.

HMS Nelson plaque commisioned for retiring First Lord of the Admiralty.

Winners plaque for the Poole to Cherbourg Power Boat Championship.

Plaque made to celebrate the centenary of the Kinson Pottery.

Army retirement gift, featuring regimental badges around the rim.

Alan White modelling the carp plate.

Carp plate modelled by Alan White and made in a limited edition of 250, 1997.

Octopus, painted plaque by Alan White, 1996.

Trellis, painted plaque by Alan White, 1996.

Fish, painted plaque by Alan White, 1996.

Barn owl, painted plaque by Alan White, 1996.

Tankard with Dolphin handle, modelled by Alan White for the Poole Collectors Club, 1997.

A typical range of hand thrown and glazed ironstone vases and candleholders designed by Alan White and made in the Pottery's craft workshop from about 1983, mark No.89. Tallest vase height $8\frac{1}{2}$ins (21.5cm).

Tableware

Java, an airbrushed and hand painted design by Anita Harris and Alan Clarke introduced 1998, shown on a range of white earthenware, mark No. 90. Diameter of large plate 10½ins (27cm).

Brunch on Earthenware, a slip trailed and hand painted underglaze design by Rachel Barker and Andrew Brickett introduced 2001, mark No. 112. Diameter of plate 10½ins (27cm).

Brunch on Terracotta, a slip trailed and hand painted underglaze design by Rachel Barker and Andrew Brickett introduced 2000, mark No. 112. Diameter of large plate 9ins (23cm).

Dragonfly a hand painted and sponged underglaze design by Zdenka Ralph introduced 1998, shown on a range of white earthenware, mark No. 90. Diameter of large plate 10½ins (27cm). A burgundy on cream version of this design was also produced.

Twintone, a revival of the Streamline shape designed by John Adams and Alfred Read and produced in semi matt sky blue and dove grey glazes from 1958. Introduced 2000, mark No. 109. Diameter of large plate 10½ins (27cm).

Latte, a slip trailed and Twintone glaze sprayed design by Janice Tchalenko and Anita Harris introduced 1998, shown on a range of white earthenware, mark No. 90. Diameter of large plate 9ins (23cm).

Tiffany Blossom, a lithograph transfer design by Joel Ulah introduced 2001 exclusively for Tiffany & Co., shown on a range of white earthenware, mark No.121. Length of oval platter 14ins (36cm).

Tiffany Rooster, a lithograph transfer design by Joel Ulah introduced 2001 exclusively for Tiffany & Co., shown on a range of white earthenware, mark No. 107. Length of oval platter 14ins (36cm).

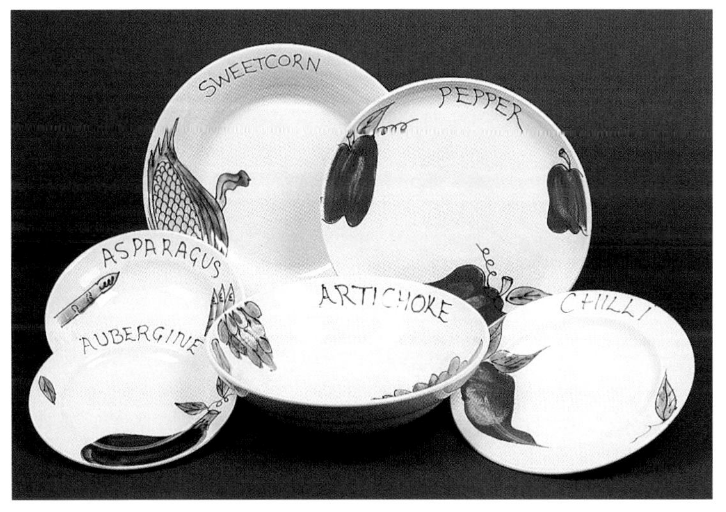

Vegetables, slip trailed and infilled with brushed colour glazes under a clear glaze, by Anita Harris introduced 2000, shown on white earthenware plates, bowls and serving dishes, mark No. 112. Diameter of sweetcorn dish 13ins (32.5cm).

Fish, slip trailed and infilled with brushed colour glazes under a clear glaze, designed by Anita Harris introduced 2000, shown on white earthenware plates, bowls and serving dishes, mark No. 112. Diameter of lobster dish 13ins (32.5cm).

Pasta dishes, slip trailed and infilled with brushed colour glazes under a clear glaze, designed by Anita Harris introduced 2000 exclusively for Liberty, shown on white earthenware dishes, mark No. 112. Diameter of dish 9ins (23.5cm).

Bamboo, a stencilled, hand painted and ceramic pencilled design by Anita Harris introduced 1999 exclusively for the John Lewis Partnership, shown on a range of white earthenware, mark No. 90. Diameter of large plate $12^{1}/_{2}$ins (32cm).

Green Leaf, a slip trailed and hand painted design by Anita Harris introduced 1998, shown on a range of white earthenware, mark No. 90. Diameter of large plate $10^{1}/_{2}$ins (27cm).

Royal Academy, a hand painted and ceramic pencilled underglaze design by Anita Harris introduced 2000, shown on a range of white earthenware including a 1950s Streamline teapot and jug, mark No. 113. Diameter of large plate $10^{1}/_{2}$ins (27cm).

Miranda, a hand painted and ceramic pencilled underglaze design by Anita Harris introduced 2000, shown on a range of white earthenware, mark No. 112. Diameter of plate $10^{1}/_{2}$ins (27cm).

Woodland White, a slip trailed and hand painted design by Anita Harris introduced 1999 exclusively for Marks & Spencer. Shown on a range of white earthenware, mark No. 90. Diameter of plate 9ins (23cm).

Omega, a slip trailed and painted underglaze design by Fenella Mallalieu. A modified version introduced 2001, shown on white earthenware, mark No. 112. Diameter of plate $10^{1}/_{2}$ins (23cm).

Collectors Club

Bluebird brooch modelled by Joe Leadbeater and colour sprayed by Alan Clarke in 1999 exclusively for members of the Collectors Club. Produced in a limited edition of 500, mark No. 64. Length 2½ins (6.5cm).

Delphis brooch designed and painted by Carol Cutler in 1999 exclusively for members of the Collectors Club. Produced in a limited edition of 200, mark No. 64. Diameter 2ins (5cm).

Corfe Castle from the Isle of Purbeck series, designed by Karen Brown and painted on Alpine white glaze. Introduced 1998, shown on a white earthenware dish, mark No. 97. Diameter 10½ins (17cm), made exclusively for the Poole Collectors Club.

Viking from the Isle of Purbeck series, designed by Karen Brown and painted on Alpine white glaze. Introduced 1998, shown on white earthenware dishes and Athens vases, mark No. 97. Large dish, diameter 16ins (42cm), made in a limited edition of 100. Athens vase made exclusively for members of the Poole Collectors Club.

Old Harry Rocks from the Isle of Purbeck series, designed by Karen Brown, and painted on alpine white glaze. Introduced 1997, shown on white earthenware dishes and Athens vase, mark No. 97. Large dish, diameter 16ins (42cm), made in a limited edition of 100. Athens vases and footed dish, made exclusively for members of the Poole Collectors Club.

Caro, based on the open air sculpture 'Sea Music' on Poole Quay by Sir Anthony Caro. Designed by Karen Brown and painted on Alpine white glaze, introduced 1998. Shown on a white earthenware vase and dish, mark No. 97. Vase height 8ins (20.5cm). Both pieces, together with an alternative version of the Lotus pattern were made exclusively for members of the Poole Collectors Club.

Lotus, inspired by the culture of ancient Egypt. Designed by Karen Brown and painted on alpine white glaze. Introduced 1998, shown on white earthenware dishes and Athens vase, mark No. 97. Diameter of large dish 10ins (26cm).

Special Productions

A recent interpretation of patterns from the 1930s painted on hand thrown white earthenware vases in a limited edition of (L to R) CBA 100, CBB 150, CBC 150 and offered exclusively for a limited period to the Collectors Club.

'Creating a brighter future', a winning design depicting the Dorset coast, sea and sky by Julie Herring, at Bournemouth University 1998. Glaze painted by Karen Brown, mark No. 106. Diameter of dish 14ins (35cm).

The Ocean Liner – 'they inspired pride, hope and realisation of dreams'. Designed and painted by Karen Brown, mark No. 97. This 16ins (42cm) diameter dish, signed by the artist 17/4/99, is one of only six made.

Vases and carafe thrown and hand painted on alpine white glaze in the style of Alfred Read's designs from the 1950s. Made exclusively for Liberty & Co., limited edition of 25, 20 and 15 (L to R) and featured in their Poole in the 50s exhibition held in 1999, mark No. 97. Height of carafe 15¼ins (39cm).

Crummles English Enamels, a display of ginger jars and pill boxes decorated with Poole Pottery Living Glaze designs and Uri Geller designs 2001, mark No. 127. Diameter of pill box 2¼ins (5.5cm).

Streamline revisited, a selection of shapes and glazes reminiscent of the post war Twintone, made exclusively for Liberty and featured in their 'Poole in the 50s' exhibition 1999, mark No. 109. Diameter of coupe plates 7ins (18cm).

Rimini and Tuscany, hand painted underglaze designs by Anita Harris introduced 1998 exclusively for Alders, shown on hand thrown white earthenware vases, mark No. 97. Height of vase 10ins (25cm).

Le Fleur, a hand painted and stencilled underglaze design by Anita Harris introduced 1998 exclusively for Alders, shown on white earthenware dishes, a prestige and Athens vase, mark No. 93. Diameter of large dish 12½ins (32cm).

Liberty year mugs 1998-2002 in white earthenware decorated with on-glaze transfer patterns based upon prints from the Liberty & Co. archive, mark No. 104. Height 3½ins (9cm).

Poole Ships collection produced exclusively for Compton & Woodhouse, from the drawings of Arthur Bradbury, in a limited edition of 4950 transfer printed plates of each design. Individually numbered, certificated and boxed, mark No. 74. Diameter of plate 10½ins (27cm).

Gemstones, Peacock, Volcano, Living Glaze painted designs reproduced as laser printed lithographs on bone china mugs introduced 2001, mark No. 122. Height of mug 4ins (10cm).

Two roller imprinted copper green vases and two midnight blue mottled flasks, designed and thrown in a white earthenware body, and decorated by Alan White. Introduced 2000, mark No. 97 and AW sprigged. Height of tallest vase 14½ins (37cm).

Commemoratives

Right: The Carterton plate illustrates some of the many facets of the life of William Carter who in 1900 provided land for the development of a small community, now a thriving town, in West Oxfordshire. Designed and painted by Karen Brown, mark No. 97. This 14ins (35cm) plate was presented to the Mayor of Carterton by Tony Carter (William's grandson) on 24th June 2000.

Far right: Russell-Cotes Art Gallery and Museum re-opening presentation plate, designed and painted in the traditional manner by Susan Pottinger, mark No. 97. Diameter 14ins (35cm).

Off-shore Grand Prix winner's trophy. A transfer printed design with hand painted inscription, mark No. 93. Diameter of dish 14ins (35cm).

RNLI Conference dish, transfer printed after an original painting by Susan Pottinger. Other items were produced in this design including a dish commemorating the 'Freedom of the Borough of Poole 23rd June 1999', mark No. 93. Diameter of dish 6½ins (17cm).

This prestigious stoneware plaque is awarded annually to schemes carried out within the borough of Poole which are judged to have made the greatest contribution to the quality and appearance of the street scene or landscape. The award in the year 2000 went to the Arts Institute for its Learning and Resources Centre. Height of plaque 10ins (25cm).

Brownsea Castle, designed and painted in the traditional manner by Susan Pottinger. One of seven plates given by Poole Pottery to the Ladybird Appeal Fund and auctioned at a Banquet held on 28th October 2000, mark No. 97. Diameter of plate 12½ins (32cm).

Daily Echo Centenary plate, transfer printed on white earthenware and made in a limited edition of 500. Trinket boxes and footed dishes were also available, mark No. 115. Diameter of plate 10½ins (27cm).

The Antiques Roadshow 21st anniversary dish designed by Laurence McGowan and decorated with an over-glaze transfer fired at high temperature. Produced in a limited edition of 150, mark No. 105. Diameter of dish 12ins (30cm), individually numbered, certificated and boxed.

Living Glaze

Promotional leaflet for living glaze, 1999.

Launched at the Spring Fair at the Birmingham NEC in 1999, Living Glaze, the inspiration of Peter Mills and Larry Ewin, was an immediate success, provoking a fantastic reaction in both admiration and in orders. Bright colours, vibrant glaze effects and abstract patterns were just what the market wanted, and Poole seemed once again to have reinvented itself as a pottery in tune with contemporary taste. The response to Living Glaze, and its rapid success in the market place, echoed in some ways the launch of Delphis in the early 1960s, and in many ways Delphis was a vital inspiration for Living Glaze, prompted by the perceived need from late 1998 to shift more production from tableware to giftware. However, Poole has never been a pottery content simply to repeat earlier successes, and so a Delphis revival was never seen as a practical possibility. Instead, Yvonne Morris, Poole's Technical Manager, research and development, experimented with reactive glazes to create bright colours from new ways of blending cadmium and solenium oxides. Some of the results seemed reminiscent of Delphis, but both the colours and the methods of application were quite different. The effects that made Living Glaze so distinct were created by combining a series of base glazes in red, yellow, orange and green with a range of top glazes designed to react with the base glazes.

The appeal to artists and designers was immediate, and within days the first patterns, Alan Clarke's Aurora and Anita Harris's Volcano, were being developed. Others quickly followed, including Galaxy, Clouds, Blue Storm and Odyssey, and it was this range of patterns that made such an impact at the Spring Fair. The resultant success demanded a close cooperation between artists, technicians and production to create a stable and marketable series.

The success of these ranges inspired artists and designers both inside and outside the pottery to use the new glaze technology in a more experimental way, and the result was an explosion of one-off studio wares, and the development of new production ranges. In-house designers involved included Anita Harris, Alan Clarke and Nicola Massarella, but also drawn into the net were two outsiders, Janice Tchalenko and Tony Morris, both with previous Poole associations. Their response to the challenge of the Living Glaze colours was exciting and dramatic, even though both used radically different styles and sources of inspiration. Janice Tchalenko's style was a blend of colour and pattern with a distinctly painterly approach, based on abstract art, natural forms and textiles. Tony Morris, well known among collectors for his earlier Delphis designs, was persuaded to return to Poole in the summer of 1999, lured by the stimulation of the new colours. His designs, progressive, strongly organic and full of movement and symbolism, drew their inspiration from nature. The work of these artists recreated the Poole reputation for innovative, individual and experimental work.

Over the next couple of years a number of other Living Glaze patterns were developed, including Peacock, Gemstones, Rain Forest, Cosmic, Strobe, Exodus, Eclipse and Safari, designed largely by Anita Harris and Alan Clarke, whose airbrush technique has been so successful for his designs. Also distinctive were Alan Clarke's limited edition Millennium and Planets series. More recently there has been a move away from the bright colours towards a softer and more subtle palette, but still based on the Living Glaze technology.

Tony Morris encouraging a member of the Collectors Club to experiment with Living Glaze.

Last days at the Quay, finding a place to work.

Alan Clarke

The Planets, a collection of nine 16$^{1}/_{2}$ins and 10ins (42cm and 25cm) dishes designed by Alan Clarke, commemorates the alignment of the planets 5th May 2000, mark No. 118. Limited to 500 of each design on each shape, the individually numbered dishes were supplied in a presentation box with a signed certificate.

Mercury.

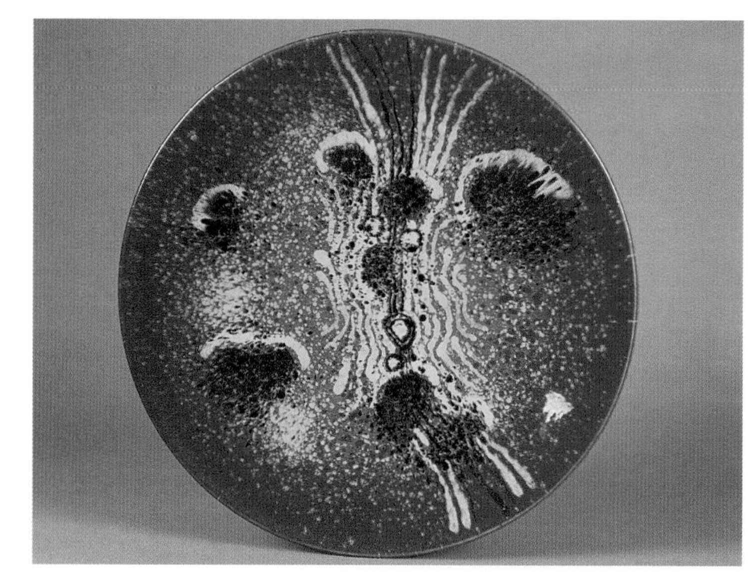

Venus.

Earth.

Mars.

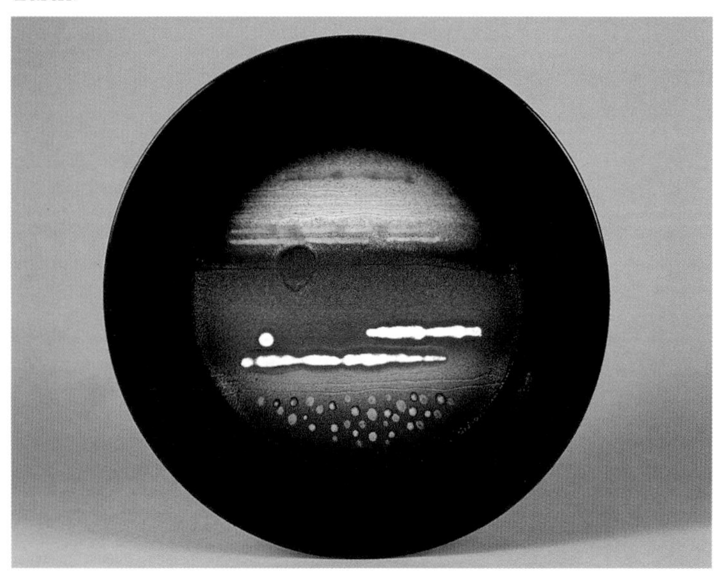

Jupiter.

Saturn.

Uranus.

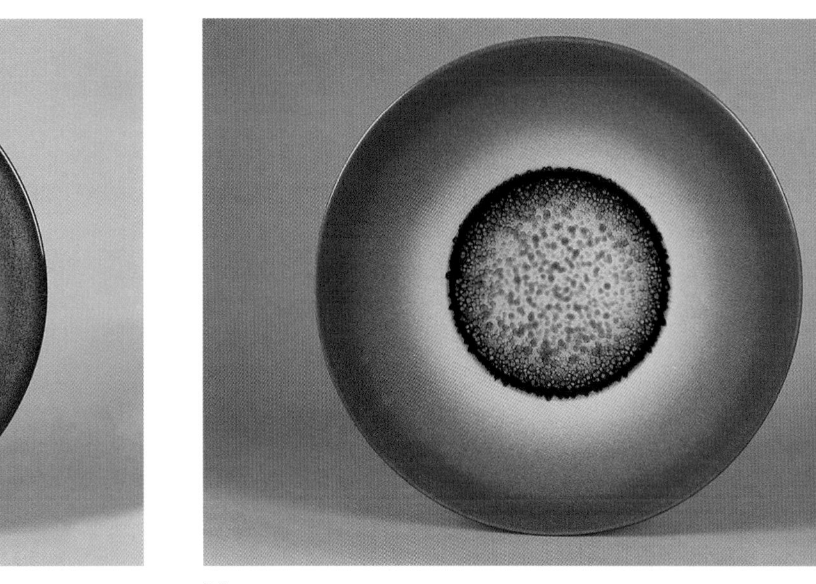

Neptune.

Pluto.

The Alignment of The Planets. Produced in a limited edition of 2500 dishes in each size, mark No. 119.

Eclipse, a glaze sprayed and painted design by Alan Clarke commemorates this rare event which took place on 11th August 1999. Three sizes of dish with an Egyptian vase in white earthenware were made in a limited edition of 1999 pieces of each shape, mark No. 108. Diameter of large dish 16ins (42cm).

Orbit, a glaze sprayed and mottled design celebrates man's first flight into space on 12th April 1961. Introduced on the fortieth anniversary of this event, a white earthenware dish was made in a limited edition of 1000 of each size, mark No. 120.

Aurora, a glaze sprayed and painted design by Alan Clarke introduced 1999, shown on white earthenware dishes, a prestige and Egyptian vase. Diameter of large dish 16ins (42cm).

Odyssey, a glaze sprayed and painted design by Alan Clarke introduced 1999, shown on white earthenware dishes, a Roman vase and ginger vase. Diameter of large dish 16ins (42cm).

Exodus, a sprayed, stencilled and painted design by Alan Clarke introduced 2000, shown on a white earthenware dish, a Roman and prestige vase and ginger jar. Diameter of large dish 16ins (42cm).

Safari, a glaze sprayed and painted design by Alan Clarke introduced 2000, shown on a white earthenware dish and Egyptian vase. Diameter of dish 16ins (42cm).

Christmas Dawn, a glaze sprayed and trailed design on white earthenware by Alan Clarke. Commissioned by Whittards of Chelsea for Christmas 2000. Made and signed in a limited edition of 100, mark No. 97. Diameter 16ins (42cm).

Reflections (left) and Aquatic Bronze (right), glaze sprayed, trailed and painted designs by Alan Clarke introduced 2000, shown on white earthenware conical vases. Both sizes of vase were made in a limited edition of 50 in each design, mark No. 97. Height of large vase 18ins (45cm).

Millennium, a glaze sprayed and painted design by Alan Clarke produced on two white earthenware dishes and an Egyptian vase, made in a limited edition of 2000 of each shape, mark No. 110. Diameter of large dish 16ins (42cm). The symbolism of this design is said to portray the resilience of life on earth and the hope which the new Millennium promises.

The Third Millennium, a glaze sprayed and painted design by Alan Clarke on a white earthenware dish. Made exclusively for the Guild of Specialist China & Glass Retailers in a limited edition of 1000, individually numbered, certificated and boxed, mark No. 111. Diameter of dish 16ins (42cm).

Red Delphis, a glaze sprayed and painted design by Alan Clarke introduced 1999, shown on a white earthenware cat and duck, mark No. 64. Height of cat $11^{1}/_{2}$ins (29cm).

A pair of Millennium glaze sprayed and painted designs on white earthenware mugs made exclusively for Marks & Spencer, mark No. 110. Height of mug $3^{1}/_{2}$ins (9cm).

Sunset, a glaze sprayed design by Alan Clarke introduced 2000 exclusively for The Guild of Specialist China and Glass Retailers, shown on white earthenware purse vases. Both sizes of vase were made in a limited edition of 2000, mark No. 97. Height of large vase 9ins (23cm).

Final Quay Edition - the Poole dolphin, a glaze sprayed and painted design by Alan Clarke produced prior to the relocation of the Pottery from the Poole Quay to its new site in 2001. Two sizes of dish in white earthenware were made in a numbered, limited edition of 1000 of each shape, mark No. 124. Diameter of large dish 16ins (42cm).

Janice Tchalenko

Cosmic, a hand painted design with lustre finish by Janice Tchalenko and Anita Harris introduced 2000, shown on white earthenware Roman and classic vases. Height of Roman vase 12½ins (32cm).

Red Magna, a sponged glaze design by Janice Tchalenko introduced 1999, shown on a white earthenware classic and conical vase. Made exclusively for the John Lewis Partnership. Height of classic vase 10ins (25cm).

Strobe, a glaze trailed design by Janice Tchalenko introduced 2001, shown on white earthenware dishes, a Roman and classic vase. Height of Roman vase 12½ins (32cm).

Janet Owen, Decorating Supervisor.

Clover, a glaze painted design by Janice Tchalenko introduced 2001 exclusively for Liberty, shown on white earthenware dishes and purse vases. Height of large dish 16ins (42cm).

Clouds, a glaze painted design by Janice Tchalenko and Anita Harris introduced 1999, shown on a white earthenware dish and ginger vase. Diameter of dish 16ins (42cm).

Velta, a slip trailed and painted design by Janice Tchalenko and Anita Harris introduced 1999, shown on a white earthenware dish, a prestige urn and prestige vase. Height of Prestige urn 9ins (23cm).

Blue Storm, a wax resist and glaze painted design by Janice Tchalenko and Anita Harris introduced 1999, shown on a white earthenware dish, a ginger jar and classic vase. Height of ginger jar 12ins (30cm).

Galaxy, a glaze painted design by Janice Tchalenko and Anita Harris introduced 1999, shown on white earthenware dishes and a classic vase. Diameter of large dish 16ins (42cm).

A metallic black version of Galaxy made exclusively for the John Lewis Partnership. Diameter of large dish 16ins (42cm).

Anita Harris

Gemstones, a glaze painted design by Anita Harris introduced 2000, shown on white earthenware conical vases. The three smallest vases in this design are made exclusively for the John Lewis Partnership. Height of tallest vase 18ins (45cm).

Peacock, a glaze painted design by Anita Harris introduced 2000, shown on a white earthenware dish, a ginger jar and classic vase. Height of ginger jar 12ins (30cm).

Matisse, a glaze painted design by Anita Harris introduced 2000, shown on a white earthenware dish, a classic and bud vase. Diameter of dish 13ins (33cm).

Green Carousel, a glaze painted design by Anita Harris introduced 2000, shown on a white earthenware dish and classic vase. Diameter of dish 13ins (33cm).

Gold Carousel, a glaze painted design by Anita Harris introduced 2000, shown on a white earthenware dish and classic vase. Diameter of dish 10½ins (27cm).

Rain Forest (left) and Babylon (right) glaze painted designs by Anita Harris introduced 2000, shown on a white earthenware classic and prestige vase, mark No. 114. Both designs are made exclusively for Marks & Spencer. Height of prestige vase 8½ins (21cm).

Volcano, a glaze painted design by Anita Harris introduced 1999, shown on a white earthenware dish, a classic vase and ginger jar. Diameter of dish 16ins (42cm).

Yellow Horned Polly 'Glaucium Flavum', a glaze painted design by Anita Harris introduced 2001 on white earthenware in a limited edition of 500, mark No. 97. Made exclusively for the Dorset Wildlife Trust. Diameter of dish 10ins (25cm).

Anita Harris

Vogue Cats, a glaze trailed design by Nicola Massarella introduced 2001, shown on white earthenware cats. Height of large cat 11½ins (29cm).

Vogue, a glaze trailed design by Anita Harris introduced 2000, shown on white earthenware dishes and purse vases. The metallic version of this design is shown on the small dish and large vase and is made exclusively for Alders. Diameter of large dish 16ins (42cm).

Sunburst, a glaze sprayed and mottled design by Alan White introduced 2002, shown on white earthenware concave vases and bowls. Height of tallest vase 12½ins (32cm).

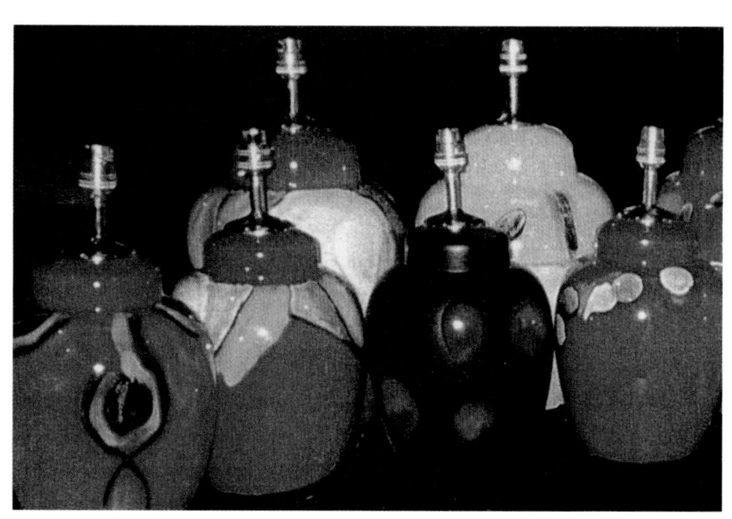

A selection of Living Glaze sprayed and painted designs on white earthenware lamp bases.

Sea Fire, a glaze sprayed and mottled design by Alan White introduced 2001, shown on white earthenware conical vases. Height of tallest vase 18ins (45cm).

A selection of Living Glaze sprayed and painted designs on white earthenware miniature vases introduced 2002, mark No. 116. Height of vase 3¾ins (9.5cm).

Furnace, a roller imprinted and glaze sprayed design by Alan White introduced 2002, shown on white earthenware concave bowls. Height of large bowl 7½ins (19cm).

A selection of Living Glaze painted designs on white earthenware powder boxes introduced 2000, mark No. 117. Diameter of box 5ins (13cm).

One-off Studio Wares

Tony Morris

Seagulls Roosting, date code B50, diameter 16ins (42cm).

Barn Owl, date code C3, diameter 16ins (42cm).

Dragonfly, date code A38, diameter 16ins (42cm).

Upton Roundabouts, date code C21, diameter 16ins (42cm).

Red Mullet, date code A9, diameter 16ins (42cm).

One-off studio decorated dish designed and glaze painted by Tony Morris. Date code H30, mark No. 97. Diameter of dish 16ins (42cm).

One-off studio decorated dish designed and glaze painted by Tony Morris. Date code H12, mark No. 97. Diameter of dish 16ins (42cm).

Red Squirrel, designed and glaze painted by Tony Morris. One of seven dishes donated by Poole Pottery to the Ladybird Appeal Fund and auctioned at the Brownsea Castle Banquet, 28th October 2000. Date code L20, mark No. 97. Diameter of dish 16ins (42cm).

Studio dish No. 2 from a group of three showing different stages in the development of Stonehenge, designed and glaze painted by Tony Morris. Date code M41, mark No. 97. Diameter of dish 16ins (42cm).

Tony Morris decorating in the Quay studio.

Studio dish No. 1 from a limited edition of 100, designed by Tony Morris and glaze painted by Nicola Massarella, mark No. 97. Diameter of dish 14ins (35cm).

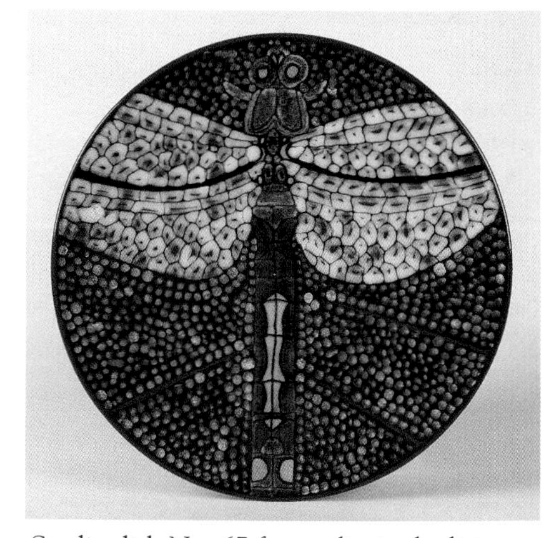

Studio dish No. 67 from a limited edition of 100 designed by Tony Morris and glaze painted by Nicola Massarella, mark No. 97. Diameter of dish 14ins (35cm).

Janice Tchalenko

Iris dish, diameter 16ins (42cm).

Oyster dish, diameter 16ins (42cm).

Chequer dish, diameter 16ins (42cm).

Janice Tchalenko

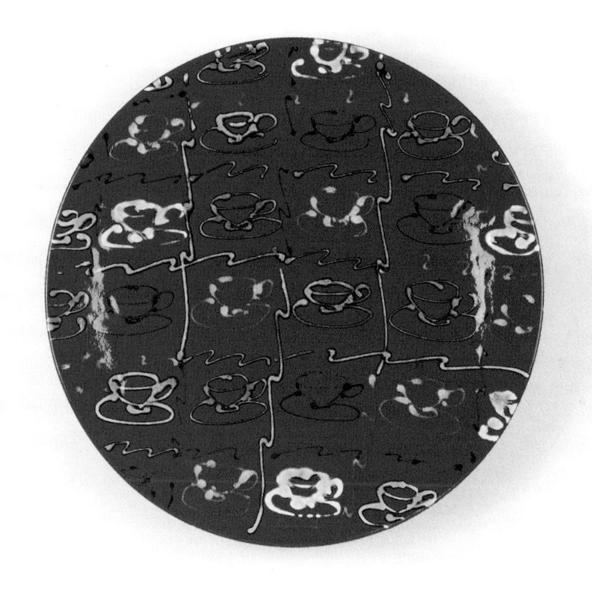

Teacup dish, diameter 16ins (42cm), 1999.

Green Strobe vase, date code HH2.

Alan Clarke

One-off studio decorated conical vase designed, glaze trailed and sprayed by Alan Clarke, mark No. 97. Height of vase 18ins (45cm).

Space dish, diameter 16ins (42cm).

Dynamic dish, diameter 16ins (42cm).

One-off studio decorated ginger jar designed, glaze sprayed and painted by Alan Clarke, mark No. 97. Height of ginger jar 12ins (30cm).

Alan Clarke's talent and techniques are ideally suited to Living Glaze ranges.

Nicola Massarella

One-off studio decorated dish designed and glaze painted by Nicola Massarella. Date code HH39, mark No. 97. Diameter of dish 16ins (42cm).

One-off studio decorated dish designed and glaze painted by Nicola Massarella, mark No. 97. Diameter of dish 16ins (42cm).

One-off studio decorated Roman vase designed and glaze painted by Nicola Massarella. Date code KK11, mark No. 97. Height of vase $12^{1}/_{2}$ins (32cm).

One-off studio decorated dish designed and glaze painted by Nicola Massarella. Date code HH19, mark No. 97. Diameter of dish 16ins (42cm).

Studio dish No. 6 from a limited edition of 50 designed and glaze painted by Nicola Massarella, mark No. 97. Diameter of dish 16ins (42cm). A companion dish with a right-hand face was also made in a limited edition of 50.

Susan Pottinger

Yellow Landscape, a one-off studio decorated dish designed and glaze painted by Susan Pottinger. Date code HH31, mark No. 97. Diameter of dish 16ins (42cm).

White Stork a one-off studio decorated dish designed and glaze painted by Susan Pottinger. Date code HH10, mark No. 97. Diameter of dish 16ins (42cm).

Susan Pottinger.

Duck dish, date code HH6, diameter 16ins (42cm).

Mini Masters, four from a series of studio decorated plates designed, glaze trailed and signed by S.M. Pottinger. Date code NN9 to 12, mark No. 97. Diameter of plates 8ins (20cm).

Anita Harris

Dancing Hares.

Dolphin,

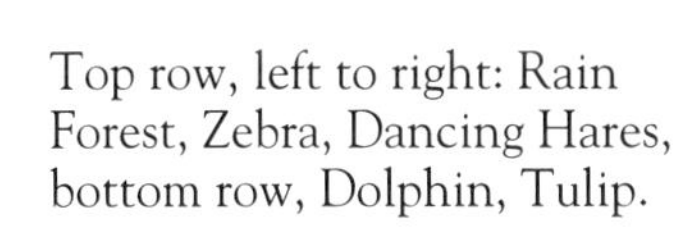

Top row, left to right: Rain Forest, Zebra, Dancing Hares, bottom row, Dolphin, Tulip.

Karen Brown

Music, a one-off studio decorated dish designed, glaze painted and signed by K. Brown. Date code MM38, mark No. 97. Diameter of dish 16ins (42cm).

Enigma, a one-off studio decorated dish designed and glaze painted by Karen Brown, mark No. 97. Diameter of dish 16ins (42cm).

The Quay frontage of the Pottery, c.1960.

Quay frontage prior to demolition, 2000.

Demolition in progress 2001.

The new complex under construction 2002.

The heart of the Pottery. Last to go, the original Pottery acquired by Jessie Carter in 1873.

Chapter Fourteen

New Beginnings

At the very end of the twentieth century, major development plans were announced that seemed likely to change beyond recognition the familiar face of Poole. Plans for a yacht marina in the harbour coincided with a scheme, first announced in 1998, for a total redevelopment of the Poole Pottery site, with a new retail village shopping complex, restaurants and flats. As owners of the quay-side site, the Pottery was, in effect, the instigator of a scheme that would involve its own relocation as a way to increase the existing shopping complex and overcome the increasingly difficult productions conditions within the old factory. After much discussion on both local and national levels, the plans for the Dolphin Quays development, variously described in the local press as 'the brave new face of Poole' and the 'St Tropez of the South Coast', were given the go-ahead. Building work began in 2000, and the following year the Pottery began the move to a new site in Sopers Lane, on an industrial site on the outskirts of Poole, a complicated £3 million process supervised by Garry Hilton, the newly appointed Production Director, that culminated in a reopening ceremony in September 2001. The end of production at the old factory was marked by a special limited edition plate designed by Alan Clarke. Once empty, the old premises were demolished, along with the Delphis restaurant and the factory museum, bringing to an end the 128-year long tradition of pottery making on the quay-side site. The famous factory museum is currently closed but discussions are underway with the council to find a new location.

Coincident with the move to the new factory was a major management restructuring operation, announced in September 2001. Peter Mills, the prime mover behind the Dolphin Quays scheme, gave up his position as managing director of the Pottery to concentrate on property development and investment. In his place as head of a new management team came Chris Rhodes. With a wealth of international marketing and business management experience to draw upon, including many years as Group Business Director with The Gillette Company, Rhodes came to Poole at a critical time in its history, a period of transition when the pottery had to move forward in its new premises while retaining its individuality, its reputation for design and the vital links with its past. .

Early 2002 introductions have included a series of limited edition plates designed by the paranormalist Uri Geller, the Zilli casual dining range created by the celebrity chef Aldo Zilli, the Wild Poppy range of expressive hand-painted plant holders, decorative bowls and up-lighters designed by Anita Harris to take Poole into the conservatory market, and Aqua, soft and pastel-coloured decorative wares inspired by the sea, but using the Living Glaze technology. These proved to be Anita Harris's last contributions to the Poole catalogue as she left Dorset in the Spring of 2002 to go to work for Moorcroft in Staffordshire.

In April 2002 the Duchess of Gloucester toured the new Sopers Lane pottery during a busy day in the Poole region. During the visit, she presented a long service award to Ken Poole, celebrating his forty-six years with the pottery, and received a pair of specially created Poole Pottery dog collar tags, for her King Charles spaniels Monty and Indie. Further changes followed the appointment during the summer of 2002 of Frances Sorrell, co-founder of Newall & Sorrell and the Sorrell Foundation, as external Design Director. Well aware of Poole's reputation as a distinctive British pottery with a history of innovation and diversity, she plans to combine the best of modern design with the pottery's heritage to create desirable dining and home products that fit the modern relaxed way of living. She introduced Charlotte Whitfield, previously with Wedgwood, to Poole who joins as Design Manager. Under Frances direction artists, designers, craftsmen and women, ceramicists and students can all contribute to Poole's creative renaissance. A new corporate identity has been established, and new designs are underway. Another part of the new look is the Poole Pottery Experience, opened in July 2002. Demonstration and activity areas, historical displays and a new shop designed by Ben Kelly in an inventive and versatile style re-establish the Poole Pottery at the heart of the new shopping complex in the Dolphin Quays development.

The Poole Pottery Experience on the Quay site, 2002.

From left to right, Chris Rhodes, Managing Director, Garry Hilton, Production Director, Alan Deves, Finance Director.

Frances Sorrell, Design Director.

Charlotte Whitfield, Design Manager.

Poole Pottery moves to Sopers Lane, 2001.

Glost kilns at Sopers Lane.

Decorating department at Sopers Lane.

Commemorative plate marking the opening of the new Poole Pottery factory. A lithograph inscription with a Gemstones painted design by Anita Harris. Made in a limited edition of 300, mark No. 109. Diameter 6$^{1}/_{2}$ins (17cm).

Golden Jubilee plate designed by Anita Harris with lettering by artist/calligrapher Roger Taylor and hand painted by Susan Pottinger. Combining past and present, the design incorporates elements which span the years between the Coronation and Golden Jubilee. Made in a limited edition of 500, each plate is numbered and supplied in a presentation box with a signed certificate, mark No. 130. Diameter 14ins (35cm).

Zilli, a transfer printed and hand painted underglaze design by Aldo Zilli and Anita Harris introduced 2002, shown on a range of white earthenware, mark No. 128. Diameter of dinner plate 12$^{1}/_{2}$ins (32cm).

A commemorative plate painted in the traditional CS pattern, marking the opening of the new Poole Pottery factory, mark No. 97. Diameter 16ins (42cm). Signed K. Brown.

Wessex Heartbeat, a transfer printed plate with hand painted inscription marking the redevelopment and opening of Ocean Ward by the Earl and Countess of Wessex, mark No. 97. Diameter of plate 9ins (23cm).

New York Toile, a transfer printed plaque redesigned by Tiffany & Co. 2002, mark No. 129. Diameter 12$^{1}/_{2}$ins (32cm). The previously designed plaque included the Twin Towers of the World Trade Center.

Uri Geller

'The Lovers' - Blue Mood and Red Mood, a glaze sprayed and mottled design by Uri Geller introduced 2001, shown on white earthenware dishes. Made in a limited edition of 1,000 dishes in each design, mark No. 126. Diameter of dish 16ins (42cm).

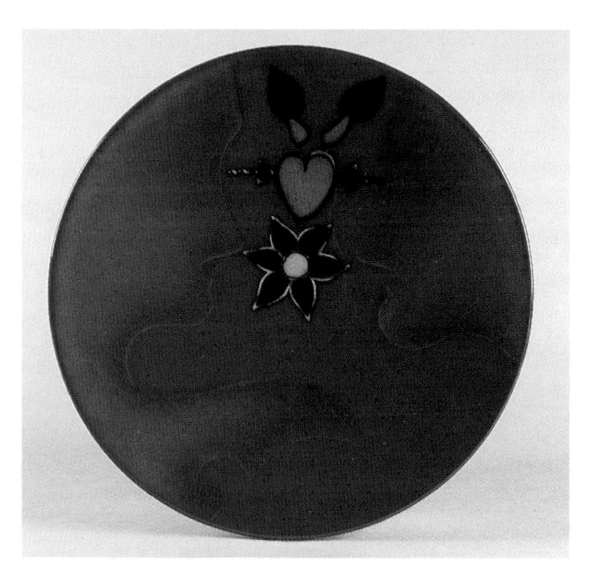

'The Lovers' – Flowers, a glaze sprayed, mottled, sgraffito and painted design by Uri Geller introduced 2001, shown on a white earthenware dish. Made in a limited edition of 1,000 dishes, mark No. 126. Diameter of dish 16ins (42cm).

Faces of the Universe and Subliminal Fish, transfer printed and hand painted underglaze designs by Uri Geller introduced 2002 on white earthenware and produced in a limited edition of 1000 plates of each design, mark No. 126. Diameter of plate 12½ins (32cm).

English Eclipse, a transfer printed underglaze design by Uri Geller introduced 2002 on white earthenware and produced in a limited edition of 1000 plates, mark No. 126. Diameter of plate 12½ins (32cm).

Creation of Earth and Healing Hand, transfer printed and hand painted underglaze designs by Uri Geller introduced 2002 on white earthenware and produced in a limited edition of 1000 plates of each design, mark No. 126. Diameter of plate 12½ins (32cm).

Himalayan Poppy, a glaze painted design by Anita Harris introduced 2002, shown on white earthenware dishes, Egyptian and prestige vases. Made exclusively for the John Lewis Partnership. Diameter of large dish 16ins (42cm).

Mosaic, a glaze painted design by Anita Harris introduced 2002, shown on white earthenware dishes and purse vases. Diameter of large dish 16ins (42cm).

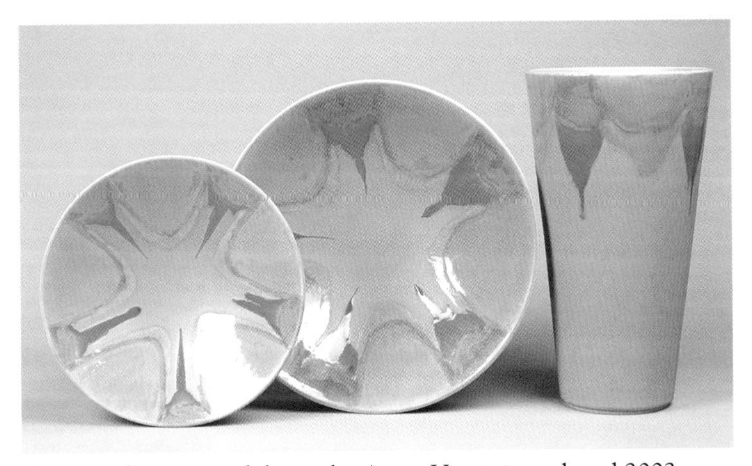

Aqua, a glaze painted design by Anita Harris introduced 2002, shown on white earthenware dishes and a conical vase. Height of vase 14ins (35cm).

Wild Poppy, a glaze painted design by Anita Harris introduced 2002, shown on a white earthenware dish, Egyptian vase, Roman vase and planter. Height of Egyptian vase 14ins (35cm).

Right: Promotional leaflet for Aqua.

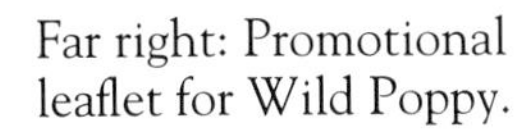

Far right: Promotional leaflet for Wild Poppy.

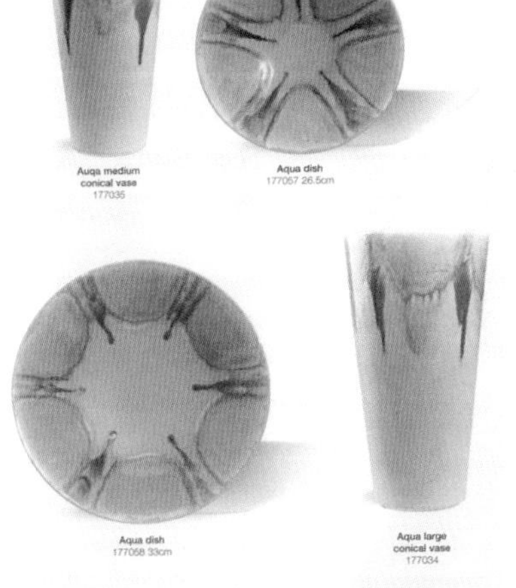

Each piece is a unique and individual hand decorated work of art. Cool, calm and tranquil, inspiring reflection.

Chapter Fifteen

Marks

Poole Pottery made between 1873 and the present day carries a variety of marks and backstamps. These include factory marks, codes used to identify patterns, shapes and glazes, and symbols used by throwers, finishers, sprayers, painters, paintresses and designers. The dates quoted against marks have been obtained wherever possible from factory records. Some have been estimated from reliable data, but from whichever source obtained, the accuracy of this information cannot be absolutely guaranteed.

FACTORY MARKS

Factory marks are listed in date order, but not necessarily to scale. Some marks were, in any case, used in a range of sizes. The earliest were mostly incised or impressed, a method still used for certain prestige products. Since the 1930s factory marks have been rubber stamped in black, or occasionally in a colour that blends or contrasts with the glaze or decoration. The name of the pattern, range or glaze is sometimes incorporated into the stamp or marked separately. There was a noted improvement in the quality of stamped marks after 1975 with the introduction of a copper plate backstamping machine. Most factory marks contain words or symbols that clearly identify Poole, but exceptions include specially commissioned wares made for organisations such as Tiffany and Altman of New York, Liberty of London, Marks & Spencer and the National Trust. Since 1972 there has been an increased use of silk screen and colour printed marks that often incorporate pattern names. Each factory mark is numbered and these numbers are used in the captions to identify the type of mark on the pieces illustrated.

PATTERN CODES

Traditional Poole patterns are identified by a two or three letter code which is painted on the unfired glaze on the base of the pot at the same time as the paintress's personal mark. When a third letter appears in a pattern code, it indicates either a prominent colour in the pattern or the colour of the ground on which the pattern is painted.

Associated but not directly related is the pink or salmon coloured slip which was brushed onto the base of painted pots when the white earthenware body was first introduced in 1934. This practice, which provided continuity with the red earthenware body used previously, was discontinued in 1937.

From 1951 until about 1966 the pattern code on the base of each pot was prefixed with the letters S M or E. This was an indication of the complexity of the pattern. These letters were not applied consistently but when used their definition was as follows:-

S = SIMPLE hand painted - a simple coloured floral sprig on a plain ground.

M = MEDIUM hand painted - sprays, bands etc., intermediate between simple and elaborate hand painted.

E = ELABORATE hand painted - multi coloured all over floral patterns, elaborate bands and motifs.

Occasionally an X will be seen above, below or sometimes in place of the prefix letter. This indicates that the pot was painted by Gwen Haskins, who was the senior paintress throughout this period.

SHAPE NUMBERS

The first identifiable range of numbered shapes, beginning at 101 and ending at 159, is illustrated in the second Hand-craft pottery catalogue issued by Carter & Company in 1921. It seems unlikely, however, that these wares were incised with the shape number, as was to become the custom with the wares of Carter, Stabler & Adams later in the same year.

The first series of C.S.A. shape numbers commenced at 201 and reached 999 by sometime in 1928 when a second series of numbers was started. The progression from this point becomes involved due to the re-issue of numbers previously used on shapes by now withdrawn from the range. The 1930 catalogue, for example, illustrated shapes from both the first and second series and even includes shape 118 from the original Carter & Company range of 1921. Later in the 1930s most of the Carter reserved numbers in the range, 101 to 200, were re-issued on modern shapes and several of these will be found in the Sylvan ware leaflet published in 1934. Despite these obvious complications, it is sometimes possible to assess the age of a piece by reference to its shape number when combined with other factors.

All shape numbers in Catalogue No.3 issued in 1922, the first to be published by Carter, Stabler and Adams, carry the prefix letter T D B or A. Margaret Holder would have made the profile and section drawings and allotted a shape number at the same time. When consulted, however, she was not able to recall the precise definition of these letters but thought they might have been represented as follows: T = Tableware, D = Decorative ware, B = Bedroom or Bathroom ware and A = Architectural ware. The letters are not prefixed to any of the shape numbers shown in Catalogue No.4 issued in 1923, which suggests that this early form of classification served no useful purpose and was therefore discontinued.

In 1947 incised numbers were replaced by impressed die stamped numbers (a useful dating point) and this method was maintained until the mid 1960s when rubber stamped numbers were introduced for Delphis and subsequent ornamental ranges.

MAKERS' AND DECORATORS' MARKS

Marks identifying throwers and stoneware sculpture finishers are impressed or incised. From 1936, sprayers used control marks consisting of dots and upright strokes stamped onto the biscuit. These were discontinued before 1950 but replaced in the 1960s and 1970s by star and diamond marks used mainly to identify the work of trainees on tablewares. Marks used by paintresses are painted directly onto the unfired glaze, while those of the sprayer are stamped underglaze onto the biscuit. Symbols and monograms used by paintresses are listed in chronological order, and the paintress is identified by her maiden name, unless she has already married at the time she started work. Married names are given in brackets. Dates given after the names indicate the period of employment. In the captions, paintresses and other female staff are usually given their maiden names.

Mark No.1
Moulded, about 1900. Found on teapot stands.

Mark No.2
Incised, 1900-1908. Found on lustre wares.

Carter & Co

Mark No.3
Incised, 1900-1908. Found on lustre wares.

Carter
Poole

Mark No.4
Impressed, 1900-1908.
Found on lustre wares

CARTERS POOLE

Mark No.5
Impressed, 1908-1921.
Found on lustre, tin glazed and unglazed wares.

Carter Co
Poole

Mark No.6
Moulded 1914-1915

KERAMIC COPY OF
BASSANO'S PORTRAIT
OF LORD KITCHENER
BY CARTERS OF POOLE
NOV - 1914 -

Mark No.7
Impressed, 1915-1921.
Found on lustre and tin glazed wares.

MADE FOR
LIBERTY & Co

Mark No.8
Impressed, 1915-1921.
Found on lustre and tin glazed wares.

LIBERTY
BRITISH MADE
LONDON

Mark No.9
Incised, 1915-1921. Found on modelled lustre wares.

CARTER'S
Co
POOLE

Mark No.10
Impressed, 1921-1922.
Found on grey semi-stonewares

CARTER
STABLER
ADAMS
POOLE

Mark No.11
Impressed, 1921-1934.
Found throughout the red eathenware period

CARTER
STABLER
ADAMS
POOLE
ENGLAND

Mark No.12
Moulded, 1921-1924. Found on garden and other moulded wares

CARTER
STABLER
& ADAMS
POOLE
ENGLAND

Mark No.13
Impressed, 1921-1924.
Found on slip trailed and other wares

CSA
POOLE
ENGLAND

Mark No.14
Impressed, 1922-1934.
Raised frame and letters

POOLE
ENGLAND

Mark No.15
Impressed, 1922-1934.
Raised frame and letters

POOLE
ENGLAND

Mark No.16
Painted, 1922-1935
Found on John Adams stonewares

POOLE

Mark No.17
Painted, 1922-1935
Found on John Adams stonewares

Poole

Mark No.18
Impressed, 1924-1950

POOLE
ENGLAND

Mark No.19
Impressed, 1924-1950

POOLE
ENGLAND

Mark No.20
Impressed, 1925-1927

CARTER
STABLER
ADAMS Ld
POOLE
ENGLAND

Mark No.21
Impressed, 1925-1934

CARTER
STABLER
ADAMS Ltd
POOLE
ENGLAND

Mark No.22
Moulded, 1925-1930. Found on 'The Ship' model

CSA
POOLE
ENGLAND

Mark No.23
Impressed, 1925-1926

POOLE
ENGLAND

Mark No.24
Impressed, c1930

MADE IN ENGLAND
EXPRESSLY FOR
B. ALTMAN & Co

Mark No.25
Moulded, about 1930. Found on bookends

CARTER
STABLER &
ADAMS Ltd
POOLE
ENGLAND

Mark No.26
Stencilled, 1930-1931

PLANE
WARE

Mark No.27
Impressed, 1930-1935.
Found on sugar sifters

CSA
ENGLAND . POOLE

Mark No.28
Impressed, 1930-1996

POOLE
ENGLAND

Mark No.29
Impressed, 1930-present

POOLE
ENGLAND

Mark No.30
Stencilled, 1931-1935

EVEREST

Mark No.31
Stencilled, 1934-1937

POOLE
ENGLAND

Mark No.32
Stencilled, 1934-1937

SYLVAN
WARE

Mark No.33
Stamped 1935-1949 and 1985-1996

POOLE
ENGLAND

Mark No.34
Stamped, 1935-1996

POOLE
ENGLAND

Mark No.35
Stamped, 1941-1950
Found on Utility wares

A
POOLE
DORSET

Mark No.36
Stamped, 1951-1955

POOLE
ENGLAND

Mark No.37
Stamped, 1952-1955

HAND MADE
POOLE
ENGLAND
HAND DECORATED

Mark No.38
Stamped, 1955-1956
Found only on Ann Read painted plaques

Mark No.39
Stamped, 1955-1959

Mark No.40
Painted 1956-1959
Found only on black glazed wares

POOLE
ENGLAND

Mark No.41
Stamped 1959-1967

Mark No.42
Stamped 1960-1969

Mark No.43
Stamped or impressed, 1962-1964

Mark No.44
Impressed, 1963-1964

Mark No.45
Stamped, 1964

Mark No.46
Stamped, 1964-1966

Mark No.47
Stamped, 1966-1980

Mark No.48
Stamped, 1967-1972

Mark No.49
Stamped, 1969

Mark No.50
Stamped, 1970-1972

Mark No.51
Stamped, 1970-1980

AEGEAN

Mark No.52
Stamped, 1972
Found on a stoneware coffee set by Tony Morris

Mark No.53
Impressed, 1973-1976

Mark No.54
Screen printed, 1974

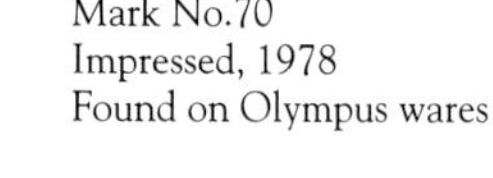

Mark No.55
Screen printed, 1973

Mark No.56
Screen printed, 1977

Mark No.57
Stamped, 1973-1974

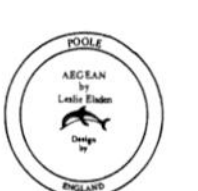

Mark No.58
Impressed, 1973-1980

Mark No.59
Stamped, 1973-1974

Mark No.60
Screen printed, 1973

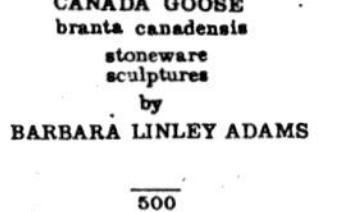

Mark No.61
Stamped, 1974

IONIAN

Mark No.62
Stamped, 1970-1999

Mark No.63
Stamped, 1970-1976

Mark No.64
Stamped, 1974-present

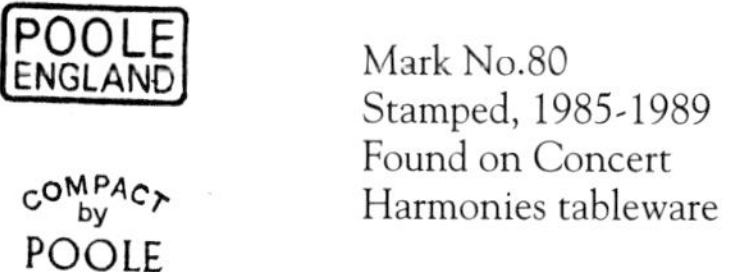

Mark No.65
Stamped, 1976

Mark No.66
Stamped, 1976-1977

Mark No.67
Stamped, 1977-1980

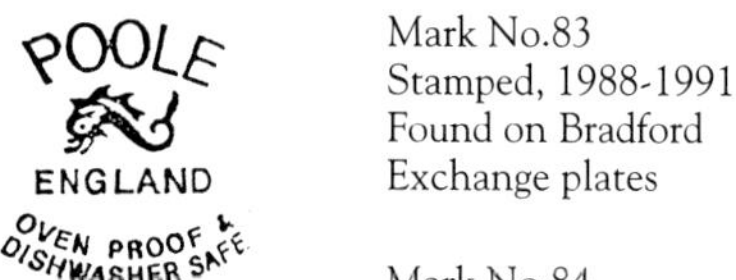

Mark No.68
Screen printed, 1978

Mark No.69
Transfer printed, 1978
Found on Camelot plates

Mark No.70
Impressed, 1978
Found on Olympus wares

Mark No.71
Stamped, 1978-present

Mark No.72
Transfer printed, 1979

Mark No.73
Transfer printed, 1979-1992

Mark No.74
Transfer printed, 1979-present

Mark No.75
Transfer printed, 1979

Mark No.76
Transfer printed, 1983-1986
Found on Flair tableware

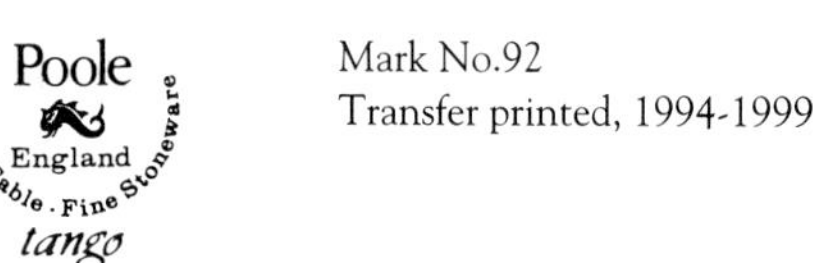

Mark No.77
Transfer printed, 1983-1994
Found on Scenic plates

Mark No.78
Transfer printed, 1983-1987

Mark No.79
Transfer printed, 1979-1990

Mark No.80
Stamped, 1985-1989
Found on Concert
Harmonies tableware

Mark No.81
Stamped, 1986
Found on sponge decorated tableware by Hinchcliffe & Barber

Mark No.82
Stamped, 1987-1999

Mark No.83
Stamped, 1988-1991
Found on Bradford
Exchange plates

Mark No.84
Stamped, 1989-1990
Found on Astral tableware

Mark No.85
Transfer printed, 1989-1991

Mark No.86
Stamped, 1990-1991

Mark No.87
Stamped, 1991

Mark No.88
Stamped, 1992-1993

Mark No.89
Impressed, 1993-1999t

Mark No.90
Stamped, 1993-1999
Transfer printed, 1994-1999

Mark No.91
Transfer printed, 1994-1999

Mark No.92
Transfer printed, 1994-1999

Mark No.93
Transfer printed, 1994-present

Mark No.94
Transfer printed, 1995

Mark No.95
Transfer printed, 1995-1997

Mark No.96
Stamped, 1995-1998

Mark No.97
Stamped, 1995-present

Mark No.98
Stamped, 1996

Mark No.99
Stamped, 1996-1997

Mark No.100
Transfer printed, 1996-1999

Mark No.101
Stamped, 1997-present

Mark No.102
Stamped, 1997-1999

Mark No.103
Stamped, 1997-1999

Mark No.104
Transfer printed, 1998-present

Mark No.105
Transfer printed, 1998-present

Mark No.106
Stamped, 1998-present

Mark No.107
Transfer printed, 1998-present

Mark No.108
Stamped, 1999-2000

Mark No.109
Stamped or etched, 1999-present

Mark No.110
Stamped, 2000-2001

Mark No.111
Stamped, 2000.

Mark No.112
Stamped, 2000-present.

Mark No.113
Stamped, 2000-present.

Mark No.114
Stamped, 2000-present.

Mark No.115
Transfer printed, 2000-present.

Mark No.116
Moulded, 2000-present.

Mark No.117
Moulded, 2000-present.

Mark No.118
Stamped, 2000-present

Mark No.119
Stamped, 2000-present

Mark No.120
Stamped, 2001-present

Mark No.121
Transfer printed, 2001-present

Mark No.122
Transfer printed, 2001-present

Mark No.123
Transfer printed, 2001-present

Mark No.124
Stamped, 2001-2002

Mark No.125
Transfer printed, 2000

Mark No.126
Transfer printed, 2002

Mark No.127
Transfer printed, 2002

Mark No.128
Transfer printed, 2002

Mark No.129
Transfer printed, 2000

Mark No.130
Transfer printed, 2002

The East Quay, Poole, drawing by Robert Jefferson.

TRADITIONAL

Anne Hatchard (Milnthorpe) 1918-1936, late 1940s and late 1950s
In use 1918 - late 1920s
In use by late 1920s

Ernest Banten, 1921-1923
Pattern designer/glaze decorator/ painter

Margaret Holder, 1921-1941
Design assistant/head of painting
Sometimes used
In use 1921-1927
In use 1925-1934
In use 1927-1941

Margaret Atkins (Stagg), 1922-1924

Gertie Warren, 1922-1927

Ethel Barratt, 1922-1927
Variations of the same mark

Truda Rivers (Mordue), 1922-1932

Winifred Collett (Howard), 1922-1935

Ruth Pavely, paintress 1922-1945, painting shop supervisor 1945-1949, design assistant/head of painting 1950-1965
In use 1922-1937
In use 1937-1965

Vera Bridle (Meads), 1923-1933

Lily Pedley (Edmonds), 1924-1932

Dorothy James (Mainstone), 1924-1935

Eileen Prangnell (Chennell), 1924-1937

Marian Heath (De'Ath), 1925-1938

Marjorie Batt (Hayward), 1925-1935 and 1946

Grace Burge (Parnaby), 1926-1929
In use 1926-1927
In use 1927-1929

Gladys Jeffery (Carter), 1926-1930

Mary Brown, 1926-1934

Doris Marshall (Atkins), 1926-1936

Hilda Trim, 1926-1942

Rene Hayes (Harvey), 1926-1940, 1945-1949

Ruth Gough (Heath), 1927-1934

Marjorie Cryer (Evans), 1927-1940

Myrtle Bond, 1927-1942

Hilda Hampton (Cleal), 1927-1945

Nellie Bishton (Blackmore), 1927-1932, 1944-1949, painting shop supervisor 1950-1976

Phyllis Way (Cattle), 1928-1934

Phyllis Allen (McHattie), 1928-1935

Gwen Dry (Rowland), 1928-1935

Iris Skinner (Adams), 1928-1937

Phyllis Ryall (Randall), 1928-1937

Joan Hartnell (Derry), 1929-1930

Clarice Heath (Drew), 1929-1940

Marian Jones (Greenham), 1930-1936

Winifred Rose (Cook), 1932-1938

Gladys Brown (Herriman), 1933-1938

Edith Jeffery, 1933-1938

Gwendoline Ponsford (Belben), 1933-1939

Vera Wills (Morgan), 1933-1950
In use 1933-1935
In use 1936-1950

Norah Preston (James), 1934-1941

Gwendoline Suckling (Williams), 1935-1939

Gladys Hallett (Hayton), 1935-1941, 1945-1948, 1954-1958

Freda Coward, 1936-1941

Christine Lucas (Neal), 1936-1941

Mollie Skinner (Harman), 1936-1940
In use 1951-1953

Esther Turner (May), 1937-1942

Audrey Miles (Osman), 1938-1942

Gwen Haskins (Lynch), 1938-1977

Annette Ball (Franklin), 1945-1949
In use 1945-1947
In use 1948
In use 1949

Jean Cockram (Wilson), 1945-1957

Margaret Best (Jones), 1946

Gwyneth Flowers (Batten), 1946-1949

Barbara Meades (Notley), 1946-1949

Eileen Selby (Hunt), 1946-1951

Gwendoline Selby (House), 1946-1951

Audrey Heckford (Bennett), 1946-1953

Hazel Allner (Tilsed), 1946-1957

Jean Best (Cluer), 1947-1951

Rachel Turner, 1947-1952

Rita Curtis (Norris), 1948-1949

Esther Meades (Stevens), 1948-1952

Phyllis Millard (Langridge), 1949-1950

Elsie Cobb (Christopher), 1949-1951

Ruth Hall (Wellstead), 1949-1952

Kathleen Riggs (Remsik), 1949-1953

Joan Shorto (Slow), 1949-1953

Mary Ives (Worsfold), 1949-1956
In use 1949-1950
In use 1951-1956

Sheila Jenkins (Drew), 1949-1961

Pat Summers 1949-1963, Design assistant 1963-1981

Rita Chapman (Lock), 1950-1955

Betty Gooby (Hall), 1950-1959

Jean Player (Cutler), 1950-1959

Susan Nunns (Russell), 1950-1952, 1977-1994

Jean Baker (Harrison), 1951-1954

Margaret West (Stevens), 1951-1954

Molly Brown (Harvey), 1951-1955

Alice Cockram, 1952-1956

Mary Cockram (Chapman), 1952-1956

Diane Holloway (Wellsted), 1952-1958

Sylvia Davis, 1952-1962

Cynthia Parr (White), 1953-1955

Pat Dightam (Burgess), 1953-1958

Iris Downton (Hosker), 1954-1961

Josephine Smith, 1955-1962

Mary Stainer (Curtis), 1955-1956, 1979-1980

Rene Brown (Blake), 1956-1958

Patricia Brown (Brilliant), 1956-1962

Josephine Sydenham (Cartridge), 1956-1962

Ann Wiffen (Miles), 1956-1962

Heather Bailey (Taylor), 1957-1959

Georgina Hare (McGregor), 1957-1959

June March (Vaughan), 1957-1961

Janet Goodhew (Poaros) 1958-1963

Variation of the same mark

Jacqueline Way (Tily), 1958-1964

Patricia Wells (White), 1959-1973

Sylvia Penney (Garcia Ruiz), 1960-1970

Mary Lowman (Wilson), 1962-1964

Carolyn Bartlett, 1962-1965

Patricia Churchouse (Roake), 1962-1965

Elizabeth Hayne, 1963

Variation of the same mark

Tessa Bailey, 1963-1964

Josephine Price (Winzar), 1963-1965, 1967-1968

Barbara March (Dunesby), 1964-1966

Susan Allen (Pottinger), 1967-1978, 1996-present

Noreen Andrews (Partridge), 1969-1971

Mariam Levers, 1972

Veronica Hanson, 1972-1975

Karen Hickisson, 1973-1982, 1996-present

Deborah Farrance (Marsh), 1975-1976

Janice Wellman (Dowding), 1975-1979

Johanna Rolfe (Allin), 1976-1981

Carolyn Davies (Beckwith), 1976-1987

Lindsey Cole (Stevens), 1979-1987, 1992-1996

Donna Ridout, 1987-1994

Kelley Dominey, 1989-1994

Michelle Knight, 1989-1994, 1995-1997

Nicola Stacey, 1989-1994

Paul Garland, 1995-1996

Emma Thomas, 1995-1997

Dilice Jackson, 1995-2000

Nicola Massarella, 1996-present

Sarah Westlake, 1996-1999

DELPHIS

Robert Jefferson, designer 1962-1966

Tony Morris, designer/painter 1963-1967

Christine Tate (Hooton), design assistant 1964-1966, Delphis section supervisor 1966-1970

Ann Godfrey (Lloyd), sprayer/paintress 1965-1970

In use 1965-1966

In use 1967

In use 1968-1970

Geraldine O'Meara (Robson), 1966

Margaret Anderson (Cooper), 1966-1967

Betty Bantten (Coslett), 1966-1967

Jennifer Wiles, 1964-1966

Thelma Bush, 1966-1968

In use 1966

In use 1967

In use 1967-1968

Shirley Campbell (Peel), 1966-1969

Jean Millership (Mathews), 1966-1969

Carole Holden (Beach), 1966-1969

In use 1966-1968

In use 1968-1969

Josephine Wall (Coulson), 1967-1968

Irene Kerton (Scammells), 1968-1969

Sally Murch (Reader), 1968-1969

Angela Wyburgh (Miles), 1968-1973

In use 1968

In use 1969-1973

Christine Phillips (Rice), sprayer/paintress, 1969-1970

Janet Laird (Parker), 1969-1970, Delphis section supervisor 1970-1974

Carol Cutler (Kellett), 1969-1976

In use 1969

In use 1969-1975

In use 1975-1976

Sarah Worrell, 1970

Loretta Leigh, 1970

Ros Sommerfelt, 1970-1971 and 1976

Pamela Bevans (Newman), 1970-1972

In use 1970

In use 1971-1972

In use 1972

Lynn Gregory (Hudson), 1970-1974

Gillian Taylor (Nakasuji), 1971-1972

Julia Wills (Williams), 1971-1972

Ingrid Hammond, 1971-1973

Rosina St. Clayre (St. Clayre-Everett), 1971-1973

Cynthia Bennett, 1971-1977

Mary Albon, 1972-1974

Anita Lawrence, 1972-1974

Jeanette Spode (Radetic), 1973-1974

Andree Fontana (Fiveash), 1973-1979

Valerie Pullen, 1974-1975

Beverley Mantel, 1974-1975

Judi Evans, 1974-1976

Wendy Smith, 1975-1977
In use 1975-1976
In use 1976-1977

Tina Fancy (Elford), 1976-1978

Susan Barfoot, 1977-1978

Elaine Martin, 1977-1979

Debbie Leroy (Garvey), 1977-1979

Faith Hole (Arnold), 1978-1979

Sarah Spreadbury, 1978-1979

In addition to their main occupations, shown in brackets, the following were also paintresses of Delphis ware.
Patricia Wells, (Traditional)
Patricia Churchhouse (Roake), (Traditional)
Elizabeth Hayne, (Traditional)
Jennifer Wiles, (Traditional)
Jacqueline Mackenzie (Leonard), (Aegean)
Linda Garwood (Denny-Conway), (Stoneware sculptures)
Diana Davis (Foreman), (Aegean)
Laura Wills, (Aegean)
Debra Squires (Hunt), (Stoneware sculptures)

AEGEAN

Leslie Elsden, designer/painter 1969-1979

Carole Holden (Beach), design assistant/paintress 1970-1974

Brian Smith, 1972

Alan Clarke, glaze sprayer/decorator 1972-1974

Julia Wills (Williams), 1972-1978

Carolyn Wills (Walters), 1972-1979

Jacqueline Mackenzie (Leonard), 1972-1979
In use 1972-1977
In use 1978-1979

Ros Sommerfelt, paintress 1972-1977

Jane Brewer, 1972-1975

Diana Davis (Foreman), 1973-1979
In use 1973-1978
In use 1978-1979

Janet Abrey, 1974-1975

Laura Wills, 1976-1980

Ann Pooles (Hudson), 1977-1978

Donna Brogan, 1977-1979

Lindsay Dean (Loader), 1978

Karen Ryall, 1978-1979

In addition to their main occupations, shown in brackets, the following were also paintresses of Aegean ware:
Susan Allen (Pottinger), (Traditional)
Sarah Worrell (Delphis)
Cynthia Bennett, (Delphis)
Andree Fontana, (Delphis)
Faith Hole (Arnold), (Delphis)

STONEWARE SCULPTURES

Barbara Linley Adams, designer/modeller 1972-1983

Linda Garwood (Denny-Conway), supervisor 1974-1984

Susan Bonsey (Campbell-Brown), 1974-1975

Hilda Smith, 1975-1978

Eunice Menke, 1975-1981

Hazel Jones, 1975-1989

Julie Miller, 1976-1978

Diane Lake, 1976-1978

Susan Dipple, 1976-1987

Debra Squires (Hunt), 1977-1979

Jane Freeborn, 1978

June Henderson-Don, 1978

Janet Stone, 1978-1981

Janet Abrey, 1978-1979

Mary Elliot, 1978-1979

Julia Mabey, 1978-1979

Carmen Levo, 1978-1979

Lesley Presswood, 1978-1979

Joanna Durant, 1978-1980

Lindsay Loader, 1978-1984

Paula Morton, 1980-1981

Nicola Massarella, 1982-present

Lindsey Cole (Stevens), 1987-1992

June Cole, 1989-1995

LIVING GLAZE

Janet Owen, Supervisor, 1999-present

Dilly Jackson, 1999-2000

Claire Lenegan, 1999-2000

Dolly James, 1999-2001

Jo Vincent, 1999-2001

Paula Watson, 1999-2001

Jane Warwick, 1999-2001

Duncan Drage, 1999-2001

Niki Lenegan, 1999-2001

Carol Bolton, 1999-present

Sue Dunn, 1999-present

Nigel Rawlings, 1999-present

Lorna Whitmarsh, 1999-present

Maxime Clarke, 1999-present

Wendy Tiller, 1999-present

Carla Singleton, 1999-present

Dawn Polden, 1999-present

Sarah Smith, 2001-present

James Lacey, 2001-present

Jane Warwick, 1999-2001

In addition to their main occupations, shown in brackets, the following also finished Stoneware Sculptures:

Karen Hickisson (Traditional)
Susan Barfoot, (Delphis)
Elaine Martin, (Delphis)
Debbie Leroy (Garvey), (Delphis)
Faith Hole (Arnold), (Delphis)
Sarah Spreadbury, (Delphis)
Jacqueline Mackenzie (Leonard), (Aegean)
Alan White (thrower)
Chris White (thrower)

In addition to their main occupations, shown in brackets, the following also worked in other departments, detailed below:

STAINED GLASS WINDOW 1972-1981
Tina Trapp
Susan Allen (Pottinger), (Traditional)
Julia Wills (Williams), (Delphis and Aegean)
Carolyn Wills (Walters), (Aegean)
Jacqueline Mackenzie (Leonard), (Aegean)
Laura Wills (Aegean)

IONIAN 1974-1975
Julia Wills (Williams), (Aegean)
Carolyn Wills (Walters), (Aegean)
Susan Allen (Pottinger), (Traditional)

JEWELLERY 1976-1983
Tina Fancy (Elford), (Delphis)
Sally Samways (Tutt), also employed in the Making Shop
Debbie Leroy (Garvey), (Delphis)
Ann Pooles (Hudson), (Aegean)
Faith Hole (Arnold), (Delphis)
Lindsey Cole (Stevens), (Traditional)

OLYMPUS 1977-1978
Tina Fancy (Elford), (Delphis)
Susan Barfoot, (Delphis)
Jacqueline Mackenzie (Leonard), (Aegean)
Donna Brogan, (Aegean)
Karen Ryall, (Aegean)
Julie Miller, (Stoneware Sculptures)
Debra Squires (Hunt), (Stoneware Sculptures)
Debbie Leroy (Garvey), (Delphis)

DORSET COLLECTION 1977-1979
Carolyn Wills (Walters), (Aegean)
Karen Ryall, (Aegean)

SIENNA 1978-1979
Jacqueline Mackenzie (Leonard), (Aegean)
Susan Barfoot, (Delphis)
Debbie Leroy (Garvey), (Delphis)
Julie Miller, (Stoneware Sculptures)
Debra Squires (Lunt), (Stoneware Sculptures)

FAIENCE BLUE PLAQUES 1977-1981
Cynthia Bennett, (Delphis)
Julia Wills (Williams), (Aegean)
Hilda Smith, (Stoneware Sculptures)

SLIP OUTLINE WARES 1980-1981
Cynthia Bennett, (Delphis)

THROWING

Guy Sydenham, senior thrower/design assistant 1951-1965
Designer/Studio potter, Delphis (shapes) and Atlantis ranges 1966-1977

Alan White, thrower, designer/decorator 1966-present
In use 1966-1981
In use 1981-present
In use 1992-present

Angela Wyburgh (Miles), 1967-1968

Michael Dowding, 1970-1971

Beatrice Bolton (Dopita), thrower/Atlantis decorator 1970-1974

Pat Notley, 1972-1974

Susan Dipple, Atlantis thrower/decorator 1972-1975

Catherine Connett, thrower/Atlantis decorator 1973-1976

Jennie Haigh, thrower/Atlantis decorator 1973-1976

Chris White, 1975-1980

Deborah Farrance (Marsh), 1976-1978

Carol Cutler (Kellett), thrower/Atlantis decorator 1975-1978
In use 1975
In use 1976-1978

Deborah Mayben (McCutchion), 1976-1979

Paul Dean, 1976-1979

Mandy Norton, 1978-1980

DESIGNERS AND DECORATORS

James Radley Young. Working 1893-1901 and 1906-1933. Tile panel painter, faience, lustre and handcraft pottery

Margaret Holder. Working 1921-1941. Design assistant and head of painting. Sometimes used
1921-1924 1925-1934 1927-1936

Ernest Banten. Working 1921-1923. Pattern designer and glazed decorator/painter.

Ruth Pavely. Working 1922-1965. Paintress 1922-1945; painting shop supervisor 1945-1949; design assistant and head of painting 1950-1965
1922-1937 1937-1965

Leslie Elsden. Working 1926-1979. Glaze sprayer, Picotee and Two-colour ranges, 1932-1949; colour spraying foreman 1949-1965; spraying shop manager 1966-1969; designer/ painter Aegean, Contrast, Calypso and stoneware plaques 1969-1979.
1936-1949 1969-1979 1969-1979

Guy Sydenham. Working 1931-1977. Thrower 1931-1949; clay shaping department foreman 1949-1951; senior thrower/design assistant 1951-1965; designer/studio potter Delphis (shapes) and Atlantis 1966-1977
1951-1965 1966-1977

Ann Read (Tibbey). Working 1952-1956. Contemporary pattern designer/paintress

Robert Jefferson. Working 1958-1966. Designer, Oven-to-Tableware, Contour, Compact, Delphis studio wares etc.

Tony Morris. Working 1962-1982 and 1999-2002. Designer, modeller, painter, faience and Delphis studio wares, Stained Glass Window/Map Plates etc.. One-off Studio Wares

Pat Summers. Working 1949-1981. Traditional paintress 1949-1963; design assistant 1963-1981

Christine Tate. Working 1964-1970. Design assistant 1964-1966; Delphis section supervisor 1966-1970

Carole Holden (Beach). Working 1966-1969 and 1970-1974. Delphis paintress 1966-1969; design assistant/Aegean paintress 1970-1974
1966-1968 1968-1974 1970-1974

Alan White. Working 1966-present
Thrower 1966-1973; throwing shop manager 1973-1978; craft section manager 1978-1982; studio potter, designer/decorator 1983-present.
1966-1981 1981-present 1992-present

Ros Sommerfelt. Working 1970-1987. Delphis paintress 1970-1971 and 1976; Aegean paintress 1972-1977; designer shapes and decorations, Olympus, Bearsdley, Dorset Collection etc.

Barbara Linley Adams. Working 1972-1983. Designer, modeller, stoneware sculptures.

Alan Clarke. Working 1972-present. Glaze sprayer and colour designer/decorator of the Dorset Fruit pattern 1989.

Elaine Williamson. Working 1977-1986. Designer tableware patterns, shapes, decorations, bone china, giftware, children's ware etc.

Anita Harris. Freelance designer working exclusively for Poole 1992-2002. Colour designer/decorator, tableware, studio vases etc, Living Glaze and one-off Studio Wares

Sally Tuffin. Freelance designer studio wares, special commissions etc. 1995-2000

Janice Tchalenko. Freelance designer, studio wares 1997-present

Charlotte Mellis. Freelance designer studio wares 1997.

Karen Brown. Working 1996-present. Isle of Purbeck studio range etc

FACTORY TRIAL AND CONTROL MARKS

DATE CODING
A date code was used by artists producing one-off studio wares from September 1999 to October 2000. This consisted of a prefix letter with A for September 1999 through to N for October 2000 and a number which equated to the number of dishes produced in that month, i.e. C16 would be November 1999 when 16 dishes were produced. Tony Morris used a single prefix letter, all other artists used a double prefix.

Index

B'MOUTH
POOLE
SECONDS
PE 69
PICOTEES
POOLE
VISITORS
POOLE